Seeking the Sacred

© Chad Sychtysz

Published by
Spiritbuilding Publishing
15591 N. State Rd. 9
Summitville, IN 46070

Spiritual "equipment" for the contest of life.

Printed in the United States of America
ISBN: 0-9821376-5-6

This book is dedicated to James Chason and Sandi Williams, fellow laborers in the Lord, who both invested a great deal of their own time and energy into refining this most important message.

Table of Contents

Introduction

My son, if you will receive my words and treasure my commandments within you, make your ear attentive to wisdom, incline your heart to understanding; for if you cry for discernment, lift your voice for understanding; if you seek her as silver and search for her as for hidden treasures; then you will discern the fear of the LORD and discover the knowledge of God.
Proverbs 2:1-5

I would like to begin with a profound and intriguing fact: whoever you are, whatever your age, and regardless of your beliefs, God is looking straight into your heart even as you read this sentence.

You cannot make Him leave. You cannot elude Him; you cannot hide from Him. His presence is everywhere all at once; there are no boundaries or circumstances that can prevent Him from seeing you. It is not a difficult thing for the omniscient and omnipotent God of heaven to encounter you and every person on this planet in this way. His ability is not limited to yours—that is why you *need* Him so much.

God is fully aware of who you are, how you conduct yourself, even what you are thinking. Nothing escapes His attention. There is nothing about you that He does not know, whether or not you choose to believe in *Him*. He knows your good deeds as well as your failures and shortcomings. He knows your good intentions as well as your wicked thoughts. He knows where you have sincerely honored Him as well as where you have profaned His holy name.

God is not looking intently at you in order to evaluate your religion. He does not want to judge you—He has the *authority* to do so, and certainly He will exercise that authority in due time (2 Corinthians 5:10)—but this is not His immediate objective. What He wants to know above all else is your answer to this most important question:

Do you know Me in the way that I want you to know Me?

Someone says, "Of course I know God! After all, I *am* a Christian!"

The decision to be a Christian is an excellent one; there is no finer vocation. However, just because one is called a Christian does not mean he automatically *knows God* in the way He *wants* and *expects* that person to know Him. This is not accomplished through a mere profession of beliefs. One cannot know God merely by sitting on pews in church buildings, listening to sermons, or randomly skimming the Bible. To really *know* God requires serious investments of time, effort, and prayerful meditation. For these reasons alone, most people who call themselves Christians are simply unwilling to commit to this.

You are someone who is obviously willing to do something about this because you have picked up this book—hopefully with the intent of reading it in its entirety. You are obviously interested in *seeking the sacred*, which means you are deeply interested in drawing near to God. This book will help you to do this—perhaps much more than you will even realize.

The fact is, however, you do not need this book to draw near to God; the Bible is the real source of that information. This book is simply an expedient toward that endeavor. It is not meant to rival or replace your Bible. Instead, you will find that it contains hundreds of appeals *to* the Bible for accomplishing this very thing. God's Word "has granted to us everything pertaining to life and godliness" (2 Peter 1:3). I cannot tell you anything more concerning your *access to God* than what the Bible has already declared. Yet sometimes people need help with this subject, since drawing near to God is not an easy thing to do—even though God has already done (and continues to do) the most difficult part.

This book has been written, designed, and produced in order to help people better understand what the Word of God teaches on drawing near to the God of the Word. Its purpose is to give *anyone who wishes* an opportunity to look more deeply into the Scriptures so that they can draw more closely to God. It is not a mere "Bible study" where we open the Bible and comment on various passages—although it certainly is a study *of* the Bible. This book will help bring Bible passages to life and illuminate the pathway to God. It is meant to stimulate your thinking *upward*, since this is the direction that seekers of the sacred always look. Indeed, this is what the apostle Paul taught (Colossians 3:1-4):

Therefore if you have been raised up with Christ, keep seeking the things above, where Christ is, seated at the right hand of God. Set your mind on the things above, not on the things that are on earth. For you have died and your life is hidden with Christ in God. When Christ, who is our life, is revealed, then you also will be revealed with Him in glory.

God has put you here upon this earth so that you might seek Him. This requires that you not just think about Him, but that you think *like* Him (Ephesians 5:1). The God of heaven is anxious for your attention; the record of His love for you is both conclusive and compelling. He has something to offer you that this world is unable to provide: *life with Him*, which is "far more abundantly beyond all that we ask or think" (Ephesians 3:20). He wants nothing more than to fill your heart with the realistic hope of being forever with Him. The full intention of this book is to show you all of these things so that you can pursue God in the way that He has always wanted you to pursue Him.

God is peering into your soul right now to see your response to His invitation to draw near to Him.

The goal of those who are "raised up with Christ" (Christians) is to "keep seeking the things above." This means, in essence: we are to be in a constant state of elevating our love, thinking, and behavior to that which conforms to Christ—not this world, and certainly not our own preferences. God *expects* this of us because we *belong* to Him: we have surrendered ourselves to His will; we have pledged allegiance to Him above all else. Even those of us who have once "discovered" God may need to *rediscover* Him and engage in fellowship with Him on an even higher level than we have enjoyed previously.

Are you in need of "rediscovering" God? If so, then this book is most certainly for you. I think you will enjoy it immensely. This book is for all those who are searching for a deeper, more meaningful relationship with God: it is for those who desire a more intimate *fellowship* with God. Whoever you are, wherever you are presently in your spiritual walk with the Lord—or even if you are interested in *beginning* that walk—this book can help you discover aspects of God that you may not have yet considered.

In order to enjoy deeper fellowship with the Lord, you must appreciate how glorious and sacred our Lord is. We are to approach Him "with reverence and awe" (Hebrews 12:28); we cannot serve passively or incidentally the One who rules over all of heaven and earth. To do this appropriately requires a proper perspective of God, as well as recognition of our own humanity. We can certainly "draw near" to Him (James 4:8), but we cannot exceed our earthbound limitations.

Then again, men *have* seen the glory of God in Jesus Christ. Christ "is the radiance of His glory and the exact representation of His nature" (Hebrews 1:3), and inasmuch as men have "seen" Christ, they have seen the Father (John 14:7-10). Jesus was God's "in-the-flesh" revelation to man; He was God literally visualized and personified. Multitudes of people *saw* Christ walk upon the face of the earth, perform miracles, and exude heavenly wisdom. Some of these people actually spoke with Him, felt His gentle touch upon their broken bodies, and experienced His divine powers heal them of their demons and diseases. A few others journeyed with Him, ate with Him, and slept around the same campfire with Him. Three of them (Peter, James, and John) actually saw Him endued with heavenly glory (Matthew 17:1-6). Christ is the closest we will ever get (in this life) to seeing the glory of God, and yet none of *us* have seen Him.

This fact appears at first to defeat the entire premise of this book. After all, this book is about "seeking the sacred"; yet I have just implied that none of us will be able to *see* the sacred—at least in this life. On the other hand, it is not necessary to actually *see* something to believe in it. We practice this kind of faith all the time: we do not see the movement of electrons, but we believe in light and electricity; we do not see wind and centrifugal force, but we experience their effects in the weather; we do not see the gravitational pull of the moon's mass upon the earth, but all life on earth depends upon the rise and fall of the oceans. Likewise, we do not need to see God in order to believe in Him. Thomas, one of the twelve disciples, vowed not to believe in a resurrected Messiah until he put his fingers in the holes of Jesus' spike-impaled hands. Jesus let Thomas wait for eight days before giving him this opportunity, upon which time He told him, "Reach here with your finger, and see My hands; and reach here your hand and put it into My side; and do not be unbelieving, but believing." Then He rebuked him for his unnecessary doubt: "Because you have seen Me, have you believed? Blessed are they who did not see, and yet believed" (John 20:26-29).

God continues to gaze unblinkingly into your heart, examining your every thought. He asks you in a whisper so quiet that only your soul can hear it: Do you believe?

So it is with us: we are *blessed* if we believe in the God whom we literally cannot see. One of the paradoxes of Scripture is that visible affirmation is not always the key to enlightenment. The apostle Paul certainly "saw the light" of his errors concerning the Messiah during three days of blindness (Acts 9:1-18). Yet this idea works both ways: those who literally see may nonetheless remain unconverted, that is, spiritually blind. Many hard-hearted Pharisees saw Jesus and many of His works yet did not believe Him to be the Son of God. As John recorded in John 9:39-41,

> And Jesus said, "For judgment I came into this world, so that those who do not see may see, and that those who see may become blind." Those of the Pharisees who were with Him heard these things and said to Him, "We are not blind too, are we?" Jesus said to them, "If you were blind, you would have no sin; but since you say, 'We see,' your sin remains."

Thus, we do not have to see to believe; we do not have to see to be blessed. This is no support for *blind* faith, of course: what we *do* believe is based upon the irrefutable evidence of the glory of God that *is* seen in the physical and moral world. We "see" the Lord through what He has made (Romans 1:20), what His Spirit has written concerning Him (1 Peter 1:10-12), and how He works in our lives, "[causing] all things to work together for good to those who love God" (Romans 8:28).

We are not interested in seeing a mere silhouette of God or a mere character sketch of His attributes (although it is beneficial to *study* His attributes, as we will do in this work). Rather, God wants us to be *seekers* of Him. This is made possible only through our faith in Him. God certainly *could* manifest His glory to us, but then we would believe only with our *eyes* and not with our *heart*. To believe with one's heart—to have faith in God—is far more difficult than to merely cognitively acknowledge His existence because of what one literally sees.

"Without faith it is impossible to please Him, for he who comes to God must believe that He is and that He is a rewarder of those who seek Him" (Hebrews 11:6). To be *seekers* of God is a far more noble pursuit than merely wanting to *see* God. This will not prevent us from desiring to see Him with our own eyes. However, it puts our longing for God and our craving for fellowship with Him in an appropriate context.

Thankfully, not only are we seekers of God, but He is also seeking us. Jesus once told a Samaritan woman that "an hour is coming, and now is, when the true worshipers will worship the Father in spirit and truth; for such people the Father seeks to be His worshipers" (John 4:23). I want to be forever with the Lord; I assume that you do too. But God *also* wants us to be with Him; He is supremely interested in our quests for deeper fellowship with Him. In fact, He actively seeks after those of us who desire to worship Him. It would not matter how deeply we desired to be with God if He did not also desire us to be with Him. If not for His making our "seeking" possible, there would be nothing we could do to bring us one inch, one day, or one thought closer to Him.

Those who seek God must accept the all-encompassing demands of this search. As with any noble pursuit, we must have an appreciation of what it means to *be* a seeker of the sacred. We must realize the purpose behind that search—what it involves and what it demands of us personally. Zeal and passion are not enough by themselves; we must also *prepare* for that search. Our mind, skills, knowledge, and courage must all be concentrated and focused in such a way that the search we perform will be effective and efficient. We must be willing to postpone or remove altogether all other searches that rob us of the energy required to conduct the *greatest* search of our lives. Furthermore, we must possess a competent approach toward our

search: where to start, how to engage in it, and *why* it is t[o]
the first place.

Any search for which the seeker has no clear purp[ose]
is doomed from the start. A person cannot properly prepa[re]
with a vague, pointless, indefinable goal. Someone searchi[ng] peace,"
for example, who has no clue what it looks like simply cannot organize his
efforts in that direction. (The exasperating search for "world peace" within
the fractured and self-serving international community is a good illustration
of this: no one can really agree objectively what such "peace" looks like,
much less how to achieve it.) One's purpose must be clear, well-defined,
and unmistakable. A vague objective will generate nothing more than a
wild and fruitless search—kind of like flailing one's arms and legs about in a
hopeless attempt to swim. A great expenditure of time and energy does not
by itself guarantee profitable results.

Christians are not above these necessary conditions, even though
what (really, *Whom*) we seek is spiritual in nature. Likewise, we are not
immune to the various pitfalls and hindrances that may plague the search
itself. Christopher Columbus and other early transoceanic explorers, for
example, did not confine their vision to a fixed point in time when they
would literally gaze upon the very object of their search. They understood
that the search itself was difficult, demanding, complicated—even life-
threatening. These men had to know a lot about ships, ocean navigation,
management of a ship's crew (which included men who probably did not
share the explorer's passion for what was being sought, but instead, looked
only for compensation for their efforts), and possess a fairly good sense of
what and where it was they wanted to find. They also had to accept the
losses and deprivations of pursuing their quest: months away from their
homes and families, poor eating and living conditions, vermin, disease,
malnutrition, and the incessant assault of scorching sun, driving rain, and
salty ocean spindrift.

Likewise, Thomas Edison—another explorer of a different sort—
searched for ways to improve upon the primitive technology of his day, but
was not oblivious to the demands of that search. He spent many, many long
hours of his life in experimentation and observation, trying to bring into

...tence devices and machines which the world has since taken for granted. We can hardly imagine the discipline of mind and diligence of principle under which he must have labored. Thankfully, he was rewarded for his efforts.

Not everyone who so labors is thus rewarded. William Tyndale, for example, worked tirelessly to translate the Latin Bible (Vulgate) into English, only to be condemned as a heretic by the Roman Church for doing so. (Catholic officials once believed that to put Scripture in any "common" language like English was to blaspheme its holiness. They believed that Latin was the only acceptable sacred language.) As a result, Tyndale's search for a Bible which the general populace could read was prematurely ended: he was burned alive at the stake in 1536.[1]

Christians today also face difficult—perhaps even life-threatening—challenges. As with seafaring explorers of old, our search will be difficult, demanding, and sometimes complicated. As with the passionate inventor, so we must have discipline of mind and diligence of principle that cannot be abandoned for lesser things. As with those who sacrificed their lives for the greater good, so we must accept the fact that our search may not *appear* to be successful in our own lifetime, or that it will meet our own initial expectations. For the many ancient explorers who were successful, whose names have become part of human history, there were countless more who were unsuccessful, whose discoveries went unrecognized, or who have simply vanished from historical memory. Our own posterity may not even care that we *were* seekers. But we cannot linger on these negative aspects. Seeking after the sacred must be a noble and sacrificial pursuit in itself; it cannot be dependent upon any other factors or outcomes.

We also cannot think that if we just look hard enough, we will always find something worthwhile. As mentioned, the expenditure of great amounts of energy does not automatically translate to success. Likewise, luck has nothing to do with salvation. No one accidentally finds divine grace; no one stumbles into heaven. Instead, the seeker must know exactly what he is seeking after and must be (or quickly become) familiar with whatever tools, resources, and processes are necessary for making that search successful.

The joy of finding what we are searching for motivates us to endure the discomfort and frustration that accompanies that search. In this way, Jesus also looked beyond the cross and its suffering and humiliation. His focus was on the joy of obedience to the Father and the satisfaction of accomplishing what was in the best interest of all mankind: "for the joy set before Him [He] endured the cross…" (Hebrews 12:2). This incentive was sufficient to overcome all the difficulties on the way to His goal. So we too must endure the hardships of the search, knowing that our obedience and God's grace will ultimately lead us where we ought to go. "For it is for this we labor and strive, because we have fixed our hope on the living God, who is the Savior of all men, especially of believers" (1 Timothy 4:10).

God, His eyes fixed intently upon your thoughts, continues to watch for signs of your submission to His will. His Spirit whispers again: Have you fixed your hope on Me?

We must also recognize the desperate *need* for this search. Without engaging in this search, we imply that God is not worth seeking, and that our present knowledge, status, and ability are all that we need to rescue ourselves from this sinful world. This is absolutely untrue. Without God's saving power, we are *unsaved people*. We are hopeless and lost without Him; without searching for God, we will not see Him in the end. Our seeking after the sacred, then, cannot be perceived merely as an exciting adventure, intriguing curiosity, or elaborate (but expendable) hobby. Rather, our spiritual, eternal future depends entirely upon it. We are not merely missing out on a great opportunity if we are not seekers, as though we have just missed a great deal on a Caribbean cruise or a new car; we are *ruined beyond redemption*. To be content with who we are or what we know presently is to consign ourselves to certain spiritual death. We cannot accept the horrible consequences of the *failure* to seek after the sacred. We cannot afford *not* to be seekers.

As seekers, we must also have personal desire and motivation. Jesus once said, "If anyone wishes to come after Me, he must deny himself, and take up his cross, and follow Me" (Matthew 16:24). I want to emphasize the beginning of that statement: "If anyone *wishes*…." In other words, *only* whoever deeply desires the Lord is of the right disposition to be His disciple.

This is the first priority; this must *precede* the search itself. All those who *do* find Christ, having made Him the object of their pursuit, will be those who had earnestly desired to find Him in the first place.

This book is designed to whet your desire for the Lord. Even more so, God's Word is designed to whet this desire, which is why we will often look into it. No one can desire Him for you; no one draws near to God by proxy.

Meanwhile, God continues to look deeply, penetratingly, and probingly into your heart. His face is ever before your face. You possess the breath of life which He gave to you—His strong desire is for you to seek the Source of that life. He longs for your awareness of Him; He stands ready to lead your pursuit of His glory; He craves fellowship with your soul.

What, exactly, is *your* desire, dear reader? Do you know the Lord as He wants you to know Him? Are you truly a seeker of the sacred? Do you wish to *begin* your quest? Or do you wish to rise to the next level *of* your quest? If so, the rest of this book will explore exactly what this means and what you must do to fully and appropriately undertake that search.

In the end, however, you will find that the information you needed in order to accomplish this search was right before your eyes all the time. In the end, you will discover that *God* was looking lovingly and intently at you all along, leading you homeward to Him.

Endnotes

1 Tyndale completed translating the New Testament in 1525 and had begun working on the Old Testament when he died. His work was resumed and completed by his colleague Miles Coverdale in 1537, and Tyndale himself was posthumously exonerated (The Origin of the Bible, ed. by Philip Comfort [Wheaton, IL: Tyndale House Publishers, 1992], 265.)

CHAPTER ONE

Becoming Seekers of God

Do not love the world nor the things in the world. If anyone loves the world, the love of the Father is not in him. For all that is in the world, the lust of the flesh and the lust of the eyes and the boastful pride of life, is not from the Father, but is from the world. The world is passing away, and also its lusts; but the one who does the will of God lives forever.
1 John 2:15-17

Just because something is important, beautiful, or transcendent does *not* mean everyone will see or appreciate it as such. Let me illustrate this at the expense of my wife, Honey (since it just seemed fitting to include her in this book *somehow*). And yes, that is her real name.

Honey and I spent our honeymoon traveling down the beautiful Oregon coast on Highway 101. We stopped at coastal towns from Astoria to Newport, visiting several parks and scenic lookouts along the way. One of the most memorable places we visited was Ecola State Park, which is a gorgeous viewpoint perched upon a huge bluff overlooking the ocean and the nearby town of Cannon Beach. It was early October, but skies were blue, sunshine filled the air, and it felt like summer.

Of course, since we were on our honeymoon, the emotions, senses, and perceptions of our travels were greatly enhanced by the thrill of our new life together. So when we first pulled into the parking lot of Ecola State Park, we were overwhelmed by our new-found freedom and the joy of sharing our life together. Thus, we just sat there in the car, soaking in the precious time we shared together, as well as the majesty and serenity of the scene around us. Gnarled, weather-beaten trees posed for us in permanent wind-blown stances. Crisp, clean, autumn air slipped in quietly through the car's partly-opened windows. The sun smiled radiantly upon the coast, its rays sparkling across the water below the cliffs. About a half mile away, a lighthouse stood proudly and bravely upon a crag of rock surrounded by roiling water.

At least that's what captured *my* attention. Honey, however, was entranced on something of a much lesser scale. A groundskeeper was cutting the park's rich, green lawns with a riding lawnmower just beyond the parking lot, and he was obviously having some difficulty navigating his machine through the soft sod. I noticed Honey's distractedness, and even though I knew what she was focused upon, I asked anyway, "What are you looking at?" It was my way of saying, "Why are you looking at *that*?"

"I think he's stuck," she said, with a tinge of genuine concern for the man.

"I'm sure he'll be able to take care of himself," I reassured her. Apparently it was not enough reassurance.

"I wonder if he'll get that thing out of there," she wondered aloud. I also wondered: was she expecting me to latch onto him with a tow-rope and pull him out with our little four-cylinder sedan?

"I can't believe this," I said, both amused and slightly exasperated by the insignificance of her distraction. "Here we are sitting at one of the most beautiful spots of the entire Oregon coast, surrounded by all this beautiful scenery, and you're wondering what's going to happen to the lawnmower guy?"

Sheepish smile, slight fidgeting. "Well, it just looks like he's stuck."

Thus began our happy life of polar opposites together. (In her defense, Honey is often much more concerned about people, whereas I am often first taken with ambiance, concepts, and abstractions. This is why people want to spend much more time with her than they do with me! Plus she is considerably more attractive than I am.)

Of course, that was just a silly illustration. Honey's distraction was harmless and my exasperation was purposely humorous and overly dramatic. But if this same scenario had been applied to spiritual matters, we would be dealing with a serious problem. For example, have you ever tried to focus someone's attention on the joy and grandeur of fellowship with God, only to have that person get sidetracked with some petty detail in his or her life—a bill to pay, vacation plans, car troubles, a TV show, a phone call, etc.? Similarly, how often have preachers tried to motivate the members of their congregation, only to have many of them sidetracked with "pressing things" that really are petty issues devoid of spiritual value?

Sometimes we can miss a *major* thing by focusing too much on a *minor* detail. This seems to be an all-too-common phenomenon: a person foregoes a deeper exploration of his eternal life because he is completely distracted with his secular life. Put another way: he is unable to become a seeker of the sacred because he does not realize that what is here on earth cannot fulfill his soul's desire. Or he does not realize how hungry and thirsty his soul is for God, since he tries to satisfy his spiritual appetite with useless scraps of the world.

Is Nothing Sacred?

We might assume that Christians naturally dwell on holiness and related subjects. However, there is nothing "natural" about dwelling on the unseen world. I myself find it difficult to sustain these thoughts over a long period of time. After a while, despite my best intentions, my humanity and secular life starts creeping into my thoughts and begins eroding my concentration. I'm not making excuses for myself, or for you; rather, I believe I am defining a common human behavior. Since we are human people living in a physical world dominated by secular thinking and "the sensual conduct of unprincipled men" (2 Peter 2:7), it is a real challenge for us to stay focused upon spiritual ideals and virtues for an extended period of time. This does not mean it is impossible, just difficult. Difficult things require much more energy and concentration than simple, mindless exercises. Let's face it: it takes a great deal less energy to watch a two-hour movie (provided you *like* the movie) than it is to engage in a half-hour meditative Bible study and then pray meaningfully for God to help you be like the Christ about whom you just read. Bible reading and prayer are certainly not the only spiritual activities Christians engage in, but if we *neglect* these, then we will soon cease to be spiritual.

In a related thought, it is hard to get people to think about the sacred when so many of us are bent on sensual or personal gratification. In our pursuit of personal pleasure, we often unwittingly (or uncaringly) forfeit spiritual values. This doesn't mean the average Joe intentionally sets out to trash everything that *is* sacred. It does mean, however, that many people never take the time or have the forethought to discern between mere entertainment and actual sacrilege. You've heard the question asked, "Is nothing sacred anymore?" It does seem that much of what used to be regarded as sacred is no longer so, or is being threatened with commonality, indifference, or intentional blasphemy.

It is easy to see why a discussion of the sacred can become lost upon a person who lives in this sort of social climate. Our perverted, voyeuristic society has not helped much. Watch a few of the trashy talk shows, purely shameless exposé shows ("The Jerry Springer Show"), or any shows where we are invited to leer at someone else's indignity and bad behavior ("Lost," "Big Brother," et al) and you will get a taste of our trampling on whatever used to be sacred. In these shows, marriage is a sham, friends are intentionally greedy and self-centered, relationships are expendable, and every dirty little secret can be divulged for a moment's glory in front of a national audience.

Fascination with voyeurism and lurid sensationalism does not exemplify the fringe element of our society, but is increasingly becoming the norm in America. Even many churchgoers, who profess to serve as the light and salt of the world, lap from the same cesspools as everybody else. The line between those who are supposed to be living as "children of God above reproach in the midst of a crooked and perverse generation" (Philippians 2:15) and those who *are* the crooked and perverse is becoming thinner and fainter. The fault, then, does not lie only at the feet of those purveyors of profit who so often promote sacrilege—media and entertainment businesses—but also every person who, once he has tasted it, goes back for seconds and thirds. In some way, on some level, nearly every one of us has a share in the guilt.

Separating the Sacred from the Profane

God does not want us to be comfortable with sacrilege but busy carrying out our sacred service to Him. This means we must "draw near" to Him (James 4:8); we must become seekers of the sacred. To become such a seeker, it is necessary *first* to gain an appreciation for the critical differences between God's heavenly world and man's secular world so that we will have a better understanding of what "seeking the sacred" means.

When we talk about the nature of God, or even the nature of the heavenly realm of God, we are speaking of the *sacred*. In this context, "sacred" indicates that which defines God or is used *by* God for carrying out His will. The realm of the "flesh"—self-serving human desires and the secular world that caters to the carnal nature of man—is *profane* in comparison to the sacredness of God. Sacred and profane are opposites: they stand contrary and opposed to one another. To illustrate this, consider what the apostle Paul wrote (Romans 8:5-9, bracketed words mine):

> For those who are according to the flesh [i.e., those who are profane to God] set their minds on the things of the flesh, but those who are according to the Spirit [i.e., those who are sacred to God], the things of the Spirit. For the mind set on the flesh is death, but the mind set on the Spirit is life and peace, because the mind set on the flesh is hostile toward God; for it does not subject itself to the law of God, for it is not even able to do so, and those who are in the flesh cannot please God. However, you are not in the flesh but in the Spirit, if indeed the Spirit of God dwells in you. But if anyone does not have the Spirit of Christ, he does not belong to Him.

To "not belong to Him [Christ]" is to belong to something else— really, to be *led by* someone other than Christ. This is what the gospel teaches elsewhere (Galatians 5:16-17, 25, bracketed words mine):

> But I say, walk by the Spirit, and you will not carry out
> the desire of the flesh. For the flesh sets its desire against
> the Spirit, and the Spirit against the flesh; for these are
> in opposition to one another, so that you may not do the
> things that you please [i.e., that our carnal-minded, human
> desires want to do]. . . . If we live by the Spirit, let us also
> walk by the Spirit.

Notice the *conflict* between the realm of the sacred and the profane world:
the one is "set against" the other; they are "in opposition to one another."
This does not illustrate a peaceful coexistence between the two realms, but
an aggressive antagonism. One is both sacred and holy or he is worldly and
profane. A person is either holy, as God is holy, or he is profane, as the world
is profane; he cannot walk a fine line between the two. Thus a "worldly
Christian" is an oxymoron, since there is no reconciling these two terms;
they are incompatible states of being.

"Holy" refers to that quality or state of being which defines and
originates only from God. It refers generally to that which God has set
apart for His use, but specifically to the distinct nature of God Himself.
Unfortunately, many Christians may have only a surface understanding
of what "holy" is. This is partly because typical Bible classes and sermons
focus more upon proper conduct rather than godly hearts, the latter of
which necessarily involves *holiness*. The difference is that visible behavior
only touches on the visible, external life, whereas holiness permeates one's
invisible soul. When we only concentrate on the external, we only change
outward behavior, not necessarily our inward being. God certainly wants
sinful and inappropriate behavior to cease, but not at the expense of *or* as a
replacement for internal conformity to Christ. If our "inner man" is truly
being "renewed day by day" (2 Corinthians 4:16), this will produce a visible
effect on the outward man.

Ideally, the more we learn about Christ, the more we are compelled
to look beyond His external behavior and begin to appreciate what motivated
that behavior in the first place. Instead of merely asking, "*What* did Jesus
do?" we begin asking, "*Why* did Jesus do that?" Christ was not just a "good
person"; He was a *holy* person. But what about you and I—can we be holy

people too? Not only can we, but we were created to serve God in that capacity. In other words, God *expects* us to be holy (1 Peter 1:16).

Unfortunately, our culture has given us a rather stereotypical view of holiness. Hollywood, for example, portrays holiness through a sanctuary-associated image—usually an ornate, classical-designed, even ominous-looking church building. Elaborately adorned priests and other clerics contribute to the holiness effect, since they are understood to be the official, ordained custodians of everything that is holy. Relics and sacred objects, which are almost always rare and antique, associated with some mysterious occurrence, and/or endowed with some almost-magical property are commonly given special attention. Thus, ornate crosses, chalices, statuettes, ancient books, basins of "holy water," special vestments, and candles—*lots* of candles—are used to create an ambiance of reverence and sacredness.

While such portrayals are supposed to emphasize the presence of God, quite the opposite is true. They all emphasize *not* the spiritual, but the worldly—not the sacred, but the secular. These depictions teach us that we need *men* to build holy shrines, craft holy images and venerated objects, ordain priests, beatify souls, and uphold an object's sacred properties. Take away the work of man and the allegedly "sacred" distinction is lost. An ordained priest is only a priest, for example, because men have conferred this honor upon him. Without man's having so recognized him, he loses all "holy" distinction. Likewise, church buildings are only considered sacred because we have deemed them as such. If the building is sold to someone who turns it into a garage or a dance hall, it loses all sense of sacredness: same building, different context. So it is with all other seemingly sacred positions, objects, and denominational beliefs. They are only sacred because man has paid any attention to them. Once he turns away, they cease to be sacred. In most cases, they simply cease to exist altogether.

What God Holds Sacred

Let's consider this thought from a slightly different angle. Suppose I have a picturesque, secluded, wooded piece of property, and in the midst of the trees is a certain spot which I have deemed sacred. It is my special place where I go to meditate, find serenity, and get away from it all. It may be only an undefined spot in the woods to anyone else, but to me it is a holy, cathedral-like sanctuary. The fact that you do not regard my special place as sacred does not make it any less sacred to me; however, without my ability to perpetuate the sacredness of this place, it will lose all such distinction. When I die, whatever is sacred only to me cannot be protected by me anymore. At that point, a developer may bulldoze my wooded property, build a dozen condominiums, and never give a second thought to my special place in the midst of the trees.

My point is: just because we privately regard something as sacred does not mean that this thing is sacred to God—or to anyone else. Our sense of holiness and God's are not automatically synonymous or interchangeable. This does not mean we cannot have our own personal sacred places, memories, or heirlooms. It simply means we cannot impose heavenly sacredness upon our subjective decisions, nor can we equate our own worldly sense of the sacred upon heavenly sacredness. What is holy to us is not always holy to God, and vice versa.

"Sacred" (or holy) in the biblical context does not merely refer to something that is important to *us*. Rather, it refers to something important to God *regardless* of us. Those things which are universally sacred are this way because God has designated them as such. Truly sacred things, concepts, or people are beyond our ability to ordain otherwise. Furthermore, these things remain sacred even though we ignore or refuse to acknowledge them. For example, God has made the marriage of a man and a woman to be a sacred union. Yet today we see people everywhere degrading marriage through polygamy, adultery, divorce, homosexual unions, and even incestuous relationships. Does this mean that because many have desecrated marriage, marriage itself no longer has any reference to a holy God? Absolutely not. The source of the sacredness of the marriage union transcends this world. God is the One who legitimizes marriage (Matthew 19:4-6); it is sacred to Him regardless of who does or does not honor this.

God does not sanctify things (or people) for any reason. He always acts with a specific purpose and according to a specific design. His will and judgment are always perfect. He has no discrepancy, no flaw, no Achilles' heel, "no variation or shifting shadow" (James 1:17). God is absolutely *perfect* in all that He is and does. He is, without any figurative speech, *the* Perfect. To refuse His perfect will, or to question His flawless judgment, is to uphold something worldly and unholy. In essence, it is to put ourselves in God's place, or even above Him—something of which we have no authority to do. To think that we *can* improve God arrogantly implies that we are in some way superior to Him. This is illogical, given the fact that we all live in subordination to His natural laws and are accountable to His moral laws.

Those who carelessly disregard what is sacred not only denigrate the sacred thing itself, but also One who made it sacred in the first place. One who profanes God's holiness also incurs His judgment: we were created to *honor* Him in whose image we are made (Genesis 1:26), not to question or disregard Him. God has the authority—both the power *and* right— to punish those who have no regard for His holiness. For example, when Moses stood in the land of Midian and stared in amazement at a bush filled with fire but that was not being consumed by that fire (Exodus 3:1-5), God told him to take off his sandals because "the place on which you are standing is holy ground." Certainly Moses did not make that ground holy; but he could not desecrate it, either, without having to answer directly to God for the offense. Likewise, whenever God tells us to *do something* in observance of His holiness, we are not to shrug off the instruction or offer what we might think is a clever counter-proposal. We are simply to respect whatever He deems sacred; we are expected to show deep reverence to the Holy God of heaven through our sincere obedience.

The Mystery of the Sacred

Even though He has revealed His will to man through the gospel of Christ (Romans 1:16-17), God Himself still remains enshrouded in *mystery*. Whatever we know about God's sacredness is completely overwhelmed by what we do *not* know. (We will examine this more closely in upcoming chapters.) The human psyche is naturally drawn toward a good mystery; thus, the mysteriousness of God does not ruin our fascination with Him, but makes Him more attractive and captivating to us.

Not only is God mysterious, but so may be those sacred things which are directly connected to Him. To continue an earlier example: marriage is a sacred union given to us by God, yet there is a certain sense of mystery concerning the union of two people becoming "one" (cf. Genesis 2:24, Ephesians 5:31). While we understand *some* aspects of this union, others exist which transcend human comprehension and defy earthly explanation. In trying to explain the intimacy of the marriage union, we ultimately are forced to reckon with the mysterious nature of God; both remain elusive and inexplicable to us. Furthermore, no matter how familiar one is with his spouse, he still does not know her absolutely. There is a certain mystery concerning that person's full identity—her soul, really—that eludes human detection. He may know all of her habits, idiosyncrasies, and even every flexure and detail of her body, but he cannot know her as intimately as she knows herself, which is still not as intimately as God knows her. There exists a definite sacred quality to the spiritual identification of each person—a quality that transcends anyone's ability to define or explain.

The gospel is sacred in this same sense: even though we know what the gospel message *says*, we do not know all the dynamics behind what makes it work or what empowers it. The Bible says "the word of God is living and active" (Hebrews 4:12)—but we struggle with what that means exactly. We will never grasp the full depth and scope of what *makes* God's Word "living and active"; this is a mystery which we are unable to solve. The Bible contains the Holy Spirit's message of redemption, which has been accurately communicated to us through inspired apostles. However, no written language is capable of conveying the full detail of God's infinite work—nor is this necessary in order for us to believe in God. Those who limit "the word of God" to a written text (the literal Bible) cannot possibly explain its "living and enduring" nature. Others attempt to constrain the ability of the Holy Spirit to what He has revealed to us, but His *revelation to man* and His *infinite deity* are certainly not one and the same. Even the sacredness of what God *has* revealed necessarily implies certain aspects that exceed human understanding.

God has only told us what He wants us to know of Him (or His Son, or His Spirit), which is what creates this aura of mystery which surrounds Him. He has the right to limit to us information concerning Him, but this does not mean He has withheld from us what we need to know. As Moses declared, "The secret things belong to the LORD our God, but the things {He has} revealed belong to us and to our sons forever" (Deuteronomy 29:29). That which is revealed *by* God is sacred *to* God; yet we still do not have a comprehensive picture of the Sacred God. Anyone who says that he "knows God" can only know what God has *revealed* to him; he cannot know anything beyond this. God's holiness prevents us from knowing anything more than what He has chosen to disclose. (I want to clarify: *we* do not create or perpetuate God's mysteriousness—*He* does.) This is part of what makes God and those things associated with Him so intriguing and attractive to us. He is real and genuine, but He is mysterious. We can have fellowship with Him, but there is much to that relationship that we simply cannot yet know.

Unfortunately, some emphasize the unexplainable mysteriousness of God at the expense of that which He has disclosed. They may be intrigued with miracles—real and imagined—but they do not always obey the God behind all genuine miracles. They want to see displays of God's power, but may be unwilling to submit themselves to the message confirmed *by* that power (Mark 16:20; Hebrews 2:4). Having fixated on the signs, they miss the substance of why the Sacred God has revealed Himself *in* those signs.

Similarly, some may be magnetically drawn to the gospel of Christ, but not necessarily for the right reasons. Many have tried, in their own ways, to solve the mystery of Christ (or what they consider to *be* the mystery) because they are unwilling to accept what has been clearly revealed. In seeking to understand what cannot *be* known, they imply that they are unsatisfied with what God *wants* them to know. They say things like, "I simply want to know God better," but what they mean is that they are unhappy with God's decision to withhold information from them, and that their quest is to extract from God more than what He intended to reveal.

On the other end of the spectrum are those who see no mystery at all in God's Word, and therefore rob it of its sacredness. Such people have approached the Bible so logically, analytically, and pedantically that it has been reduced, in their eyes, to a mere clinical study of ancient texts and languages. Thus, the Bible has all the intrigue of, say, a wiring diagram for a new car. The Bible is a "sacred" text to them only because it came from heaven, not because questions remain. There is nothing to solve because there was nothing unknown in the first place which higher education and a doctorate in theology could not make known to them. They have heaven all figured out because they are among the elite and the enlightened.

So then, we have people on either end of the spectrum: those who are trying desperately and often fancifully to *solve* the mystery, and those who are convinced that there really was nothing mysterious to begin with. Both positions assume too much and believe too little; both positions do not express *faith* in God, but actually rely on human ability. The first position assumes that every heavenly secret must be exposed, and that this should be the chief endeavor of Christians everywhere. The second position assumes that higher knowledge and exhaustive dissertations will overcome all the obstacles to knowing God. Thus, we have fanciful dreamers (people who are caught up with intrigue—and perhaps little else) and modern-day Gnostics (people who have reduced salvation to the mere possession of human knowledge).[2]

Somewhere in the middle is the voice of reason, the person who is not seeking to solve the unsolvable nor deny that a mystery does exist. While some are trying to *remove* the sacred, there are others—like you, I trust—who are content with the fact that many questions concerning the heavenly will never be answered in this life. Why then did God leave us with unanswered questions? In order to make a point: we are *not* complete here and were *never* meant to be complete here. We *are* to study the Word in order to present ourselves approved to God (2 Timothy 2:15), but never with a smug anticipation of knowing all that the Holy Spirit knows. We will spend the rest of this book investigating how we *are* to live as seekers of the sacred, but we simply cannot know for certain what God has not told us. Even our profound understanding of this present world is inherently dwarfed by our inability to understand God and His world. On the other hand, God does not need to answer all of our questions or satisfy all our curiosities in order to be God. Faith in God means that He does not have to explain everything to us.

God is not a mystery that will *never* be solved, however. By doing what He says and living as He has prescribed, someday He will reveal Himself to us as He actually is. As Paul said, "For now we see in a mirror dimly, but then face to face; now I know in part, but then I will know fully just as

I also have been fully known" (1 Corinthians 13:12). This will not make those things or God Himself any less sacred, but will give us an entirely new appreciation and definition *for* what is sacred.

Escape from the World

God wants us to appreciate the sacredness—and even the mystery—of His existence and His Word. This, of course, requires a great deal of our time and energy in order to overcome the unrelenting allure—or the incessant bombardment—of the world. The gravitational-like attraction of the secular life is extremely powerful and not easily overcome. For example, in order for a rocket to leave the earth's gravitational field (a.k.a. "escape velocity"), it must travel over 25,000 miles per hour. That requires a tremendous amount of power (thrust) and energy (fuel). Even though men have learned how to produce such power, no man is capable of producing that power *himself.* No man, no matter how strong or zealous he might be, is powerful enough to escape the earth's gravity *alone.*

This example is analogous to the type of power and energy that is required for a person to overcome the pull and draw of the secular life so as to live in a spiritual life with God. This is power and strength that you and I are *unable to exert* on our own, since it supersedes that which we are even capable of producing. This does not mean that this is a hopeless pursuit; however, it means that we need God to help us, and that we are unable to be helped by anyone or anything else. God's grace—whatever power He provides or blessing He extends to us for the sake of our salvation—is what we must have in order to overcome the satanic, worldly clutch on our souls. Think about this idea with regard to what Peter said (2 Peter 1:2-4):

> Grace and peace be multiplied to you in the knowledge of God and of Jesus our Lord; seeing that His divine power has granted to us everything pertaining to life and godliness, through the true knowledge of Him who called us by His own glory and excellence. For by these He has granted to us His precious and magnificent promises, so that by them you may become partakers of the divine nature, having escaped the corruption that is in the world by lust.

23

God's "divine power" is able to extract us from the grip of the secular world and bring us safely into the realm of spiritual life with Him. Through His Word, His power, His knowledge, His glory, and His excellence, God provides us the ability to be "partakers of the divine nature, having escaped the corruption" of this secular world.

How important is it that we escape this corruption? This world is temporary and offers no refuge for the soul. Every person who does *not* seek after the sacred becomes engulfed in the quagmire of the world: all such people forfeit their souls and gain nothing in exchange. Or as John declared, "The world is passing away, and also its lusts; but the one who does the will of God lives forever" (1 John 2:17). Given this, it is extremely important that we escape the destruction of this world.

God does not want us merely to escape the world and its lusts. He wants us to find refuge and spiritual completion in *Him*. These two things, then, must go hand in hand: in order to escape the world's corruption, one must become a seeker of the sacred. Put another way: the *only way* to escape the destruction of this world (and everyone who chooses to remain identified with it) is to find salvation and fellowship in the Lord Himself. There is no other way to escape one's total and irretrievable loss; there is no other way to gain total and absolute *fulfillment* of everything one's soul needs and craves. There is no heaven but God's heaven.

Before we go on dreaming about heaven, however, we must be realistic as to how to get there. We will not achieve heaven by wallowing in the human-inspired thinking and gratification of this world. The apostle Peter wrote, "As obedient children, do not be conformed to the former lusts which were yours in your ignorance, but like the Holy One who called you, be holy yourselves also in all your behavior; because it is written, 'You shall be holy, for I am holy'" (1 Peter 1:14-16). This means: you must be *seeking the sacred*—not just something sacred, but the One who *defines* sacredness.

You must seek after God Himself.

Endnotes

2 Gnosticism refers to a first-century philosophy that taught that the route to true enlightenment was through secret and privileged knowledge which only certain people (Gnostics) possessed. It assumed that those who do not know the secrets of God cannot partake in the salvation of God. (It is widely believed that the First Epistle of John, for one, was a direct rebuttal to this elitist doctrine.) Gnosticism has since been repackaged in many different forms, and seems to be alive and well today in seminaries and theological academia.

CHAPTER TWO

Peering into the Sacred Realm

"My kingdom is not of this world. ...My kingdom is not of this realm."
John 18:36

Imagine yourself going into one of those large home improvement stores (like Lowe's or The Home Depot) and looking for a certain device—say, a drill press. The natural place to go in the store for something like that would be the power tool department. You would not be able to find such a thing in the lighting department, plumbing, or flooring. Your search for a specific *tool* would require you to search in a specific *department*. (We should also mention that you first have to be in the right *store*. I would not recommend looking for a drill press in a Rite-Aid drugstore or a Kroger's grocery.) And even when you find the right department, your search is still not over; you have only narrowed it down considerably.

This same process is applied to the search for whatever spiritual treasure one desires to discover. After knowing *what* it is one wants, and having the right details and disposition to *engage* in the search, one must know where to go to *find* it. A person seeking Eastern mysticism ought to visit a Buddhist temple, or travel to India, Thailand, or Japan. One seeking fulfillment in the Mormon religion ought to immerse himself in the writings of its founder, Joseph Smith—i.e., the Book of Mormon, *Doctrine and Covenants*, *The Pearl of Great Price*—as well as membership at a Mormon Temple. But one seeking after Christ and His salvation must look into the Bible in order to discover where He dwells: the realm of the sacred.

Just as you will never find a drill press in a grocery store or in the paint department of a hardware store, so you will not find Jesus in the secular world. By this, I do not mean that Jesus' *presence* is not all around us (I will discuss this later). I mean that if you wish to know Jesus—to *find* Him, *commune* with Him, have *fellowship* with Him—you must ascend in faith to the world where He dwells—*His* world. Remember what the angels said at Christ's empty tomb: "He is not here, for He has risen, just as He said" (Matthew 28:6). This implied more than the obvious fact that Jesus had resurrected from the dead; it anticipated His ascension to an existence that transcends both physical life and the death to which physical life eventually succumbs. (His *literal* ascension came weeks later, but the spiritual implication still remains.)

If we are looking for the Christ today, we cannot look among living men or the tombs of the dead—"He is not here." We will not find Him in church buildings, our personal sanctuaries, or in some esoteric communion with nature—He is not there. We will not find Him in sermons, Bible classes, spiritual counseling, or psychotherapy sessions—He is not there, either.

If you wish to seek after Christ, you must turn your spiritual eyesight upward, to "the right hand of God," for that is "where Christ is" (Acts 2:33; Colossians 3:1-3). His kingdom is not an earthly one (John 18:36); His church has no physical headquarters (Hebrews 13:14); His gospel is not a man-made message (Galatians 1:11-12). Christ is exactly where He is *supposed* to be: at the center of all power, authority, and majesty. However, He has promised us that He will bring us to where He is, but only *if we seek after Him now.* "In My Father's house are many dwelling places," He said. "... if it were not so, I would have told you; for I go to prepare a place for you. If I go and prepare a place for you, I will come again and receive you to Myself, that where I am, there you may be also" (John 14:1-3).

Before you or I ever can find God (for Jesus Christ *is* God), we must have an understanding of the realm in which He lives. I'm not talking about a physical interpretation of a place called "heaven" with winged angels hovering and whispering above streets of literal gold. I'm talking about the *spiritual realm* in which His life, presence, and activity are real and factual, a realm not defined by men's wishful delusions. We must have an understanding of the *sacred*, for everything about God Himself and everything about His world *is* sacred. It is worth our time to explore more precisely what this means.

The Secular and the Sacred Realms

The secular world and the spiritual world are certainly related, but are independently defined. "Secular" comes from the Latin *saecularis*, which refers to the known or present (visible) world. It encompasses all the different spheres and tangents of human existence which (initially) appear to have nothing to do with spiritual concerns. This includes one's blood relations, marital obligations, family life, occupation, recreational activities, trips to the grocery store, excursions to the coffee shop, the society in which one lives, etc. It is true that these things may be *influenced* or *conditioned* by one's spiritual beliefs, but the fact of the matter is that more often than not these are simply products of and functions within the physical world.

One's association with the secular is limited to his walk upon this earth. Physical death severs all ties with this visible, physical world (cf. Ecclesiastes 12:7; Hebrews 9:27). Nothing from the secular ever enters into the spiritual world, except for one's own record of his life *in* the physical world (2 Corinthians 5:10). "...Flesh and blood cannot inherit the kingdom of God; nor does the perishable inherit the imperishable" (1 Corinthians 15:50).

The spiritual world is the nonphysical, intangible, invisible domain of life which we know of and participate in—deliberately, through faith; intuitively, through our consciousness— but cannot experience directly. The ancients referred to this realm as the "third heaven" (cf. 2 Corinthians 12:1-4): the first heaven is the earthly atmosphere; the second, the cosmos; the third, where God dwells. One's association with the spiritual world *begins* in the physical domain, but most certainly transcends this existence. To live in God's world while still living on this earth requires one to follow after God's heart, submit to God's will, and obey God's commandments (1 John 2:4-6; 5:2-3).

Life in the secular realm is not necessarily defined by moral connotations. Just because we call something "secular" does not mean we automatically refer to it as evil or immoral. A basketball game is a secular pastime—not an evil affair (unless *your* team is losing?), but simply something non-religious or non-spiritual. We could say the same about going to college, buying tires for the car, painting the house, and a great deal of other non-religious, non-spiritual, human activities. We sometimes refer to these things as "mundane" (from Latin, *mundus*, "world"), which literally refers to any ordinary earthly activity.

While secular does not immediately imply anything evil, a person whose life is irreligious—void of any participation in or reverence for the spiritual—is, from God's perspective, an evil person. Someone might find this to be a rather harsh judgment, but it is merely a factual observation. A person does not have to be a thief and a murderer to be evil; he just has to be *unlike* God. In God's sight, any thought or behavior which is not *like* Him is opposed to Him (Matthew 12:30; Romans 8:5-9; 1 John 5:12; et al). Furthermore, one's evil life is the result of that person's own decision to *be* exclusively secular and not godly. No one is forced to be one way or the other; both godliness and ungodliness are choices, not impositions. It is true, one's circumstances or environment may *incline* a person to choose one over the other, but the ultimate choice is still one's own. Therefore, there is nothing judgmental in simply acknowledging someone else's own decision.

A secular person is one who has his heart set upon this life, as opposed to having his heart set upon heaven (Matthew 6:19-21). He is a man of the world, as opposed to a disciple of Christ and a "man of God" (2 Timothy 3:17). One man has his vision, future, and completion in this physical life; the other, in the life to come, that is, in God. We might say one man's *identity* is entirely defined through the visible world, whereas the other's identity is ultimately defined in the invisible heaven (Philippians 3:20).

The comparison between spiritual and secular persons—for our discussion, between the man (or woman) of God and the man (or woman) of the world—is not a passive one. These two people share completely different perspectives, pursue completely different interests, and operate with completely different objectives. Of course, both people live on the same planet, breathe the same air, may enjoy the same sunsets, and may even be of the same family. In the context of our present discussion, however, they are aliens and strangers to each other, regardless of any blood-ties or marriage commitments. The spiritual person follows the heart of God, whereas the secular person follows the heart of man. This "heart of man" involves a spirit of antagonism against whatever is heavenly and spiritual (Galatians 5:16-17).

The World of Satan

As a side note, even though Satan and his league of dark angels are technically regarded as "spiritual" (in nature and by definition), we are not lumping him (or them) in with the heavenly realm of God in any way. There is simply no agreement between the two realms and we should be careful to make a clear distinction between them. At the same time, we ought to be realistic about Satan's power. Just because we pledge our allegiance to Christ does not make Satan disappear or make us immune to his influence. Such influence may be direct (as when he actively preys upon spiritually-minded people; 1 Peter 5:8) or indirect (as when he simply promotes godlessness and deceit through others; 2 Corinthians 11:13-15). As Paul wrote, "For our struggle is not against flesh and blood, but against the rulers, against the powers, against the world forces of this darkness, against the spiritual forces of wickedness in the heavenly places" (Ephesians 6:12). Satan, though he is a spiritual being, heads the mentality of the world and all that it includes, whereas Jesus is the reason for all that is godly and just. As active as Satan is, God is even more so. Let us never assume that because Satan's activity seems so much more prolific in our physical world, he eclipses all the work of the Holy Spirit among men. Let us never assume, either, that Satan and Jesus are equally-powerful opponents. This is absolutely false. Jesus has been made King over *all* powers and authorities, including Satan's (Colossians 1:15-18). This does not mean that Jesus dictates the activity of Satan's kingdom (within the secular realm), but that He most certainly limits the scope or jurisdiction of Satan's power. In other words, Jesus does not tell Satan what to do, but He does allow Satan to do only so much.

Whatever is of *man* (i.e., of human design or intent) is actually of

Satan, since "the whole world lies in the power of the evil one [Satan]" (1 John 5:19). I'm not talking about harmless, non-moral ideas of men, like the invention of an internal combustion engine or the making of a beautiful quilt. I'm talking about the *exaltation* of man through his thoughts, ideas, or inventions. Satan is the driving influence behind all self-exaltation and self-serving arrogance. This does not mean Satan is *responsible* for one's sins (as in, "The devil made me do it!"); it means that Satan *inspires, tempts,* and *coaxes* one to sin. In *this* context, even an internal combustion engine can work as a tool of Satan if it tempts man to place more confidence in his own creation than in his Creator. Likewise, a beautiful quilt—while benign or spiritually-neutral in itself—can invoke the smug arrogance of Satan if the person who made it praises her own talent and ability rather than giving thanks to the One who *gave* her these.

This spirit-of-man/power-of-Satan relationship manifests itself in passages like Matthew 16:21-23, where Peter challenged Jesus' prediction of His own death, burial, and resurrection. Jesus spoke with a view toward the spiritual world; Peter responded with a disappointing secular perspective. Jesus' heart was completely in heaven; Peter's heart, while striving to accept the heavenly, was nonetheless susceptible to Satan's spell. Thus, while Jesus spoke directly to *Peter,* He actually implicated *Satan:* "Get behind Me, Satan! You are a stumbling block to Me; for you are not setting your mind on God's interests, but man's." God's interests (the sacred heavenly realm) are completely contrary to Satan's interests (the worldly realm of physical man). There is no cooperation or shared allegiances between the two. As Jesus said before Pontius Pilate, "My kingdom is not of this world. ...My kingdom is not of this realm" (John 18:36). Jesus also said of those who follow Him, "They are not of the world, even as I am not of the world" (John 17:16).

The secular "world" (as Jesus and John used the term, John 15:18ff and 1 John 2:15-16, respectively) breeds, feeds, and supports its own. "They [those who malign the doctrine of Christ—MY WORDS] are from the world; therefore they speak as from the world, and the world listens to them" (1 John 4:5). The "world" hates God as well as anyone who is associated with God through His Son, Jesus Christ. Anyone whose heart is fixed upon this world is "hostile" toward God; anyone who chooses friendship of the world over fellowship with God makes himself to be an enemy of God (Romans

8:5-9; James 4:4). The heavenly realm of God is the holy sanctuary of the sacred; the godless, secular world of man (really, of Satan) is the God-forsaken crypt of the sacrilegious.

God's Sacred Distance from Us

Of course, with God being so holy—and ourselves being so imperfect and inadequate on our own—there is a certain sense of *detachment* automatically implied with respect to our relationship with Him. It is not so much that God is remote from us distance-wise, as though literally a certain number of miles or light-years from us, for we are told that God is "over all and through all and in all" (Ephesians 4:6). Technically, it is impossible to escape God's unseen presence or for Him to be too far away from us. We cannot apply earthly measurements, time constraints, or dimensional boundaries to a Personage who is not bound or even explained by such attributes.

"Detachment" is meant in a spiritual sense, that is, in God's *sacred distance* from our corrupted humanity. In other words, there is a difference between God's omnipresence in His Creation and one's having fellowship with God. His power and energy (His "presence" in this respect, He being the source of all life and sustenance) are what make our world functional and alive. His omnipresence does not require any submission or even acknowledgement on our part; it is simply a fact of our existence—really, of His supernatural involvement with whatever He has created. Fellowship, however, *demands* our submission and allegiance; it is not a given fact, but is contingent upon our *moral response* to God's offer of grace and mercy. Certainly fellowship offers far greater enjoyment and rewards than the first; however, such fellowship is removed from us if we choose to remain defiant sinners since God can have no fellowship with sin (Isaiah 59:1-2; 2 Corinthians 6:14-15). Fellowship, in the context of our discussion, involves an intimate communion between two persons based upon common goals, common effort, and individual participation. You can see how this is impossible between people who live in rebellion to God (regardless of how subtle that rebellion is) and the holiness of God Himself. No one can have fellowship with God who chooses instead to embrace the lusts and behaviors of a satanic world.

We are sinful people, and because this physical world has become corrupted by our sins, this realm is not a proper dwelling place for God and (left to ourselves) we are not a proper people for God's fellowship. In ancient times, God *did* allow Israel to build temples to carry out Jehovah worship, but not because God has need of such things. King Solomon, in the benediction of his grand temple, admitted this (1 Kings 8:27), as did much later the apostle Paul (Acts 17:24-25). God allowed men to construct a temple in His honor only to symbolize His presence among His people, contingent upon their moral fitness. Centuries later, when Israel and then Judah sank into the quagmire of apostasy, God removed His glory from this temple and had it leveled to the ground (by King Nebuchadnezzar of Babylon, 586 BC).

God has come to us more recently in the "tabernacle" of His Son (cf. John 1:14), but this world was not worthy of such glory. We crucified the Son of God—every one of us who has sinned against the Lord had a hand in this—and rejected God's fellowship. Contrary to what Satan had led us to believe, we gained nothing worthwhile in the process. God is still God, for He cannot change and is incorruptible; but we, having fallen from His glory (Romans 3:23) and died in our moral transgressions (Ephesians 2:1-3), gave away everything that was once good about us. Having broken fellowship with God, we were left a broken people. Left to ourselves, we had absolutely *no hope*.

Thankfully, God is willing to extend mercy and grace to save us from our self-inflicted demise. (Divine mercy saves us from deserved condemnation; divine grace gives us undeserved salvation.) Thus, God has given us an Intercessor—Jesus Christ—in order to bridge the gap between our pathetic, ruined state and God's perfect holiness. As the apostle Paul wrote (Colossians 1:19-23),

> For it was the Father's good pleasure for all the fullness to dwell in Him, and through Him to reconcile all things to Himself, having made peace through the blood of His cross; through Him, I say, whether things on earth or things in heaven. And although you were formerly alienated and hostile in mind, engaged in evil deeds, yet He has now

33

reconciled you in His fleshly body through death, in order
to present you before Him holy and blameless and beyond
reproach—if indeed you continue in the faith firmly
established and steadfast, and not moved away from the
hope of the gospel that you have heard...

What this tells us is: God the Father is behind all that God the Son
has accomplished; He has desired our fellowship from the beginning. Those
who are not "in Christ" are *alienated* from God, even hostile to Him; if we
are *in* Christ then we are brought into holy fellowship with God through
the voluntary, effective sacrifice *of* Christ (Romans 8:6-9). Because of His
unfaltering obedience, atoning sacrifice on the cross, and His Father's full
authority, Christ is able to make all who "call upon His name" (Acts 2:21)
"holy and blameless and beyond reproach." What *that* means is: we are,
because of such mercy and grace, able to enjoy spiritual fellowship with the
Father. Not a single one of us is worthy to receive such privilege, but anyone
and everyone who believes in and obeys Him *can* receive such fellowship.

Such fellowship, however, depends upon our appropriate response
to His offer of mercy and grace. As Paul said, our presentation to God
through Christ's mediation is possible only "if indeed you continue in the
faith firmly established and steadfast, not moved away from the hope of the
gospel...." God's love for us is unconditional—He loves us regardless of
whether or not we respond rightly to Him—but His salvation is conditional.
Grace is a free gift to us, but the failure to prepare our heart to receive it—
to fail to act as proper recipients of God's love—forfeits all the benefits of
Christ's saving grace. Let us never think that spiritual salvation is accidental,
automatic, or assumed.

Unfortunately, even though we are blessed with spiritual fellowship
through Christ's intercession, the fact remains that we are still *human*. We
are still flawed, less-than-perfect, inadequate creatures living in a profane,
unholy, and corrupted world. We still must combat the temptations and
unholy passions of a world infected with greed, selfishness, and ungodly
appetites. Even on our best days, our goodness is limited to "days," not
months, years, or decades. It is inevitable: given enough time, even the
very best of us will succumb to the daily assault of Satan's influences. In all

likelihood, we are even unaware of how unholy—and therefore, *unsacred*—we are simply by dwelling in the midst of such ungodliness. This is why we must humbly and regularly petition Jesus Christ for the forgiveness of our sins—not only sins we acknowledge, but even those which escape our detection.

In sharp contrast, God in all His glory is surrounded by nothing less than flawless angels, fantastic heavenly beings, and perfect symmetry, beauty, and architecture. There are no pockets of evil or dark corners in His sacred world, "no variation or shifting shadow" (James 1:17). His world knows no erosion, decay, deterioration, or death. There are no time-worn features of the passing of countless ages, since there is no time in His world and nothing there ever grows old. Likewise, there are no evidences of physical decline or the weakening of strength or glory, since it is a spiritual realm in which nothing physical or man-made exists. We have a difficult time trying to fathom a world in which everything and everyone is perfect, since *our* world is filled with limitations and imperfections. The sacred realm of God is so far removed from us that it exceeds our earthbound ability to properly understand it, much less appraise its worth. God Himself is so beautiful, powerful, unique, and transcendent that we struggle with even trying to relate to Him.

For this very reason, a person may shrug in resignation or give up in despair over the idea of spending the rest of his life seeking the sacred. "If God is so different from us, then why bother?" he might ask himself. Indeed, God *is* so different from us: this is what makes Him "God" and underscores the fact that we are *not* God (or anything resembling divinity). Another person might think in another direction: "Regardless of how holy or Sacred God is, I know that I need salvation, and so for that reason I will consent to His wishes." This person consents to seek after the sacred, but only because he desires to save his own neck, and not for the joy of fellowship with God Himself.

Both perspectives fall short of the appropriate one. First of all, God is not just "different" from us: He is the absolute *perfection* of us. If we could remove every one of our human limitations—of time, strength, ability, authority, knowledge, etc.—then we *would* look like God. Since we are made in God's image (Genesis 1:27), we have the potential of "looking" like Him—not by our own power, but certainly with our deliberate consent. (This does not mean we would *be* God, since He is the Source of our perfection and therefore is exempted from any challenge or comparison; cf. 1 Corinthians 15:27-28.) Thus, in seeking after the Sacred God, we are really seeking after the epitome of what it means to *exist*, since no one's existence is perfected apart from Him. In seeking Him, we are not pursuing a mere intriguing distraction from the monotony of mundane life. Rather, we are allowed to glimpse at the Source of life, the Perfection of love, the Wellspring of all that is good and beneficial, and the Priceless Treasure of all that is special and worthwhile. God is all of these things: His sacredness *guards* these things, not to prevent us from experiencing them, but so that these qualities and gifts will never be diminished in the slightest sense. In other words, when it is time for us to behold Him face to face, we will behold Him in His absolute fullness. As we *behold* Him in all His glory, we also will be entirely *filled* with this glory and thus brought to absolute completion.

The other perspective ("What does it matter how 'sacred' God is? I need Him for salvation, so I must oblige...") fails to appreciate the intimate *love* that God has for all those who are made "in His image." Certainly there exists a sacred distance, so to speak, between Him and us right now, but that does not mean that we cannot *draw near* to Him. (We will expound upon this thought more thoroughly in a later chapter.) Obedience is necessary in order for love to have any *meaning*; likewise, love is necessary in order for one to obey for the right *reasons*. Our obedience to God is not a mechanical, pragmatic response to our need for salvation; rather, it is supposed to be a joyful expression of our tremendous gratitude for *being able to have fellowship with Him*. God is worth our obedience; His sacredness is worth seeking. To obey Him for any other reason is to fail to understand why He has offered us salvation in the first place. He does not merely want to rescue us from our demise: *He wants us to be with Him.*

This is the crowning emphasis of our search for the sacred. We have an indescribably wonderful God who is fascinating, captivating, mysterious, and transcendent—and who has invited us to live forever in His perfect, sacred realm. This gracious God has also promised us that if we *do* seek after Him, we will not be disappointed in the least, nor will we regret for a moment whatever losses must be incurred for such an existence. In the end, not only will our search be entirely fulfilled—not only will we have escaped all the pain and profanity of this secular world—but we will be with *Him*.

CHAPTER THREE

Engaging in the Search

O God, You are my God; I shall seek You earnestly; my soul thirsts for You, my flesh yearns for You, in a dry and weary land where there is no water.
Psalm 63:1

Have you ever lost something that, well, you didn't care that you lost? In other words, the lost thing was of such little value, it wasn't worth finding. All of us have lost business cards, telephone numbers, mementos, combs, loose change, and things like these. Few of us give such losses much thought. We may be irritated over our benign irresponsibility, but the objects are easily replaceable and never meant much to us in the first place. To engage in an aggressive search for any of these simply is not worth the time and effort.

However, when something is of value to us, the situation is much different. One might say that the intensity of the search is directly proportional to that which is being sought. As the value increases, so the search intensifies. "Value" is not always measured by monetary worth; some things are valuable simply because we crave them so badly. Such things—though possibly small and insignificant to someone else—might be extremely valuable (as in important or gratifying) to the one who appraises them highly. For example, a few months ago I found in my change an old penny—a 1918 Lincoln wheat cent. You don't find one of *those* everyday! I know it's just a penny, a small scrap of metal to someone else. But to me, a lifelong amateur coin enthusiast, it was quite a treasure! Shortly afterward, however, *I lost it*—I simply could not remember where I had put it. My family still snickers and rolls their eyes as they recall me searching frantically through the wardrobe, dresser, closet, cupboards, bathrooms, and anywhere else that I might have dropped it or set it down. I spent an entire hour frantically searching for a penny—at least, that's how *they* saw it. To me, I was searching for a special and nostalgic piece of American history. I finally did find it, thankfully (it was, um, in my pants pocket), and was quite relieved.

Now that coin sits in a pile of other old coins I have found in my change and elsewhere. The coin was important because it was *old* (and therefore irreplaceable) and because it was *rare*, but it was more important that I knew where it *was* rather than to make it a special part of my life. Isn't that how we all are at times? We may be more interested in finding something just to know where it *is* rather than to incorporate it into our lives. Put another way: we may have a strong emotional attachment to something (or someone)—not always because of what it *is* (like an old penny), but because of what it *represents* to us (a rare, irreplaceable treasure)—but this may be the extent of that attachment. We do not always want to have a *relationship* with the new-found thing we had lost. It's hard to have a relationship, for example, with an old coin; there are some insurmountable limitations to such an object that hinder anything *more* than an emotional or sentimental affection.

In another example, suppose you had lost contact with a dear family who helped care for you as a child—a couple you had not seen for 20 or 30 years. Due to the advantage of the Internet, however, you are able to locate them and establish a place of meeting. Finally you see them—my, how everyone has changed!—and you sit down to coffee to talk. You share at length your times together as well as where you are now in your lives. After your tearful good-byes, however, you realize that there is little else that will become of your friendship. You had nothing in common but your past, a relatively brief overlapping of your lives' paths; you are unable to build upon what you had once shared together. You and your rediscovered family are, for all intents and purposes, estranged people. Nonetheless, you may feel a great deal of emotional satisfaction in simply knowing *where they are*, and that they are doing well.

Perhaps some of these thoughts help to illustrate some perspectives concerning one's search for the sacred. First, sufficient admiration and respect for God is required to engage in the search at all: He is worth the search; His fellowship is not something we can afford to "lose." If the intensity of the search is proportional to the value of the thing "lost," then this makes our search for intimate fellowship with God—because His fellowship is the most valuable experience and existence in all of Creation—the most active, aggressive, and all-encompassing search of our entire lives.

Second, God cannot be merely important to us because there is a void in our lives, like trying to fill a void in our coin collection. Jesus used a parable of a lost coin (Luke 15:8-10) to describe the intensity of His search for *us* who are lost (i.e., severed from His fellowship), but the point of that illustration was to highlight the active, persistent nature *of* that search, not to reduce our worth to Him to a monetary value. In the parable, the coin was extremely valuable to the woman who lost it; likewise, we are extremely valuable—priceless and irreplaceable!—to God. The woman's aggressive search for that coin was not just because she had a void in her coin collection; she sought the coin because it was meaningful and significant to her. Thus, God is not a "lost coin" to us, nor are we "lost coins" to Him. His search for us involves all the business and focus of heaven; our search for Him ought to encompass our best efforts and greatest resources.

Third, we cannot search for God only to know where He is, so to speak. I believe some get frustrated when they think they've "located" God, and now the search that was supposed to last a lifetime and to which they had devoted so much time and energy is already *over*. Now there is nothing left to do; they know where God is, and now they need to search for something or someone else. Granted, there is a certain amount of satisfaction they experience in having discovered Him, but they are not interested in pursuing Him any further. In other words, they were interested in *finding* God, but they were not interested in having an intimate, lifelong, ever-deepening *relationship* with Him. God is tossed onto the pile of other lost-and-now-found treasures, but He is not necessarily more important than any of them.

On the other hand, God is not seeking *us* only so that we can be found, and so He can know where we are. We are not an elusive catch, or a runaway favorite pet, or an escaped convict to Him. We are His *children*, and He cares for us more than we could ever comprehend in this life. He has given up His own dearest treasure—His Son—in order to find us and bring us back to Him. We were created to live with Him forever: we were never meant to be lost; He was never meant to be abandoned. Imagine losing a dear child to some horrific monster—a child molester, torturer, and cannibal all in one—and this is much closer to what God feels for every soul that is seduced by Satan to follow *him* rather than to remain with the Father of Life. No, God's search for us is not a passive, obligatory one. He does not simply want to know where we will be for eternity; rather, He wants us *in the closest fellowship ever possible* with Him, in His own "house," forever and ever. This is the God who is searching for us; this is also the God we ought to be seeking.

Who Is Lost (and Who Is Not)

This chapter's focus is on the nature of that search for God. Just as a person must read the rules of a game before playing it, so we must know what is expected in our search before engaging in it. To do so properly requires a clarification of the objectives, methods, and perspective of the search itself. (In the next chapter, we will discuss more in detail the characteristics of the One for whom we are searching.)

We must understand first that we are not searching for God because He is *lost* or because He needs to be *found* in order to be God. We are not trying to plaster a poster of God's "face" onto a utility pole; we're not assuming the role of a search-and-rescue party, as though we ourselves are already safe and secure but are now looking for someone who is in distress. No, *we* are the ones who are lost without God. We are seekers of the sacred only because we are nothing *without* the sacred; yet regardless of what happens to *us*, God is still God.

It is not as though the roles are reversed, either—that is, it is not as though God is the divine Search Party and we are the missing hikers or seamen or flight crew. We have not fallen off the radar; God has not misplaced us. He knows exactly where we are—He always has and always will. If we are "lost," it is because we have failed to be found; we have deliberately foiled our own rescue; we have sabotaged our own salvation. Thus, anyone who is "lost" has not disappeared from God's all-seeing vision, but has purposely or negligently wandered away from "the Shepherd and Guardian" of our souls (cf. 1 Peter 2:25). Our search, then, is for ourselves more than anything. I don't mean that generically, as though "Our search is for people everywhere" because it's not: on the contrary, it is intensely private and personal. We are not searching for God on behalf of others or "people everywhere." We are searching for God because *each one of us personally and individually* needs to "discover" Him in order to join in fellowship with Him.

We must realize, too, that our search is not some "touchy-feely" experience that we "sense" through yoga exercises, chanting, burning incense, and maybe some so-called transcendental meditation. Our God is not some divine fakir, swami, or mystical guru with a turban wrapped about His head; He is not "discovered" by trying to read something in the lining up of the planets or the lines on someone's hands. Crystal balls, tarot cards, palm readings, and psychic mediums are useless in searching for the sacred. In fact, God has specifically condemned any appeals to spiritism, mysticism, or sorcery in an attempt to obtain secret information or a portal to future events (cf. Deuteronomy 18:10-12).[3] One who seeks after anything through demonic or illicit means manifests unbelief in God. A person cannot seek after the sacred through unsacred means.

Our search for God, then, must be real, logical, and practical. It cannot be a search that works only for *you*; it must be a search that works for *any* person and is qualified by God Himself. It must also be *scriptural*: using the Bible to discover God is not optional but is an absolute requirement. In fact, we can know nothing *factual* about God *except* through Scripture. Everything else remains conjecture and opinion. Much of that conjecture and opinion may be itself the product of long-held traditions, predetermined agendas, and subjective "This-is-what-I-want-God-to-look-like" expectations. We all have these to begin with and they never disappear entirely; however, we must do our best to abandon these as much as possible. We will never seriously or aggressively search for God if in the back of our mind we think we've already "discovered" Him (as we *want* to discover Him, not as He really is).

Resistance and Resignation

Not everyone appreciates the value of knowing God, however—much less of discovering Him. While this is a common problem, it is nonetheless unwarranted and terribly sad. After all that God has done to make Himself available to each one of us, why would anyone forfeit such an opportunity? The fact that the Creator is regularly and carelessly rejected by most of His highest creation must cause Him pain and grief beyond description.

Nonetheless, many simply refuse to make a connection with God. He is useful, they surmise, for granting absolution, receiving prayers, or rescuing them during times of desperation, but getting to know God on a more intimate level is not on most people's agendas. Some do not care; others are oblivious to the opportunity; still others are so intoxicated with their self-serving lives that they refuse to abandon them. Even some who call themselves Christians may not be really interested in knowing God on anything more than a surface, clinical, "religious" level.

A brief examination of some specific excuses for failing to seek after the sacred would be appropriate here. Some feel that their lack of religious education hinders them from even participating in the search. God would never want to enter into anything deeper than an "acquaintance" relationship with them, they suppose, because they do not have the right credentials. They have never been to seminary, do not have a Doctor of Divinity (DD) degree, never attended a so-called "Christian" college, are not ordained, etc. God is only concerned, they reason, with the academic intercourse of scholars, rabbis, and priests; the only reason He listens to laity is because of clergy. A related excuse might be that, because the official clergy *does* exist (I'm using others' terminology, not mine), it is unnecessary for them to pursue anything beyond a "standard" or "practical" relationship. Church officials can and will take care of more pressing details, including these people's relationships with God—that is their job! Of course, such reasoning is unfounded: God is impartial and is not interested in seminaries or divinity degrees. We are all "clothed with Christ" the same way and are put into the same spiritual body—His church (1 Corinthians 12:12; Galatians 3:26-29). From God's perspective, all who are "in Christ" are equals, regardless of worldly status or human opinions.

Another deterrent for seeking the sacred—among Christians and non-Christians alike—is a debilitating feeling of unworthiness. Guilt, both real and imagined, can reduce people to a subhuman status. Some believe they cannot overcome the tremendous power of their guilt and shame. Having accepted Satan's accusation ("You'll never be worthy enough to enjoy meaningful fellowship with God—don't bother trying!"), they meander uncomfortably through the rest of their lives on the most superficial level, never able to reconcile how God could possibly *want* an intimate relationship with *them*—yet all the while desperately hoping that God will receive them in the end. Their objective is really not seeking the sacred, but is sheer, desperate survival. They do not long for intimate fellowship with God as much as they simply do not want to be *destroyed* by Him. They fail to realize that anyone who *is* in fellowship with God has no need to fear being destroyed by Him. As John wrote, "Now, little children, abide in Him, so that when He appears, we may have confidence and not shrink away from Him in shame at His coming" (1 John 2:28). If we walk by His Spirit (Galatians 5:25), we ought not to cringe in fear at meeting God; rather, we ought to joyfully and confidently anticipate this meeting.

Then there are the critics. Ah, the critics. It is not as though these people are irreligious, always on the outside of Christ's church looking in. The outsiders are often so ignorant of spiritual matters they cannot adequately appraise what it even means to be a Christian (cf. 1 Corinthians 2:11-14). Those who pass judgment on Scripture while they themselves are ignorant *of* Scripture only make themselves look foolish—and so do those who listen to them.

No, but the dangerous ones are on the inside, critiquing—even cannibalizing—their own kind. These freely call themselves Christians; they attend church, perhaps even regularly; they may well occupy functional roles within congregations; in a denominational structure, they may be on boards or committees. Often self-appointed, self-serving, and self-sufficient, these people do not really *need* the grace of God, but feel that their mission upon earth is to evaluate and censure, if necessary, all who *do*. They are vocal, prolific, and not afraid of confrontation and controversy.

They are the newspaper columnists who chastise Christians everywhere for not embracing the social changes of the day, however perverted or counterproductive these changes might be. They are the editors of so-called "brotherhood newsletters" who strain out a gnat but swallow a camel (cf. Matthew 23:24), looking for someone to castigate in order to feel smugly pious—and sell more subscriptions. They are the outspoken ministers who are more interested in making people feel good rather than helping people be right with God. They are the church "activists" who spend their lives jumping from one bandwagon to another, always eager to support a "cause," always salivating at another opportunity to "make a difference" regardless of what that difference is or whether it is even relevant. They may be otherwise inactive members of a congregation who do little, share little, contribute little, and live small, petty spiritual lives—until someone rubs them the wrong way or some important decision needs to be made that apparently demands their immediate input. Or they may champion some underdog, victim, abusive situation, perceived injustice, etc. only as a means of gaining personal notoriety.

It gives me no pleasure to acknowledge that such people are even remotely associated with Christ's church. Nonetheless, they are in every city, every community, and every congregation. While I may at times admire their courage, tenacity, and/or outspokenness, in the context of our present discussion they pose a terrible threat to promoting a closer, more intimate fellowship with God. Yet an open, liberating, and self-disclosing relationship with God is a threat to their self-asserted opinions and independence. The last thing critics (especially professional ones) want is to lose control over those whom they critique. After all, what often drives their criticism in the first place is the insatiable desire for *control*. When one places himself completely under God's control, he (or she) no longer has to answer to the critic. When one appeals to the absolute authority of Scripture for his decisions, he no longer conforms to the opinions of others. When one places absolute confidence and trust in the love, grace, and promises of God, evaluations of the self-serving critic are irrelevant to him (1 Corinthians 4:3-5). In other words, when a person lives for God, he no longer has to live for the approval of men—and that is a maddening situation for the critic.

Jesus said, "If anyone is thirsty, let him come to Me and drink. He who believes in Me, as the Scripture said, 'From his innermost being will flow rivers of living water'" (John 7:37-38). Paul said, "Whoever believes in Him [Christ] will not be disappointed" (Romans 10:11). Peter said, "God is not one to show partiality, but in every nation the man who fears Him and does what is right is welcome to Him" (Acts 10:34-35). James said, "Draw near to God and He will draw near to you" (James 4:8). Through these inspired men, the Holy Spirit has thus stated His own position. Those who think that searching for a deeper, more meaningful relationship with God is unnecessary (or that this should be left to the clergy) are terribly mistaken. Those who feel too guilty, unworthy, or inferior to engage in a quest to discover God beyond a superficial relationship do not understand the grace of God. They do not yet know (or believe) that divine grace is more powerful than a multitude of sins. Those who cower before the self-appointed critics need to realize that it really does not matter what people say, so long as you do what *God* says. Even critics are in constant need of God's forgiveness, and we should pray that they would humble themselves before Him just as is expected of all of us (Ephesians 4:1-3).

God created us to worship Him and to thoroughly relish the experience. Thus, He seeks after and wants to be sought by "true worshipers" (cf. John 4:23-24). He wants us to spend time, energy, and even money searching for Him. He wants us to sacrifice our own comforts and temporary pleasures in order to seek Him. He wants us to put our desire—and thus our search—for Him above all other desires and searches. He promises to more than compensate all those who believe in Him. He has already proven His ability to follow through with such promises.

Methods and Procedures

Now we will turn our attention to the process itself of seeking the sacred. Seeking after deeper fellowship with God is not like seeking after anything else: it is a unique, special, and life-altering search, just as God Himself is unique, special, and life-altering. It is not like looking for your lost wallet, a nice place to live, or answers to difficult questions. It is more like finding inexpressible and irrepressible joy in the midst of a monotonous and mundane life. It is like discovering priceless wealth in the midst of one's own poverty and insignificant circumstances. It is like inheriting indescribable glory and honor in the midst of one's own humility, ridicule, and shame. It is like finding the perfect friend—one who will never be anything *but* a perfect friend—in the midst of liars, backstabbers, and hypocrites. Seeking the sacred is *like* discovering these things, but in fact it produces joy, wealth, glory, and fellowship that supersede our ability to define these things.

Of course, people utilize a variety of approaches in seeking the sacred, but the ones will not work that do not properly take into account the sacred *nature* of this search. For example, there is the "private investigator" approach: someone feels compelled—by guilt, peer pressure, a call to duty, etc.—to "look" for God, and considers himself some kind of spiritual detective. Now, we must admit, all Christians are "detectives" of sorts; we all have to do our fair share of investigation, research, critical analysis, etc. The person I'm describing, however, has taken his detective work to the extreme and thus has adopted a detached, professional approach to his work. His search is not personal, it's just business. He is not looking for intimacy or fellowship—just clues, telltale signs, and traces of secret information. His methods are clinical; his procedure, forensic; his disposition, mechanical, scientific, and dispassionate. "I'm a Christian, so therefore I must seek God," he says, but doesn't really *desire* the search, he only feels compelled to *participate* in it.

Another person may be far too *emotional* in his (or her) conception of God. God is not a distinct Divine Being, Father, or Creator, but is Someone with whom he can have a feel-good relationship, an emotional epiphany, a rhapsodic but abstract connection. Faith, to him, is a feeling, not a realistic, fact-based, demonstrable way of life. He wants euphoria, not endurance; he seeks after a spiritual high, not holiness. This person usually does not want to be bothered by facts, citations from the Bible, or definite theological constructs; he just wants to *connect* with God on an emotional level, nothing more. He is fond of gushing things like, "Isn't God an awesome God!" but what really turns him on is the rush of *awesomeness*, not necessarily living in obedience or taking up his cross (Luke 9:23).

A third person views God—and everything about God—with such

mysteriousness and intrigue that he becomes obsessed with such things. True, God *is* mysterious and intriguing; this is part of His sacred nature. It is *not* true that everything we know or learn about God has to be so mystifying and inexplicable that we simply regard Him as a complex puzzle or an elaborate enigma, and not a personable and loving Father. This person is nearly a fanatical extremist, a conspiracy theory-driven individual who cannot just accept what he discovers and enjoy it, but must uncover the great conundrum or riddle that has been posed to him through his discovery. Therefore, every news event is interpreted as a "sign from God." Every passage has some ominous, surreptitious "clue" that unlocks the secret of yet another enigmatic passage. Every spiritual conversation has (or is expected to have) some sort of cryptic "message" which he must decipher and then incorporate into his giant puzzle. He is not interested in actually finding God; he is only interested in the thrill of the search itself.

Granted, these are all extreme views, and they illustrate improper, ineffective, and inefficient ways of enjoying a realistic and enjoyable relationship with God. God is not a crime scene which needs to be labeled, dissected, examined under a microscope, and then shelved in some forensic police lab. God is not a bundle of emotions, waiting to stimulate someone to an intense level of moving, poignant affectation—and ultimately to some euphoric emotional experience—and that's it, that's all He has to offer. God is not to be reduced to a mere puzzle to be solved, leaving secret hints, textual clues, anagrams, cryptograms, and whatever else someone subjectively "sees" in Scripture and elsewhere so that He can be discovered in that sense.

God is a Divine and Holy Being, a personable and affectionate Father, as well as an omnipotent and omniscient Lord over all the heavens and earth. Looking for Him might seem daunting at first, especially when we will never see Him in His *full, expressive glory* in this lifetime. Someone says, "But Jesus was God; all we have to look for is Jesus, and we will have found God!" This is true, in a very real sense, but then, what did Jesus look like? No, I'm not talking about Jesus' physical features—shape of His face, hue of His eyes, curvature of His nose, color of His skin—but I'm referring to His *identity*, what constitutes His actual nature. Besides, Jesus has been alive forever; His incarnation is only *one aspect* of His otherwise eternal existence. "He was in the beginning with God. All things came into being through Him, and apart from Him nothing came into being that has come into being" (John 1:2-3). That says something of the omnipresent, ever-existent quality of what it means to be "God." Jesus Himself said, "Truly, truly, I say to you, before Abraham was born, I am" (John 8:58). Jesus (God) did not just "exist" before Abraham, as though He viewed existence in a linear, straight-line perspective (i.e., this person was *first*, then this other person, then further along the line, this third person, and so on). Jesus has always *been*, now *is*, and will *be* forever.

At the same time, Christ is our most familiar and visible link to the Father. As He Himself said, "He who has seen Me has seen the Father; how can you say, 'Show us the Father'?" (John 14:9). We know, then, that the Father "looks" like Jesus—that is He has His character, nature, grace, mercy, compassion for people, etc. We don't have a face to associate with God, but we have the factual, historical person of Jesus Christ to know that the way to the Father is *real* and *possible*. For this reason, Jesus said, "I am the way, and the truth, and the life; no one comes to the Father but through Me" (John 14:6). No one can seek after the sacred without submitting himself in obedient faith to Christ. There is no *other* access to the sacred.

Remember too that everything we can *truly* know about God comes from His own revealed Word. The only way we can know about the supernatural is if Someone who *is* supernatural reveals Himself to us. For example, in response to Peter's famous declaration of Jesus' identity as both "the Christ" and "the Son of the living God," Jesus admitted that "flesh and blood" (i.e., human effort) did not reveal this to Peter, but the supernatural intervention of God Himself (Matthew 16:16-17). No, God did not literally compel Peter to respond this way by placing some foreign thought in his brain. Instead, Jesus referred to the *supernatural evidence* Peter had seen: the miracles performed by Christ. Peter never would have arrived at the conclusion that he did *logically* without divine proof—nor could he. Being a natural man, Peter could not have accurate knowledge of anything or anyone supernatural without being revealed *by* the supernatural. Even Jesus said (John 14:10-12),

Do you not believe that I am in the Father, and the Father

is in Me? The words that I say to you I do not speak on My own initiative, but the Father abiding in Me does His works. Believe Me that I am in the Father and the Father is in Me; otherwise believe because of the works themselves. Truly, truly, I say to you, he who believes in Me, the works that I do, he will do also; and greater works than these he will do; because I go to the Father.

Jesus did not merely *claim* to represent the Father, He *proved* such representation by the performance of genuine, irrefutable miracles. Such power indicated the Spirit of God was with Him, since no one could perform such works apart from God's Spirit (cf. John 3:2). Likewise, Paul wrote, "...no one speaking by the Spirit of God says, 'Jesus is accursed'"—because the Spirit would never lead one to such a conclusion—"and no one can say, 'Jesus is Lord,' except by the Holy Spirit" (1 Corinthians 12:3). Thus, if *we* are going to learn of God, it must be through the supernatural evidence already provided us: miracles, heavenly teaching, and prophecies of the future, all of which are recorded and preserved in the Word of God.

Realizing Our Limitations

If one is truly sincere about seeking the sacred—that is, in seeking the Sacred God of Heaven—then he will find Him. As Paul wrote, "...He is not far from each one of us" (Acts 17:27), not in distance or accessibility. However, we cannot assume that God will look like us. We also cannot assume that God's ethereal presence is limited to a human form, or a single person's body, or a single point in history. He has chosen not to reveal Himself to us entirely, but only in a limited, discreet manner. There are good reasons for this:

☐ We cannot comprehend His glory; it is "unapproachable" for us in our present existence (cf. 1 Timothy 6:16). "The Light shines in the darkness, and the darkness did not comprehend it" (John 1:5): as enlightened as we may be, we still live in a darkened existence and cannot escape our limited perception of God.

☐ Even if we could survive the experience of gazing upon the glory and majesty of God, we would not believe our eyes; we would fail to comprehend or appreciate what we beheld. Men looked upon Jesus Christ—God in the flesh—and were not impressed with Him (cf. Isaiah 53:1-3) even though He exhibited perfect human qualities and sublime wisdom that surpasses anything the world has ever seen before or since.

☐ We are unprepared to stand in God's presence on our own. As holy and righteous as we may strive to be, we are still prone to sin and tainted with human pride. Even in our best behavior, we are still "unworthy slaves" (cf. Luke 17:10) not fit to have God share His full glory and presence with us in our present condition.

☐ God wants us to believe in His existence and power through *faith*, not through literal, visible affirmation, "for we walk by faith, not by sight" (2 Corinthians 5:7). God does not want us merely to *see* Him; He wants us to *believe* in Him even without having seen Him. Besides, it is a tremendous privilege to be able to behold God; He is not going to openly disclose Himself just because we want Him to; He has no need to prove anything to us beyond what He has already proven. He will only fully disclose Himself to us when and because we belong to Him *forever*.

☐ It would not change anything. The fact of God's supernatural, sovereign existence is not diminished in the least because we have not seen Him; likewise, we would not have to believe in His love, grace, and power any less if we *did* see Him. God's full disclosure to us would not require anything less of us as His disciples.

Nonetheless, He has made Himself available to us in the way that we *need* to know Him for the purpose of our fellowship with Him. It is enough that we have seen Jesus through the testimonies of others; it is enough that we have seen God's power demonstrated through the physical glory and earthly majesty of His Creation; it is enough that we have experienced God's presence in our lives through His divine providence, the answering of our prayers, and the guidance of His Word. Besides, God declares that His *grace* is sufficient for us, not the literal manifestation of His existence (2 Corinthians 12:9). God's grace is whatever He does for us that we cannot do for ourselves with regard to our salvation. He does not leave us empty-handed but fills our outstretched arms with grace, mercy, and the swelling anticipation of actually *someday standing in His very real and visible presence.*

Therefore, the one who asks, seeks, and knocks in his search for God will certainly not be disappointed. He will find God, since God wants to be found by those who seek Him (Hebrews 11:6).

And yet, try as we might—try as *I* might in the pages of this book—we still struggle with searching for a heavenly, supernatural, spiritual Being from our earthly, finite, and physical-based perspective. We may think that if we pray harder and study our Bibles more that pretty soon we will come to "see" Him more clearly. In one sense, this is true: through prayer, study, and fellowship with God's people, we do appreciate deeper aspects of His love, personality, grace, and power. In another sense, we cannot assume that nearness to God is directly proportional to the hours we spend in prayer and study. Prayer, study, and fellowship are tools and opportunities by which to draw closer to Him; they are not numbers to plug into an equation to calculate the exact progress of our journey. On the other hand, it is impossible for a person to engage in the search for the sacred by purposely *refusing* prayer, study, and fellowship.

Our human knowledge of God will always be limited to this life. But this is not a constrictive idea so long as we keep it in its appropriate context. The whole of one's life simply cannot contain all that God has already revealed to us, much less discover it all. Since God is infinite, it is illogical and presumptuous to think that our finite self, during our brief walk upon this earth, can allow us to know Him in His fullness. Just as we cannot fit the ocean into a drinking cup, or cram the entire Milky Way into a single solar system, so we cannot expect to accumulate—much less digest—God's endless and timeless knowledge.

This is not meant to discourage us in the least. On the contrary, the fact that we are able to enter into an infinite fellowship with One who *does* exceed our comprehension is absolutely fantastic in itself. Just because we cannot (in this life) "see" Him entirely should not dampen our enthusiasm one bit: the God whom we are seeking is forever a great and awesome God. He is most certainly worth all the time, effort, sacrifice, and self-denial that are required to seek after Him. He is indeed worth the search.

Remember: it is not God who is lost; that is not why we are

searching for Him. Instead, *we* are lost without *Him*, and if we never embark on such a search, or if we abandon it in order to search for something so much less, we will always *be* lost. There is no more wretched existence than one where God is *not*. Thank God—literally—that He has given each one of us time, patience, and mercy so as to seek after Him and thus begin our eternal fellowship with Him even while we are still here upon this temporal earth.

Endnotes

3 The fact that this prohibition was given to Israel under a different covenant than the one offered through Jesus Christ does not make it any less binding: this is a moral issue and therefore is a constant in every covenant of salvation with the Lord (see Acts 19:18-19, for example).

CHAPTER FOUR

What God Looks Like

Then Moses said, "I pray You, show me Your glory!"
…But He said, "You cannot see My face, for no man can see Me and live!"
Exodus 33:18, 20

Suppose that instead of putting *pictures* of missing children in post offices, milk cartons, and your IRS tax guide, police officials just asked us to *search* for those children. In this hypothetical scenario, the authorities provide no description of what the missing children look like—no physical characteristics, height, weight, gender—not even a sketch. When questioned about this, they simply reply, "It's really not important what these children *look* like, but it's critical that we *find* them!"

Of course, any person of reasonable intelligence would say, "What! How can we search for children when we do not even know what they look like? That's an impossible search!" *Exactly.* We cannot search for someone without knowing some of the details of that person in the first place. This makes sense; it is logical, rational, and expected.

We should apply this same logic, then, to our search for the sacred. It is pointless for us to seek after God if we do not know what He "looks" like. Neither can we implore others to seek God under these same circumstances or with those same limitations. Decades ago some Soviet cosmonauts, having returned from their orbit around the earth, arrogantly announced something to the effect of, "We looked for God in space, but we did not see Him." Of course not, gentlemen: you obviously did not even know what to look for in the first place. So it is with every person who claims to "find God" but has no clue of that for which he is looking. He will certainly be disappointed—not because God is not worth discovering, but because of his own failure to adequately prepare for the search.

Putting a Face on God

Our approach to visualizing God, so to speak, will be straightforward and logical, but not dispassionate and unrewarding. God has given us intelligence and He expects us to use it rightly; but this search must be personal and cannot be reduced to a scholastic exercise. Factual conclusions about God must be based upon Scripture, our only authentic and authoritative source of information about Him. We will also appeal to factual observations of life, human nature, and the physical world which give us insight to the Creator of those things. We're not trying to paint a mere portrait of God as though we were simply trying to construct a two-dimensional reproduction of an infinite Being. God is omni-dimensional; even our most ambitious attempts to describe Him will be seriously lacking. We must confess that there are qualities and characteristics of God that are beyond our ability to define, explain, or even comprehend.

To begin, we should ask ourselves: what makes God "God"? How can we describe Him—really, how does He describe Himself to us—as a Divine Being and not merely a glorified *human* being like ourselves? The Greeks, Romans, and many other ancient cultures imagined gods that possessed immortality and supernatural advantages. Other than these traits, however, these gods had the same loves, jealousies, ambitions, flaws, and vanities as mortal men and women. The Sacred God of heaven, however, has none of our shortcomings, vices, selfishness, or limitations. *We* are made "in His image," but at the same time *He* is nothing like us. This paradox is explainable—it does make sense, in its appropriate context—but we must appreciate it up front. The point is that we cannot search for a divine, immortal, omni-dimensional God who ends up being nothing more than the product of our own wild imagination, One who is nothing more than a glorified extension of ourselves.

Having said all that, let's examine some of the characteristics of this Sacred Person whom we know as God:

God is alive. This may seem to be a rather trivial observation. Someone might already be saying, "Of *course* God is alive! So are we—and so are all other creatures—but that does not make us 'God.'" This is true. The fact that God *is* alive does not by itself *make* Him God. But we are not looking for a sepulcher, mummy, or corpse, either. We are looking for a "living and true God" (1 Thessalonians 1:9). This fact rules out all searches for someone who is dead, or for a non-living or inanimate object.

The point is not a meaningless one. Many ancient peoples served, worshiped, sacrificed to, and even gave up their lives for lifeless gods. Pagan worshipers carved their own gods out of wood, stone, or iron, and then bowed to them as though those idols had given life to *them*. This is, of course, entirely backward logic which God Himself mocks (see Isaiah 44:9-20). Men give life to idols, not the other way around. The only life an idol has is what a person gives to it; once he abandons it, the idol is nothing more than the lifeless object or material that it was at first.

In sharp contrast, the God of heaven does not depend upon our worship or even our acknowledgment in order to be alive. He is alive without our having given Him life; He is unchanged in nature whether or not we conform to His will. This means that *no one gives life to God* because His existence is self-sufficient and self-perpetuating. God was "in the beginning" (Genesis 1:1), and His existence endures throughout the eternity to come. He Himself has said, "I am the Alpha and the Omega...who is and who was and who is to come, the Almighty" (Revelation 1:8). Furthermore, God is the Source of all life: *our* lives are fully dependent upon *His* life. Inasmuch as God has created all living things, so He is the giver of life to all things that live. Just as He breathed the breath of life into Adam (Genesis 2:7), so He breathes life (so to speak) into *all* things that are alive.

God is not a mere intellectual concept, a lifeless idol, or a ghost-like apparition of some great power that once was but now is not. Anyone searching for such a god will not find the God of heaven, but only a projection of his own imagination. The Sacred God of heaven is very much alive: He cannot age, He cannot change (diminish or improve), and He cannot die. The fact of His living existence may be fundamental, but it is absolutely necessary that we appreciate it.

God is self-sufficient. Many people like to think of themselves as "self-sufficient." By this they imply that they do not depend upon anything or anyone else for advancement but themselves. While this sounds lofty and utopian, it is impossible to achieve. Every person on earth depends on someone or something outside of himself in order to survive. For example, someone might be self-employed, but he still has to obey the laws of the land, pay his taxes, and ultimately rely upon the revenue that other people provide for his support. He also must rely upon the inventions, products, and services of others to provide what he needs to sustain his life. The very concept of money implies a dependence upon a system of exchange or commerce that is mutually agreed upon. Money has no value unless there is a higher power that declares and enforces its worth. Even if a man lives on his own sovereign island, grows his own food, and draws his own water, he still relies upon the ocean, weather, soil, and seed to contribute to his success. The failure of such provisions—all of which are outside of his ability to control—spells doom for his survival. His existence may be isolated from direct contact with men, but it is not a truly *self-sufficient* one. In the end, he (and everyone else) is still dependent upon his health, time, and the biological and spiritual aspects of life itself. He cannot override any of these things nor can he prevent them from running their course. He may boast about his resourcefulness, but not even his most creative resourcefulness can overcome his human and earthly circumstances.

God, on the other hand, is truly self-sufficient. This is one characteristic of His *being* God. His existence is not dependent upon any outside intervention, favorable variables, or uncontrollable factors. Whereas our lives require the cooperation of numerous conditions, circumstances, and other people in order to survive, God's survival requires no such cooperation. He does not need your support, cooperation, participation, or approval in order for Him to exist in the absolute sense of the word. There is nothing that we are able to provide for God—as a contribution to His nature, identity, or survival—that He does not already self-generate. "'Heaven is My throne and the earth is My footstool. Where then is a house you could build for Me? And where is a place that I may rest? For My hand made all these things, Thus all these things came into being,' declares the LORD" (Isaiah 66:1-2).

Not only is God alive, but there is nothing that can threaten or remove His life. Jesus Christ, as God in the flesh, manifested His power over earthly elements, people, distance, time, and even supernatural beings: nothing could overpower Him, since He is over "all things" (Ephesians 1:22-23; Colossians 1:15-18, et al). Even Jesus' own physical death was something that He *orchestrated*—He was put to death, but not killed against His own will. Not even death itself was able to overpower Him (John 10:18).

Anyone seeking God must search for One who needs nothing from anyone else for His survival. Any other being, human or otherwise, that is not truly self-sufficient cannot be God. Any religion that depends upon a person or thing that is not truly self-sufficient is not worth our attention. Any worship of any person, being, or concept that cannot exist apart from man's support of it is hopeless and pathetic. There are many man-made religions in the world that rely upon man-made doctrines, man-appointed leaders, and man-supported beliefs; these are designed to seek after God through man-made means. In light of God's absolute self-sufficiency, this is not only foolish but threatens the spiritual life of anyone who pursues them. God did not give life to such things, and whatever is not of God will not endure beyond this life (cf. 1 John 2:17).

*   *   *

God is sovereign. Whereas self-sufficiency refers to one's independent *ability*, sovereignty refers to one's absolute *authority*. A sovereign is a sole, independent, and supreme ruler who does not answer to anyone for his actions. King Nebuchadnezzar of ancient Babylon (6th century BC), for example, was a sovereign ruler: he answered to no other man or body of men, and his word was law. However, Nebuchadnezzar was not a god, and even he answered to the God of Heaven (see Daniel 4). Anyone who must answer to anyone else cannot be God since the One who is truly God answers to no one. This fact rules out all men, angels, demons, and even Satan himself: all of these are put under Christ's feet by the divine, irrevocable, sovereign decree of God the Father.

Since this is true, our search for the sacred must take us beyond the confines of this world and all worldly authority. Men, regardless of how independent they think themselves to be, ultimately answer to each other. For example, after World War II the Nuremberg Trials made men answer for their "crimes against humanity," holding them accountable to a world tribunal. The judges and juries of these courts recognized that all men are accountable to one another and that no one is above (the) law. God, on the other hand, *is* above the laws of men and even the laws which He has imposed upon the physical world (laws of thermodynamics, electromagnetism, gravity, motion, time, etc.). To say that God is above the law does not mean that God is lawless, reckless, or acts without purpose. God is accountable only to Himself, since there is no law or standard of accountability higher than Him (cf. Hebrews 6:13-18). God's holy nature is our morality; His holiness determines what is truly sacred. Whatever is truly moral, just, lawful, pure, and good is that which is consistent with His perfect nature.

We cannot prosecute God according to our own man-made laws, or require that He stand trial in human courts of law. It is ridiculous to even think that we can—yet this does not stop people from trying. It is not uncommon for people to find God "guilty" of violating their expectations— as though this were a moral crime in itself. Such law-making (on our part) is without authority in the first place; therefore such verdicts are entirely illegitimate.

God *does* have the authority to bind divine decrees upon us, however. Not only this, but He has the authority (and ability) to reward us for obedience and punish us for disobedience. This is a significant aspect of His sovereignty: we can neither reward nor punish God, regardless of how innocent or guilty we think Him to be. Yet God can reward us with that which we do not presently have for our faithful obedience to Him. He can also prosecute and punish us for our faithlessness, not only in this life but also in the one to come. No person can literally curse God—He is above all human ability to do so—but His curses are absolute and irrepressible, as are His blessings. As He told Abraham, "I will bless those who bless you, And the one who curses you I will curse" (Genesis 12:3). No human being can enforce such a pronouncement, but the Sovereign God of Heaven can and does. No wonder Jesus warned us, "Do not fear those who kill the body but are unable to kill the soul; but rather fear Him who is able to destroy both soul and body in hell" (Matthew 10:28). Only a sovereign God is capable of such power.

Human justice is biased, prejudiced, and self-serving; we are limited in authority, knowledge, and (therefore) justice. Without perfect knowledge and wisdom, we cannot render perfect decisions. God, however, is self-governing and unchallengeable; He does not require our approval; He is not threatened by our disapproval. We cannot bribe, extort, blackmail, intimidate, or coerce Him in any way. He does not answer to us and His life is not contingent or dependent upon ours. Therefore, we can die—physically or spiritually—and He remains infinitely alive.

*   *   *

God is spirit. As an experiment, try defining a person without any reference to his physical body. I'm not referring to describing someone, either from portraits or photographs, whom you have never literally seen. I'm talking about describing a person who has never *had* a body: What does that person look like? How would you describe him? What features or characteristics does he have? When a person dies, we may say something like, "But they live on in spirit"—yes, that describes their present *existence*, but it does not describe either how we knew them or how they were known on earth. Ultimately, we always assign a physical form to everyone who has ever existed. If a living being has never had a flesh-and-blood existence, then (according to our perception of life as we know it), we must conclude that that being is *not human*.[4] In the absence of a physical body or without evidence of a literal existence (e.g., through divine revelation), we cannot know with any certainty that such beings even exist.

Heaven does not conform to the rules and boundaries of earth or of our own mental constructs. God the Father does not have a physical body, and yet He exists. His identity is not constrained or defined by a three-dimensional, tangible, earth-bound body like the rest of us, but this only means He does not exist like *us,* not that He does not exist. The *proof* of His existence is universal and irrefutable. The undeniable implications drawn from the intelligent and systematic design of our physical world, the human body, and our moral consciousness are conclusive enough. If we had never seen God in the flesh, we would still be able to prove (by necessary inference) His existence.

The fact is God (as Jesus Christ) *has* manifested Himself in the flesh (John 1:1, 14). Even so, in becoming "flesh," Christ did not cease to be a Divine Being. The Greek word rendered "became" in John 1:14 means to become one thing while retaining the original identity. Similarly, Abraham became a father to Isaac without ceasing to be a husband to Sarah; he simply took on a new identity. Aaron became a high priest of Israel without ceasing to be Moses' brother. David became king of Israel without ceasing to be the son of Jesse. And God became Jesus the man ("in the flesh"; 1 John 4:2-3) without ceasing to be God the Spirit.

This is not easy for us to understand, but then it wasn't meant to be easy or even humanly understandable. It's like saying, "The circle became a square without ceasing to be a circle," or "The apple became a zucchini without ceasing to be an apple," or other mind-boggling illustrations. God does not explain Himself to us as we *want* to know Him but only as we *need* to know Him. For anyone who is truly interested in searching for Him, He has provided sufficient information. We must not impose upon Him features common only to mortal man, however; we cannot look merely for a glorified human being. Even Jesus, while in the form of a bond-servant (Philippians 2:6-8), never intended to disclose the full manifestation of God. Paul did declare that "in Him [Christ] all the fullness of Deity dwells in bodily form" (Colossians 2:9), but this meant that the divine attributes and nature of God were manifested in Jesus the human being. As for God's heavenly, spiritual glory, He dwells in "unapproachable light" and cannot be seen by mortal men (1 Timothy 6:16; see also John 1:18 and 1 John 4:12).

God is spirit (John 4:24) which means that the full nature and existence of God can never be reduced to mere physical or fleshy characteristics. Flesh and blood cannot enter into God's world (1 Corinthians 15:50); therefore, God cannot be defined by flesh and blood. Likewise, "even though we have known Christ according to the flesh, yet now we know Him in this way no longer" (2 Corinthians 5:16). Our search for the sacred, then, must be spiritual in nature. We are not looking for sacred amulets, chalices, crosses, books, cathedrals, or so-called Holy Lands. Physical objects, man-made relics, humanly-designated places, etc. cannot be the object of our search. Instead, we must search for the sacred in the spiritual realm since that is where God dwells.

God is omniscient. God, in order to *be* God, must know more than anyone else. If He only knows what we know (or what we can discover over time), then He really is no different or better than we are. It is true that men can learn new things, even profound and wonderful things, through studying the world around them (i.e., via data acquired through empirical evidence, experimental procedure, observation, chemistry, physics, mathematics, statistical information, etc.). Such knowledge is gained only by having walked upon this earth; it is not knowledge which transcends this earth or one's individual capacity for knowledge.

Ask a man about things which he has not studied or investigated—knowledge he cannot know intuitively—and he will only be able to give you an opinion at best and a helpless shrug at worst. Even very intelligent people—scholars, professors, brilliant scientists, members of Mensa—may have a lot to offer in the way of acquired knowledge and learned discernment, but they are hardly gods. They only know what they have absorbed from the world around them; they cannot know anything beyond this. They may be better at *processing* or *retrieving* information than the rest of us, but they do not have any unique *access* to information. Ask them about the distant past and they will only tell you what historians and archaeologists have told them. Ask them about the distant future and they will be offering mere opinions. Ask them about the spiritual realm and the best that they can tell is what God has already told *all* of us. Whatever knowledge we have of God has been given to us by God, whereas God's own knowledge is hardly dependent upon what we have shared with Him.

People are not all-knowing, but God *must* be. In order to be the Creator of the physical world, God must possess full knowledge of everything *in* the physical world. Inasmuch as He has created man, so He knows everything there is to know *about* man. God knows what we think, our intentions, even our innermost secrets (Acts 1:24; Romans 2:16; Hebrews 4:12-13). Jesus, as God in the flesh, "knew all men" and "knew what was in man" (John 2:24-25). On the other hand, no one knows God's thoughts unless He reveals them (1 Corinthians 2:11). God can read our thoughts, but we cannot read His; He can judge our heart with perfect wisdom, but we are unable to accurately judge His.

Even when God reveals knowledge to men, they do not always understand what they are given. Consider Jesus' response to the Sadducees, for example, when they posed to Him the seemingly irresolvable dilemma of a woman with seven husbands, as to which of these would be her husband in the hereafter (Matthew 22:23-33). Jesus' profound response to these well-learned, well-scripted men was: "You are mistaken, not understanding the Scriptures nor the power of God" (verse 29). In other words, even when men have access to divinely-provided knowledge, they still may not get it right. Only an all-knowing God could rightly determine who is right and who is mistaken. What man-made idol has ever criticized or corrected the thoughts of the one who has molded it? Yet God has every right to challenge the thoughts and conclusions of men because He is not bound by the limitations of our knowledge.

Jesus said, "If you continue in My word, then you are truly disciples of Mine; and you will know the truth, and the truth will make you free" (John 8:31-32). Only Christ, because He *is* God, knows the real truth about what lies beyond us. We can accept His authority on this too since He has proved with powerful miracles—especially His own bodily resurrection—that He knows what He is talking about.

Of course, we cannot limit our description of God merely to "knowing everything." While it is true that God *does* know everything, we cannot reduce God merely to being the Divine Almanac of all facts and data, the Spiritual Accumulation of every shred of information that exists. A person who is very knowledgeable is not always the sharpest knife in the drawer; having knowledge is not necessarily equal to being wise and discerning. Wisdom is not the mere accumulation of facts and figures; it includes being able to *use* that knowledge most effectively and efficiently in the best interest of all those involved.

In being all-knowing (omniscient), God also has the ability to use that knowledge in the absolute best possible way. His decisions are based on perfect knowledge *and* He exercises perfect wisdom. He does not have to ponder over what would be the best course of action or the most intelligent response to whatever problem is set before Him. God does not "think" about things; He does not need time to weigh evidence and deliberate over verdicts. He does not "take things into consideration," for He does not need to "consider" anything. God did not have to sit down and sketch blueprints for the Creation of the world, the design of man, or the content of Scripture; these things already existed as perfect, completed, flawless plans in His infinite mind. While men may store up thoughts in their head, God does not have to store up anything.

"Yes," someone insightfully remembers, "but God has retracted His earlier decisions in the past, which suggests a recalculation and reconsideration of even His own divine knowledge." Such a person would likely cite God's regret over having created mankind (Genesis 6:6-7), or His change of mind over destroying the Israelites (Exodus 32:9-14). These instances appear on the surface to contradict God's perfection of knowledge: surely He should have known that men would sin—even His *own* people! But we must remember the context of these situations. Never did God say or imply, "Whoops! I made a mistake" or "I never saw *that* coming," nor did Moses ever charge God with such a crime. However, God must react to man's decisions, and He is indeed "sorry" whenever He must destroy those who have made foolish decisions. In other words, God may let man "do his thing," and will react or respond accordingly, but He also has perfect knowledge that His responses will ultimately serve the very best interest of His entire creation (Isaiah 55:8-11).

*　　　*　　　*

God is omnipresent. This idea is quite intriguing, which is why I spend so much time on it in a forthcoming chapter ("It's God's World—We're Just Living In It"). Because of this, we will keep our comments here brief. The essential point to consider with regard to the qualities and characteristics we ought to expect in a divine and supernatural Being is that God is not bound by the same spatial limitations that we are. We live in a three-dimensional world: length, height, and depth are all that our physical senses can accommodate. Some want to regard "time" as a dimension, but even our concept of time is entirely based upon physical things: the rotation of the earth, the earth's orbit around the sun, the sun itself, cycles of the moon, and clocks themselves (which are man-made inventions measuring time according to man-made calibrations). Thus we speak of "physical time" as opposed to the mere concept of time which, unless it is measured or acknowledged, does not really exist.

While it is true that our metaphysical abilities—the mind, conscience, spiritual awareness, etc.—can perceive of things beyond the physical dimensions of our earthly life, we still cannot voluntarily escape from our three-dimensional boundaries. To think of ourselves as being in more than one place at a time immediately boggles the mind and is, of course, physically impossible. A god of our own making that is bound to these same constraints is a god with no more power or ability than we already possess.

If we were gods, then we would simply dictate the scope of our existence. We would not purposely limit ourselves, except by our own choice; thus we must conclude that these limitations have been imposed upon us. This draws our attention to the source of such limits—i.e., the One who made us. To claim that the natural world imposed these limitations is to conclude that the natural world made intelligent and necessary decisions for us. However, "nature" is bereft of any intelligence or decision-making processes, and therefore does not have the capacity to make decisions, much less the ability to execute them. In other words, by appealing to the Theory of Evolution and its "blind forces of nature" as satisfactory explanations for such limitations, is not only illogical but insults *our* intelligence.

Our search for God, then, forces us to look for One who *does* have the ability to make intelligent decisions *and* has the power to execute them regardless of our input or protest. One who is truly God must not be confined to the three-dimensional constraints of space, the imposition of time, and the scope of our own thoughts; He must be One who absolutely transcends our finiteness and natural limitations. He must not be restricted to our world but must have free access to and control over *all* worlds, whether visible or invisible (Colossians 1:15-17). He must be "the Alpha and the Omega" (Revelation 1:8), the first and last, the beginning and end, the summing up of all things (Ephesians 1:9-10). He must be the *Creator* of our world and not merely another *subject* of it (Genesis 1:1; Isaiah 40:25-26; 45:12, et al).

God is omnipotent. "Power" has several different meanings associated with it: authority, control, command, rule, strength, force, ability, etc. We refer to sovereign political nations as "powers"; those people or agencies that govern our lives are referred to as "the powers that be"; in mathematics, something can be raised to a certain power; in optics, power refers to the ability of a lens to focus light. In its most common usage "power" is an aspect of physics that has to do with the measurement of *work* being performed in a given period of time. For example, electrical power (as wattage) refers to the work that is being performed as electrical current meets resistance; "horsepower" measures the strength of, say, an internal combustible engine (i.e., as foot-pounds of pressure).

What is common to all of these definitions—from politics to mathematics to electricity—is this: power indicates the execution of *applied force* to accomplish some *form of work*. This requires several things: energy, the ability to harness that energy for a given purpose, a clear and productive objective (work) for the use of that energy, and a standard by which this work can be measured. Consider this on a cosmic scale: how much power (applied energy) do you think it would have taken to produce the universe and everything in it (a given work)? How much power would it take to create a single atom, not to mention an entire galaxy? Evolutionism claims that this happened automatically, even accidentally. To accomplish a single work of creation, then, "power" had to come out of nowhere, be harnessed by nothing, have no clear objective (or purpose), operate without a blueprint, and be only hypothetically or subjectively measured. Somehow, despite all of these illogical factors, intelligent life *and* systematic design came into being. This is not only absurd, but once again it makes a mockery of our own intelligence—not to mention *God's* intelligence.

The Bible, however, claims that an intelligent and all-powerful God created everything in the universe: He provided the energy, He harnessed that energy perfectly, He used that energy to perform a work according to a plan that exceeds our ability to comprehend, and He measured that work by His own perfect and supernatural standard (Genesis 1:31, "God saw all that He had made, and behold, it was very good"). All energy has to come from somewhere (or Someone); likewise, all energy must be used according to specific laws and conversion processes. Work cannot exist without power;

if no power exists, then no work can be accomplished, which is to say that *nothing* would happen. Without work there cannot be movement, velocity, gravity, heat, light, or anything else that requires any application of energy. Thus, before God created the heavens and the earth (Genesis 1:1), what we know as the universe could not possibly have existed since *no work existed by which the universe could be defined*. The universe was not just dark, quiet, and still; it was unable to *be*.

In order to *be* God, One must be the Creator of all these things, because God Himself cannot be created by anything or anyone else. If (since) God *is* the Creator of all that exists, then by necessary inference, He also is above all *power* that is exercised within His Creation. God cannot create a power more powerful than Himself! Likewise, God cannot be controlled by a greater power than Himself and still be "God." Only God, by definition, is all-powerful; otherwise, He is not *the* God but only "a" god. If there is a power that exists that God cannot control, overcome, ordain, supersede, or annihilate, then there is a force in this universe that is stronger than God—one to which even God Himself must submit. This would mean, too, that whatever God declares to be "sacred" is only sacred as long as this higher power *allows* that condition to exist. Thus, in seeking the sacred we could not seek after God, if indeed God is not the epitome of our search. God must be the sole source of sacredness (holiness) since there cannot be anything or anyone more sacred than He.

If one is going to search for God, then he must search for One who is *all*-powerful (omnipotent) and not merely possessing power. People are powerful; governments are powerful; gravitational forces are powerful; but *none* of these are *all*-powerful. There cannot be *any* power in the universe if there is not (first) a *source* of that power and (second) a *management* of that power. As stated above, power cannot just pop itself into existence; it cannot be used (applied) without the proper vehicle to utilize such energy. These things require that *someone be in control* of everything. This Someone is God; there can be no other "someone."

*   *   *

God is not stuck in your perception of Him. Given God's

supernatural attributes, it is impossible for us to describe or explain Him *fully* according to our own small, finite perspective. But what really must be a source of endless annoyance to God—even as it is to some of us here on earth—is when someone claims to possess some "unique," "exceptional," or "privileged" view of God that the rest of us do not (or cannot) have. There's always someone who wants to think of himself (or herself) as a special conduit of divine insight—a modern-day prophet, a contemporary seer, a new "messiah."

The truth is: such privileged access does not exist. The Bible does not allow for this, there is no need for it, and, quite frankly, all those who claim to have such revelatory information have no more proof to offer than their own testimony, which is insufficient to substantiate their claims. Even Jesus said, "If I alone testify about Myself, My testimony is not true" (John 5:31). In other words, if believing in Christ depended only upon His own statements, then that is insufficient evidence by itself. If Jesus, being God, applied this criticism to Himself, then surely we can apply it to ourselves and others. What Jesus *did* appeal to was a myriad of evidence outside of Himself—prophets, prophecy, Scripture, miracles, the audible testimony of God Himself—to justify His claims. In doing so, He has provided us with a reason to believe in Him (John 20:31; see also John 5:32-47; 10:37-38). The point is: unless someone has more credible evidence than his own testimony to support his (or her) claim to know, see, or understand God more clearly than is possible for the rest of us, we must politely ask that person to hold his tongue and keep his visions (or whatever) to himself.

This perception thing does not apply only to alleged private revelations from God. Many people claim—with all sincerity—to "know" God in some particular way that actually defies Scripture and (thus) the Holy Spirit's own revelation of God. For example, I have listened to people explain how God will forgive even ungodly people, or will save those who defiantly reject Jesus as the Son of God, or will reward those who are "good" people just because we deemed such people "good" in the first place, and similar Bible-contradicting statements. People may have good intentions and still be in serious opposition to the God of Scripture. Others may choose to portray God according to their own liking rather than according to how He has revealed Himself to us in prophecy, the written word, and His historical activity among men. No doubt all of us have done this, consciously or not, at some point in our lives. This does not make it right but only acknowledges a tendency of human nature.

The apostle John, who knew Jesus in the flesh, wrote, "No one has seen God at any time; the only begotten God who is in the bosom of the Father, He has explained Him" (John 1:18). I cannot explain or describe God whom I have not seen or met in person, but Jesus can—and did. I have no better source than Him to which to defer: whatever Jesus (and those to whom He revealed Himself) says about God is true and accurate; whatever I say about God must conform to His testimony. If I say something about God that is not specifically detailed in Scripture, then it is either to be regarded as my own personal opinion (and left in the *context* of opinions) or it must agree in principle with or be a necessary inference about God. Certainly God is not stuck in my own paradigms; He is not trapped in my own personal opinions concerning Him. God is sovereign and independent of my finite impositions regardless of how confidently or passionately I defend them. Similarly, He exists as He is regardless of your opinions otherwise. We cannot subjectively define God according to our own liking.

This is not meant to be critical or judgmental against us but liberating and refreshing. In other words, thank goodness God is not only who we think He is! He is infinitely better, greater, wiser, and more powerful than we allow Him to be even in our most creative imaginations. The Scriptures already provide a beautiful and irrepressible picture of God that far exceeds our ability to describe Him according to our earthly or human conceptions. Everyone is supposed to "know the Lord" (cf. Hebrews 8:11), but we are to know Him as He presents Himself to us, not as we determine according to our own expectations.

Attributes of God's Sacredness

The above characteristics briefly expound upon the attributes of a supernatural God. If we are going to search for God, He must be:

- **Alive**—not merely existing, but *full* of life and the *source* of life.
- **Self-sufficient**—dependent upon nothing besides Himself in order

to exist and survive.

- **Sovereign**—answering to no authority above Himself, since no such authority can exist.
- **Spirit**—and therefore not a part of or constrained by the physical world.
- **Omniscient**—not only having full knowledge of all things, but able to use that knowledge in the most effective and efficient manner possible.
- **Omnipresent**—and thus not bound by earthly or human constraints of any kind.
- **Omnipotent**—possessing absolute creative and destructive power, as well as overseeing the use of all such power *within* His creation.
- **Above your perception of Him**—free from your or my expectations of Him.

There is another aspect to this search that is related to and yet exceeds everything discussed above. God's *sacredness* is also an inseparable part of who *God* is. This fact compels us to consider some different characteristics or expressions of what it means to be perfectly *holy*, which further defines aspects of God's *nature*.

God's sacredness is not something to be taken lightly; likewise, our search for the sacred must be conducted with the utmost respect. Unfortunately, it is not uncommon for people, in their desire to become "closer" to God, to regard Him as a casual friend or a sort of grandfatherly pastor. People imagine themselves having casual conversations with God, as though shooting the breeze with Him over coffee or plying Him with questions or—even worse—their own personal views. Yet God is not a casual friend; there is nothing casual, simple, frivolous, or light-hearted about God. He is not someone's divine "buddy"; He is not "one of the guys"; He is not "the man upstairs"; He cannot be reduced to any such human characterizations. His sacredness cannot be confused with mere niceness, politeness, formality, or gentlemanliness. We cannot regard Him ceremoniously, either, as though He were merely some high official with whom we must conduct ourselves according to strict protocol. A brief glimpse at His sacred attributes will reveal just how unique and special God is:

His eternality: God's *eternal* existence is part of His *sacred* existence. God is not sacred only because He is eternal, but because He is the source of all that is sacred, He must be eternal. He cannot cease to be, since all that is sacred is dependent upon His ever-existent, ever-present life. Of course, eternity not only supersedes earthly comparison, it defies human comprehension. Solomon wrote that God "has also set eternity in their [man's] heart, yet so that man will not find out the work which God has done from the beginning even to the end" (Ecclesiastes 3:11). What I believe him to be saying, in context, is this: God has allowed us to understand the *concept* of eternity even though we are unable to *experience* eternity in this finite, time-bound existence. Since our entire universe is filled with deterioration, decay, and death—i.e., it is a universe in which nothing really lasts forever—we cannot really grasp what "eternity" means. In this same way, we can understand the *concept* of sacredness, but we will never be able to fully *experience* His sacredness while in this life. God has always been and always will be; there is nothing that can interrupt or even threaten His perpetual existence. Likewise, "Jesus Christ is the same yesterday and today, yes and forever" (Hebrews 13:8). Jesus *is* God—He is not God the Father, but He is a Person of the Divine Godhead—so whatever qualities we might observe in God generally, we can also apply to God the Son, God the Father, or God the Spirit specifically (see also John 1:1-3; 8:57-58; Hebrews 1:1-4, et al).

His immutability: This refers to the unchangeableness of God. No one can alter who He is, what He wills, or whom He loves. This also is a dimension of God's *sacredness*: the quality, intensity, mystery, and wonder of God's sacredness cannot be increased or diminished whatsoever since it is already fully perfect and complete. No one has the authority or ability to change anything about God's sacredness or whatever God deems sacred. Not only are people unable to change God, but no other angel, spirit, demon, or rival god—not even Satan himself—can alter God's nature. He is not merely above us all; He is above everyone and everything. This is comforting for us who have entrusted our souls to God's care who are thus protected by God's unchangeableness. As Christ has said, "My Father, who has given them [Christ's "sheep"] to Me, is greater than all; and no one is able to snatch them out of the Father's hand" (John 10:29, bracketed words mine). This means that God's sacred promises concerning our future with

Him will never change. As Paul wrote: "…if we died with Him, we shall also live with Him; if we endure, we shall also reign with Him; If we deny Him, He also will deny us; If we are faithless, He remains faithful, for He cannot deny Himself" (2 Timothy 2:11-13). God cannot be anything less than what He is now.

His infiniteness: If God is spiritual in nature, omniscient, omnipresent, and omnipotent, then He is *infinite*. While these other qualities speak of who God *is* or what He *does*, His infiniteness speaks to God's *holiness*. His holiness has no limits—in time, space, scope, expression, glory, or magnitude. Naturally we struggle with this since the concept of "infinity" is only understood in an abstract or perhaps mathematical level. Our mundane existence knows no such thing as infinity, timelessness, or anything that cannot be contained or quantified with some kind of physical, voluminous, or spatial measurement. If you've ever wrestled with a concept of, say, how "big" God is—is He our size? Is He one hundred feet tall? Does He literally hold the earth in the palm of His hand?—you know what I'm talking about. To refer to His "size" is to assign to God human or earthly attributes. A wedding ring is endless (so ministers tell brides and grooms) since it is a circle without beginning or end, but it is still a limited circle with a certain beginning in time and a certain lifespan, so to speak. We simply cannot conceive of something or Someone being absolutely immeasurable in every sense of the word. Because God is absolutely sacred, He is also absolutely *deep*: there is no end to God in any respect. He "is able to do far more abundantly beyond all that we ask or think" (Ephesians 3:20) because His sacredness cannot be measured or restrained by anything or anyone. God's glory fills the "whole earth" (Isaiah 6:3); likewise, "The heavens are telling of the glory of God; and their expanse is declaring the work of His hands" (Psalm 19:1). Whenever the Bible speaks of God's *glory* or *excellence* (as in 2 Peter 1:3), it speaks of His *sacredness*. Just as there is no end to His glory, so there is no end to His sacredness (and vice versa). Men cannot create infinity; we cannot exceed our finite limitations. Men are not sacred (unless God *makes* them so), and God is not of men. He is not constrained by what we cannot be or how we cannot perform.

His indestructibility: One thing we may not consider when speaking of the attributes of divine sacredness is God's inability to be destroyed. The concept may have never even entered your head; indeed, it is an astounding thing to consider. Imagine God being "killed," or dealing with the corpse of God, or even reducing His power to something less than all-powerful. Such thoughts are, for those who genuinely worship God, incomprehensible—even blasphemous, if taken seriously. Yet God's holiness cannot be destroyed or compromised in any way. He is inexhaustible, irreducible, and unassailable. All that is unholy, including this sacrilegious, profane world, will be destroyed by God (1 John 2:17); but nothing and no one can destroy God. As a supremely holy Being, He will not permit anything unholy (including sinful souls) to coexist with Him forever (see Genesis 6:3 and Ezekiel 20:9, 14, 22, for example). Out of mercy He has been patient with us; through divine grace He has provided a means for fellowship with us through Jesus Christ. Still, the opportunity for this fellowship is limited, and those who forfeit God's gospel of grace will be destroyed by His wrath (John 3:36).

His separateness: This does not refer to God's unwillingness to have fellowship with us for indeed He desires our fellowship. Nonetheless, God maintains a sort of "sacred distance" from us. His holiness demands this; He will not compromise His absolute perfection and purity with any form of corruption. Jesus Christ, as God in the flesh, was not an exception to this, but His situation was certainly unique. Through the incarnation of God the Son, the Father is able to interact with men; but mere men still cannot stand in the holy presence of God. Not only does He dwell in a humanly-inapproachable existence (1 Timothy 6:16), but the Son is our only access to Him (John 1:18). No one can come to the Father except through the Son (John 14:6); no one is called to Christ apart from His gospel (2 Thessalonians 2:13-14); and no one will ever see God apart from faith (Hebrews 11:6). These may be difficult concepts for us, but just because we cannot fully appreciate them does not nullify what we *do* know of God.

*   *   *

Just as we cannot search for a person whose likeness we do not know, so we cannot search for God if we do not know His "likeness." This does not mean we will literally "see" God just because we do draw near to Him, but it does mean God will become increasingly clearer—and more special—to us as we strive to learn more about Him. Many people are content with having access to what God *has*—forgiveness, peace of mind, answers to prayers, etc.; but those who are determined to seek after the sacred are interested in who God *is*. Fellowship with God is to be more important to us than merely being involved in a religion, church, or ministry. Seeking the sacred is hardly some esoteric spiritual "journey" that has no specific objective.

To draw closer to God is not something He only *desires* us to do, it is something He *expects* us to do—something he expects *you* to do. God has made you "in His image," and He earnestly craves your communion because He has imparted His own Life into your soul. As James wrote (4:5), "Or do you think that the Scripture speaks to no purpose: 'He jealously desires the Spirit which He has made to dwell in us'?" If you are "in Christ" (cf. 2 Corinthians 5:17), then God has anointed you with His Spirit (cf. 2 Corinthians 1:21-22). This means God has blessed you with an opportunity to know Him intimately, as much as is possible in our earthly state.

The things that are of men—theories, philosophies, fantasies, or utopian dreams—are not worth seeking after. The origin of such teachings cannot overcome the inadequacies of those who promote them nor can they rescue from spiritual destruction those who listen to them. Seeking the sacred, then, is *not* about seeking after men, or the teachings or practices of men; rather, it is seeking after God Himself. And God most certainly is worth seeking, as we shall continue to see.

Endnotes

4 Humanness and personhood are not necessarily the same things: one who is a human is always a person, but one can be a person without being human. Angels, spirits of those who have died, and deity are all examples of this. We may speak of a dead person as a human spirit, but we are imposing a quality upon them that no longer has real application. A person's spirit in the spiritual world is no longer human, but is in a different context altogether.

CHAPTER FIVE

A God Worth Seeking

The God who made the world and all things in it, since He is Lord of heaven and earth,... [has] made from one man every nation of mankind to live on all the face of the earth, having determined their appointed times and the boundaries of their habitation, that they would seek God, if perhaps they might grope for Him and find Him, though He is not far from each one of us...
Acts 17:24-27

One of the fascinating aspects of the Bible is the sheer intrigue that it inspires within us. To say that the Bible is a unique book is like saying the Eiffel Tower is a unique structure, or the Taj Mahal is a pretty building. Such pithy comments simply do not do justice to the subject at hand. The fact is: there is no other book of religion or literature comparable to the Bible. Even religious books which claim similar status cannot come close to competing with the clarity, thematic uniqueness, and lucidity of the Bible— not to mention the sheer drama and fascination it contains.

No other book makes such profound and life-altering claims as the Bible does *and* supports those claims with historical and irrefutable evidence. Miracles and supernatural intervention are corroborated by physical proof and a host of eyewitness accounts. The credibility and remarkableness of its sacred text do not rest upon one or two fantastic miracles, but with hundreds and thousands of supernatural acts. Since God's very existence is miraculous by definition (when compared to our mundane existence), His every activity upon the earth or within the human soul is also miraculous in nature. The greatest of these miracles on earth is indisputably the resurrection of Christ. The greatest miracle within the soul is the born-again experience of the one who is made a "new creature" when he obeys Christ's gospel (John 3:3-5; 2 Corinthians 5:17; 1 Peter 1:3).

The Bible serves as the connective link between secular history and the theocracy of Israel. It blends together the physical world of man with the reality of heaven. It unites the humble smallness of man with the majestic greatness of God. It magnifies the weakness of man's frail and self-destructive nature *and* the infinite power of Christ's saving grace. It contrasts the self-serving pride of the human spirit with the unstoppable and inexhaustible power of the Holy Spirit ("the zeal of the Lord"). The Bible speaks, works, and inspires on a level that far transcends the mundane world of man.

The God of the Bible

We could continue to talk about the Bible's unique character, but we really want to draw our attention to something even greater than the Bible itself: the One who *wrote* it. "All Scripture is inspired by God" (2 Timothy 3:16), which means that the message which has been preserved through the ages is not only in agreement with God but *originated* with Him. God did not necessarily oversee every word the Bible writers chose to use; He did not prevent their own personalities or writing styles from influencing the expression of their works. But God *did* make sure that the Creation account, Israel's history, prophecies of His Messiah, and the gospel of the Savior Himself would all be accurately recorded, preserved, and uncorrupted (Galatians 1:11-12; 2 Peter 1:16-21). Thus the Bible is a product of God's mind, not a mere collection of men's writings or recollections of history.

In reading what has been preserved in the Bible, we are made to wonder: what kind of God is this who not only *desires* to communicate with us but also has the *ability* to do so? Men have been seeking contact with "extraterrestrial intelligence" for some time now, but nothing can be more extraterrestrial or intelligent than an omnipotent, omniscient Creator! This Creator has not sent us blips and beeps on an astral radar screen to identify Himself (like what we think we will receive if intelligent life *was* trying to contact us), but He has communicated with us through an intellectual, logical, poetic, and life-transforming message. He has told us things we could not have known otherwise; at the same time, He has not gushed with intellectual smugness, like we would expect from an all-knowing human genius. God's great *restraint*—in knowledge, power, and reaction to men's provocations—is as impressive as that which He *has* revealed.

God's timelessness, His transcendence, and His flawless knowledge of the future are some of what makes the Bible story so impressive and amazing. God is not a glorified man; He is not a spiritual Superman with superhuman powers—or kryptonite-induced weaknesses. His power cannot be depleted or exhausted; He cannot be conquered or killed. God has no equal or comparison. We cannot say, "God is like such-and-such," because there is nothing in this world or in our imagination that God is *like*. As Isaiah has recorded (44:6-7),

> Thus says the LORD, the King of Israel and his Redeemer, the LORD of hosts: "I am the first and I am the last, and there is no God besides Me. Who is like Me? Let him proclaim and declare it; yes, let him recount it to Me in order, from the time that I established the ancient nation. And let them declare to them the things that are coming And the events that are going to take place."

Who else is able to scan all of human history in a single view? What man or idol has ever been able to accurately foretell the future? Not only does God *see* all of history from beginning to end, He also *directs* it according to a predetermined purpose (Ephesians 3:11). While He allows man to make moral choices on his own, no man can usurp *God's* choices. This is one of the primary lessons of Genesis: God's promises to Abraham continue on course, unaffected by the pitfalls of the story's characters. God's will is going to be accomplished; His purpose is going to be fulfilled; there is nothing that men, time, or circumstances can do to alter this. As God has said (Isaiah 55:10-11),

> For as the rain and the snow come down from heaven, And do not return there without watering the earth and making it bear and sprout, and furnishing seed to the sower and bread to the eater; So will My word be which goes forth from My mouth; It will not return to Me empty, without accomplishing what I desire, And without succeeding in the matter for which I sent it.

We are unable to control the events of our own lifetime (or a single day), but God is able to control the events of *all history*. This does not mean that God is responsible for every single thing that happens, but that *nothing* happens without His knowledge and nothing can overwhelm His overall purpose. His *ultimate* purpose is the salvation of all those who believe and obey Him (John 3:16; 1 Timothy 2:3-6).

God not only exercises divine control over the world, He has *created* it. Every living creature, every mountain, every jungle, every ocean, every weather pattern, and every ecological system was originally made and ideally designed by God the Father through the agency of God the Son (see John 1:1-3; Colossians 1:15-18; Hebrews 1:1-2). Every atom, proton, and electron—as well as every constellation, galaxy, and quasar—was brought into existence by the very *utterance* of God's mind.

Not only does He oversee the physical world, but God also has absolute control over the spiritual realm. All authorities and dominions, whether on earth or in heaven, have always been under the authority of God the Father; He has since put these under the authority of God the Son (1 Corinthians 15:27-28; Colossians 1:15-16). This means God presides over *our* spiritual realm, the unseen dimensions of our unseen existence. He is able to peer into the folds and crevices of our secret lives, even the most private recesses of our souls. Nothing escapes His view; no one can remove himself from under His authority. The Bible tells us (Hebrews 4:12-13):

> For the word of God is living and active and sharper than
> any two-edged sword, and piercing as far as the division of
> soul and spirit, of both joints and marrow, and able to judge
> the thoughts and intentions of the heart. And there is no
> creature hidden from His sight, but all things are open and
> laid bare to the eyes of Him with whom we have to do.

What other person can know our thoughts unless we divulge them (cf. 1 Corinthians 2:11)? Yet God knows not only our thoughts themselves but also the *intentions* of those thoughts—the motives that inspired them. In other words, He not only knows the "what" of our thinking, He knows the "why." There is no thought that we can hide from Him, no motive that He cannot expose; and in the end, "God will judge the secrets of men through

Christ Jesus" (Romans 2:16).

The more we learn about God the more we realize that He is *not of human invention*—He is not even within human reach.   We are not dealing with a molten image that sits on a man-made pedestal gathering dust in some ancient temple.   We are not admiring a god of our own making, indirectly praising *ourselves* through the work of our own hands or minds.   We are not dealing with a "God" of some denominational religion that tries to dictate our beliefs through charismatic men, human creeds, and human effort.   We are not hoping in a questionable or vague spirit whom we can never really trust or place any confidence.   We are not waiting for a god who may fail, has never proven his performance, or has not been deemed worthy of our faith.

In light of all that we have discussed thus far, we must ask ourselves: *Is this a God worth seeking?*   If not, then what other god *is*?   Should we seek instead after a god that has nothing to offer, is incapable of love, and does not even truly exist?   This makes no sense.   In light of all that the God of Scripture has to offer, all other choices are rendered pointless. Yet whenever people seek completion, satisfaction, or salvation in anything else other than the God of heaven, they are seeking after such a god.   Instead of seeking after the sacred, everything these people do ultimately is "futility and striving after wind" (Ecclesiastes 2:17).

The Object of Our Search

We have discussed how important it is that one first understands the very nature *of* the sacred before commencing one's search for it.   We must not succumb to what so many have done in the past, which is to seek after something "sacred" simply because it is *deemed* sacred.   Seeking after an object of curiosity or person of intrigue is hardly a noble endeavor in itself. This is merely an expression of idolatry and can never equal or replace one's search for God.   Seeking after any god—or object of veneration—other than the God of heaven has always been condemned *by* God (Exodus 20:3-5; Romans 1:21-25, et al).

Furthermore, it is not enough to believe that a Sacred God exists;

we must also actively seek Him. Read this again: *we* must actively seek *Him*. We are not merely to seek a religion that involves God, or embark on a search that seeks only the gifts of God. Our goal is to draw near to *Him*, not merely to a congregation of those who *belong* to Him, or to a church that uses His name. While many seek "truth" or "religion" or "a church that I feel comfortable with," these people often fail to understand that their search is supposed to be for the One who calls *us* to Himself. When we focus our search for God on *His* terms, then our religion, worship, and focus become very productive and personal. If we fail to understand this, then these things will always remain on the periphery of our lives. Our religion will at best be an emotional experience; at worst it will be a purely mechanical one.

This anticipates the question, "Why do I need to 'seek' after God? Isn't it enough that I simply recognize His holiness and acknowledge His supremacy?" While these actions are absolutely necessary, they are not the goal of our moral responsibility. Worshipping the Sacred God must not be reduced to a mere worship of the sacredness *of* God. God does not want to be merely "recognized," as though nodding respectfully in His direction while gorging ourselves with self-indulgence. God wants to be *loved*, just as you and I want to be loved. He wants to be *admired*, just as you and I want to be admired. He wants to be *obeyed*, just as you and I want to be obeyed by those whom we oversee. His supremacy really is not "acknowledged" at all if He is not given His due respect as One who is supremely worthy of all these things.

Let us now consider some other reasons why God must be *sought* and not merely acknowledged:

He is a part of us and we are a part of Him. We are His own Creation, and He is our Father. We cannot exist without God, and God's love cannot be demonstrated without an object of that love. This demands a certain *relationship* between the two parties, that is, between you and the God who gave you life. This relationship factor is crucial to understanding *why* you should seek God. "The fear of the Lord is the beginning of knowledge" (Proverbs 1:7) which means that before one can become enlightened *by* God he must first have a proper respect *for* God.

Our destiny (ideally) is to be with Him, just as He wants

fellowship with us. God does not create a human life to destroy it, but to give that person an opportunity to choose Him as his God—in essence, so that God can enjoy his fellowship endlessly. This takes the relationship factor to the next level. It is not enough to honor God as our Creator or as the Father of our souls (cf. Hebrews 12:9); it is necessary to become part of His *family*, "the household of God," through Christ's church (1 Timothy 3:15). This requires that certain conditions be met—namely, that one's heart will surrender and submit to Christ's gospel. God's love is unconditional; salvation (which is found only "in Christ") is most certainly conditional.

 This world is empty, vain, helpless, and hopeless on its own. This world creates problems but cannot solve them. It identifies limitations, but cannot overcome them. It ridicules the sacred, but cannot find peace and solace apart from communion *with* the sacred. Each one of us is incomplete without God. This may not seem to be a significant problem up front (after all, we have become accustomed to living with inadequacy and incompleteness), but it is our incompleteness that will prevent us from being *with* God in the hereafter. We cannot complete ourselves, however; it is only "in Christ" that we are made complete (Colossians 1:28). There is no other way to the Father except *through* Christ (John 14:6).

 This world is not supposed to be our final dwelling place. Rather, it is supposed to make us appreciate a *better* dwelling place. When the Bible talks about a "new heavens and a new earth" (such as in Isaiah 65:17 or 2 Peter 3:13), the context always describes a new dwelling place for man—a new state of existence—not a refurbished physical planet: "the former [heavens and earth—MY WORDS] shall not be remembered or come to mind." Those who believe that Christ is going to live on this overhauled earth for a thousand years miss the point: God is not going to live among *us* on this planet, but the redeemed are going to live with *Him* in His heaven. This has been His intention ever since He created us. We begin in the physical realm, but anticipate life with God in the spiritual (cf. 1 Corinthians 15:46-50; Philippians 3:20-21, et al).

Seekers by Nature

It is not unusual that God asks us to be seekers of the sacred, since He has made us seekers by nature. We are always searching for something whether or not we recognize this. We are all seeking answers (sometimes it's just "the" answer), reasons, knowledge, and enlightenment in one form or another. We seek forgiveness, vengeance, apologies, and closure. We also seek fame, fortune, acceptance, love, physical or sensual gratification, and pleasure in whatever form we can find it. Despite this, no other search is going to produce the absolute joy, completion, and reward that the search for the sacred will most certainly produce—*if* one conducts it properly.

Unfortunately, some focus upon a certain *object* or *achievement* as their lifelong quest with a "search for the holy grail"-kind of mentality. (We must question how productive or useful such a search really is.) Others become absorbed and even obsessed with the search itself; whether or not they actually accomplish anything in the process seems almost secondary to the thrill of the pursuit. For example, you will hear people use phrases like, "It's been my lifelong passion to . . ." or "My vision is to . . ." or "The purpose of my existence . . ." is to do or discover something or other. You hear it from the numismatist that is always searching for the perfect coin to add to his collection. Or listen to the big game hunter who is ever seeking that perfect hunt for the ideal prey. Or there is the mountain climber who forever has his sights on that euphoric mountain climbing experience upon the perfect peak. More close to home, there is the man or woman seeking to find—or become—the ideal wife or husband. Or there is that lonely person seeking after companionship and the warmth of someone else's presence in his life.

Certainly we should have dreams and we should pursue them. That's all part of the human experience. My point is that all of these searches—and any search for something that can only be found on this earth, or even worse, only in one's imagination—are ultimately disappointing. This is because they are *limited* to the human experience. All such searches end once a person dies, no matter how passionate his pursuit was when he was alive. Even if a person is successful in his pursuit, there is still emptiness at the other end of it all. Once a person finds what he is looking for, then what? Now that he has discovered his priceless reward, what is there to look forward to? Worse yet, what if that person never finds the object of his quest at all? If someone has put all his life into looking for some fabled Fountain of Youth, for example, but never finds it, he has *spent* all his youth and all those productive years for nothing. This is beyond disappointing; it is a total loss.

The search for the Sacred God is entirely different, however. Such a pursuit is not a useless, pointless venture. For one thing, God is not a figment of someone's imagination. He is not an urban legend, myth, fable, or fantasy. Heaven is not El Dorado, Xanadu, Nirvana, or the Lost City of Atlantis. Holiness is not some comic-book "power" which only a superhero can possess, nor is it some kind of spiritual aphrodisiac designed to create the ultimate euphoric experience.

Secondly, *anyone* can join in this search and *everyone* who sincerely and appropriately does so *will indeed find what he or she is looking for*. The search for God is not limited to a privileged few, the rich, or the powerful. No one stumbles into completion accidentally, salvation cannot be purchased with money, and no one is invited into heaven because of earthly status. In fact, "many who are first will be last; and the last, first" (Matthew 19:30).

Thirdly, no one who "finds God" is ever done with the search. Discovering God is like discovering math: you might think that simple arithmetic is fascinating in itself, until you realize that simple math leads to more complex math, then to math that can hardly be described with human language. In another sense, you might relate to math first on a purely numerical level; then you realize that math can be expressed through variables and non-numerical symbols. Ultimately, you may realize that math ascends to a virtually conceptual level which cannot be expressed in mere numbers *or* variables, but requires actual written explanation, three-dimensional models, or . . . who knows what else.

God, even more than mathematics, is infinite. He is not merely a mathematical expression, however; He is a Living Being who is impossible to fully know or "discover" in this lifetime. Which leads to a fourth point: the search for the sacred is not limited to this earth, a particular time in one's life, or even to this life at all. The search is not consummated until we leave this world and actually enter into God's own world, where we will meet Him face-to-face. Even then, one has to wonder if we will not spend the rest of eternity still "discovering" God. Since He is infinite and since His Life has no end or boundaries, then to think we will spend every moment of eternity drawing ever closer to the sacred is not a far-fetched one. In fact, it is perfectly logical.

The Distance to God

Jesus once told a man who had answered Him well that he was "not far from the kingdom of God" (Mark 12:34). Jesus was not speaking of the length of travel or of geographical proximity. He was not telling the man how far it was to the nearest "sound congregation," if you know what I mean. He was talking about *attitude*. Jesus meant, in essence, "Your attitude is very close to that which is expected in the kingdom of God." Similarly, someone else once said, "The distance to heaven is not a matter of altitude, but attitude." Paul wrote that Christ's salvation is not too high, nor too deep, nor at all inaccessible to the one who believes; rather, He is *in your heart*, which is as close to a person as anyone can get (Romans 10:5-10).

Searching for God is not like searching for treasure on a treasure map where "X" marks the spot. However, there is a certain obvious parallel. The *Bible* is like a treasure map, in the sense that one must follow God's instructions in order to enjoy the riches of God (Ephesians 1:18, et al). Indeed, the *cross* marks the "spot" where God is centrally located—not the physical wooden crucifix upon which Jesus was literally crucified, and not the literal location where that crucifixion occurred, but what that cross symbolizes in expressing the very heart of God's love for man.

Someone says, "Well, if the cross marks the location of the treasure, then why do I need the rest of the Bible? You've already given away the secret!" First of all, there are no secrets to which I or anyone else is privy that you yourself cannot know. Anyone and everyone can "know the love of Christ which surpasses knowledge, that you may be filled up to all the fullness of God" (Ephesians 3:19) provided they search for this knowledge and fullness through prayer, study, and fellowship. Christ's church is the church of the elect, not the elite. Anyone can be a part of it and no one has a good reason *not* to be a part of it.

Secondly, one is mistaken if he thinks that by learning key Bible verses or becoming an expert on biblical concepts is a replacement for the rewarding search for the sacred. Whoever has access to a Bible can learn of God's sacred plan of salvation, and this plan always leads one to the cross of Christ. In fact, the more one studies the Bible, the more one realizes just how powerfully and perfectly the cross consummates the grand picture which God has revealed to us. The cross is the opening of the treasure, so to speak; indeed, it serves as a kind of wooden key that opens up the doors of heaven to the seeker of God. However, discovering the full extent or depth of that treasure is an endless, exhilarating, and completely worthwhile adventure.

The Object of Our Existence

To seek after the sacred means to put all other searches and pursuits secondary to this one search. Whatever else we seek here upon this earth cannot be considered equal or superior to our search for God. This mindset requires, especially in the beginning, an abrupt yet critical shift in our thinking. Our jobs, careers, spouses, children, different seasons of life, etc. are all part of what we call our "life," but your life is not complete with any one of these things or all of them combined. Jesus once told a crowd, "not even when one has an abundance does his life consist of his possessions" (Luke 12:15). We may not categorize our family and careers and such as "possessions" *per se*, but I don't think Jesus was limiting His discussion only to things you can buy at the store either. I understand the context to refer to whatever one has or possesses in the most general sense (think of Matthew 10:37-39, for example). Not ironically, His statement about possessions is in the context of a general warning against succumbing to greed, which is naturally and frequently present in the raw, unrefined, and unspiritual human life.

This thought forces us to clarify the true object of our existence. It is not to possess things; it is not merely to have or enjoy human relationships; it is not to have control over things or people. Furthermore, we were not put upon this earth merely to make a living, produce offspring, and have a good time. From God's point of view, we were *created*, and therefore we have *purpose*: we were created *for* a purpose. The highest purpose of *every* person is to seek after God—to be a seeker of the sacred. Consider the words of Paul in his speech on Mars Hill in Athens (Acts 17:25-28, emphasis mine):

> He [God] Himself gives to all people life and breath and all things; and He made from one man every nation of mankind to live on all the face of the earth, having determined their appointed times and the boundaries of their habitation, **that they would seek God**, if perhaps they might grope for Him and find Him, though He is not far from each one of us; for in Him we live and move and exist...

God is the beginning of our existence. Ideally, we are to regard Him as the substance, desire, and *consummation* of our existence as well. People, possessions, or positions are not the objects of our existence. I realize that for many this is all they have, but that is not the way it is supposed to be— this was never God's intention. Furthermore, if this is all that one has, then it is only a thin veneer of "substance" which barely masks a vast expanse of emptiness and darkness. Such emptiness will be painfully evident once that person's physical life is taken from him.

Jesus admonished us to store our treasures in heaven—in essence, to recognize that our treasure is *in* heaven, where God is—versus accumulating treasures here upon this earth (Matthew 6:19-21). This is such a simple spiritual concept, but it ushers in an absolute and monumental truth: we have so little control over the things of this world and no control of the things beyond this world, *if left to our own power*. This is the ultimate context in which Jesus had revealed this truth. He was not merely talking about property and possessions, but power and control—i.e., the human inability to exercise or sustain power and control over the things of this world. In contrast, God's power and control cannot be touched by the deteriorative or corrosive elements of this world or by the greed and wickedness of men (as illustrated by rust and moths, intrusion and thievery). Trying to place any sort of permanent value upon earthly things or relationships is ultimately self-defeating.

This does not mean that this world is useless to us or that we must abandon people in order to have a proper relationship with God. Quite the contrary, a person who has forsaken all worldly connections and has divorced himself from all personal relationships will hardly be able to relate to the world in which he is supposed to exercise Christian virtues. One can hardly be a light to the world or salt of the earth if he is holed up in some (literal or figurative) monastic cave (cf. Matthew 5:13-16). He will not be a "fellow partaker of the gospel" if he is unable to be all things to all people (cf. 1 Corinthians 9:23). He cannot be useful to the kingdom of God if he cannot functionally interact with this world.

What God gives us to enjoy in this life are *blessings*, not cargo to jettison. (It is true that *God* can give or remove these blessings according to His will [cf. Job 1:21]; it is *not* true that we have the right to insist that He does one or the other.) God does not bless us with marriages, children, material possessions, jobs, etc. just so that He can have something with which to criticize and condemn us. Imagine a father who gives his son a nice car, a great job in the family business, and a college education—then turns around and berates the son for actually accepting those gifts instead of denouncing them all as excessive! What a hypocrite that father would be to his son. Not only that, but such a man would be impossible to please since his son is condemned no matter what decision he makes.

Our God is not a God of contradiction or double-minded intentions. God does not tempt us with evil (James 1:13) nor does He give us evil things to bring about our ruin. God does not attempt to confound our seeking Him by throwing all sorts of obstacles and stumbling blocks in our way; He does not beckon us to heaven and then plant land mines in our path. Christ admits freely that our path is narrow and fraught with danger, predators ("wolves"; Matthew 7:15-20), distractions, and sensual temptations, but Christ does not *put* them there. These things exist in the world due to the sin of man, and anyone who is in the world—no matter how godly that person may be—will be confronted with them.

We must also recognize just how important *sacrifice* is in our seeking after the sacred. (We will discuss this much more thoroughly in an upcoming chapter entitled "Drawing Near to God.") Jesus taught that whatever causes us to stumble we are to cut, gouge, or rip out of our lives (Matthew 18:8-9).

The context refers to whatever tempts us to *sin* and yet is within our power to remove from our lives. The implication is clear: when Jesus speaks of a stumbling block, He refers to *whatever interferes with our search for God.* Such obstacles must be removed; we cannot be passive toward them. The search for God is worth sacrificing whatever would compromise that search. God is worth seeking; therefore God is worth the sacrifices we would render to Him. Jesus Christ deserves our full attention; therefore, He deserves our uncompromising allegiance. Our future with God cannot be jeopardized by (comparatively-speaking) a few moments of pleasure or distraction.

Enhancing Our Search for God

Let's turn this subject on its head for a moment: suppose we considered all that we have in our life as part of the search, if viewed properly. From God's bird's-eye perspective, every earthly blessing is supposed to enrich our *spiritual* life, not ruin it. In fact, if we step back and look at the big picture, we can realize that these things, while not part of our final objective, most certainly ought to whet our appetite *for* it. In essence, rather than serve as stumbling blocks, our circumstances and possessions can actually point us heavenward. Think about the following:

Physical wealth, regardless of how much or little it might be, can help give us a foretaste of what God has prepared for us. If we have much, then we can always remember that God has far more, and He will share *all* of it with us so long as we do not cling too tightly to what we have now. If we have little, then God's unlimited wealth will also be ours, as long as we do not despise what we have been denied here upon the earth.

Personal relationships, if we find them to be enjoyable, will be infinitely more so in heaven. Fellowship there will have no bounds, no inhibitions, and no end. All the limitations of time and distance, all the interference of human emotions and others' intrusions, and all the hindrances of human imperfections will be gone. All who are in heaven will be in love with Christ and thus in love with one another. I'm not talking about some sappy, emotional love, but the "great love with which He loved us" kind of love (cf. Ephesians 2:4). Even if our earthly relationships are joyless—i.e., we endure them out of obligation, duty, previous commitments, etc.—then we can anticipate a "time" with God when all such relationships will have ceased to exist. This does not mean that all those with whom we have such relationships will be lost just because we do not enjoy such people. It means that in heaven *no one* will have an unpleasant relationship with anyone else. Such experiences will not exist; the very idea is unthinkable there. We will all be kindred spirits; no one will be overwhelmed or overlooked.

Health problems, physical flaws or imperfections, aging and disease—all of these should remind us that our stay here is temporary and ultimately unsatisfying. We were not intended to remain upon this earth forever, but we are here only for a brief stay until we can always be with the Lord. Every day—perhaps every hour—that we must endure the pain and discomfort of this physical existence can be looked upon as one day closer to our eternal rest with God. One needs only to view his earthly struggle one day at a time; one's suffering only has to last 24 hours until that day is done. In contrast, life in God's "day" will be one of perfect health, without decline or deterioration of any kind.

Suffering—not the mere deprivation of desired comfort, but the assault of wrongs and injustices of this world upon our innocence—can also whet our appetite for the world to come. In God's world there are no tempters or oppressors, and no person, power or thing can ever change any of that. In heaven God will maintain the protection of His people forever; having made them innocent with His Son's blood, He will preserve their innocence and security eternally.

Wickedness in general, whether or not we are directly touched by it, can inspire a powerful hope for an existence in which there is no wickedness. The more we see of the wickedness of this world, the deeper our longing for a world without wickedness becomes. After all, Jesus came as a brilliant light into a darkened world (cf. John 1:4-9, 8:12); His brightness was paradoxically amplified and magnified *by* the extreme moral darkness of fallen humanity. The darker the picture into which the Light enters, the more brilliant the Light will appear—and the greater the contrast between the two will be.

Death itself can provide a powerful incentive for a search for God.

The fact of our impending death forces us—if we are willing to confront our mortality at all—to appreciate the wonderful experience of simply being alive. An imperfect life is much more enjoyable if we believe that it will not last forever; death can be much more acceptable if we know that it serves as only a transition to a perfect life that will *never* end. Every day which is lived to the fullest can be viewed as only a faint glimmer of the kind of endless life that God has prepared for us with Him. The loss of dear friends and loved ones, while causing unspeakable pain and sorrow here, can still point us toward the God to whom all souls return after this life is over. Those who "die in the Lord" (cf. Revelation 14:13) will ultimately be rejoined with all who are believers in an inexpressibly wonderful existence with the Lord Jesus forever. There will be no more separation from those who love God. Even with regard to those who have chosen a different end, we will not grieve over them forever. When we are with the Savior, we will have sufficient knowledge and perspective to understand what has happened. With such understanding, we will find closure in what cannot be resolved here; we will find straightened whatever seems crooked and unfixable here; we will find completion to whatever is lacking here (cf. Ecclesiastes 1:15). Death, while appearing to be a symbol of irretrievable loss to us here will, in the end, provide for a rebirth into something better, brighter, and more beautiful than anything we could have ever known in this life. Death, paradoxically, leads us straight into the arms of Jesus, directly into the very real presence of God.

*   *   *

The point here is not merely to provoke a rhapsodic, "How beautiful heaven must be!"— although I, too, believe heaven will be beautiful. However, if we focus upon heaven as a mere *place* or *experience* that is filled with good things (or void of bad things), we miss the central theme of the Bible, the intent of Christ's ministry, and the ultimate fulfillment of man's very existence. This ought to evoke from us not merely, "How beautiful heaven must be!" but "How beautiful *God* must be!" It is God, after all, who is at the center of every portrayal of heaven—heaven exists only by His authority, power, and majesty. God is the source of the very *concept* of heaven; even here everything we call "good" mirrors the very nature of God Himself. God is also the giver of all that is good: everything we call "good" ultimately finds its origin in God Himself since "Every good thing given and every perfect gift is from above, coming down from the Father of lights, with whom there is no variation or shifting shadow" (James 1:17). The entire Bible is a tremendous testament to the glorious God of heaven. Through a study of it, we cannot help but become enthralled with a deeper, fonder, and more thrilling picture of this great God.

So once again we are confronted with the question: Is this beautiful, majestic, and transcendent God not worth seeking? I believe He most certainly is, without question. There is nothing in this world that can compare to the sacred glory of God. To search for Him is to be filled with the rhapsody of life, love, and joy. To become a seeker of the sacred is the most fulfilling, rewarding, and intimate journey upon which anyone could embark. All other searches or pursuits are doomed to fail; if nothing else, death destroys them all. Yet God is "not the God of the dead, but of the living" (Matthew 22:32). Furthermore, Jesus Himself declared that He is "the living One; and I was dead, and behold, I am alive forevermore, and I have the keys of death and of Hades" (Revelation 1:18). Not even death can end one's search for the sacred.

Just because I have come to this conclusion does not mean that you will automatically be convinced of it. Nonetheless, the evidence of these things is compelling and irrefutable; not only this but ultimately you have everything to gain by engaging in such a search. In this life, even if you gain the whole world but never find God, you still lose everything (cf. Matthew 16:26); but if you find God, even though you *will* lose the whole world, you will be blessed beyond earthly calculation in the end. With that in mind, I trust that you will continue with me in seeking the sacred. We will not be disappointed in what we discover.

CHAPTER SIX

It's God's World—We're Just Living in It

Where can I go from Your Spirit? Or where can I flee from Your presence? If I ascend to heaven, You are there; If I make my bed in Sheol, behold, You are there. If I take the wings of the dawn, If I dwell in the remotest part of the sea, Even there Your hand will lead me, And Your right hand will lay hold of me.
Psalm 139:7-10

Have you been in the presence of God? Could God be in *your* presence right now— perhaps without you even knowing it? Do you *believe* He is that close to you?

The gospels record some unsuspecting encounters with God. When Jesus spoke to the Samaritan woman at the well, she stated, "I know that Messiah is coming," and Jesus responded, "I who speak to you am He" (John 4:25-26). After Jesus healed a man's congenital blindness, He asked him, "Do you believe in the Son of Man?" And the man replied, "Who is He, Lord, that I may believe in Him?" And Jesus said, "You have both seen Him, and He is the one who is talking to you" (John 9:35-37).

Someone says, "Those people encountered *Christ*, not God." But Jesus has said otherwise. In John 14:8-11, Philip asked Jesus, "Show us the Father, and it is enough for us." To which Jesus replied, in essence, "Inasmuch as you have seen *Me*, you have seen the *Father*." He had already declared, "I and the Father are one" (John 10:30). This did not mean that Jesus *was* the Father, but that His identity as Son of God is inseparable *from* God Himself (John 1:1-2). The point is: anyone who has come into contact with Jesus Christ has, in a very real sense, been in the presence of the God.

You and I have not had this privilege, however. We have seen Jesus in the Scriptures (cf. Luke 24:27); we have seen Him in the testimony of others (1 John 1:1-3); but we have not seen Him in the flesh. Indeed, "even though we have known Christ according to the flesh, yet now we know Him in this way no longer" (2 Corinthians 5:16). Therefore, we must "walk by faith, not by sight" (2 Corinthians 5:7); we are compelled to *believe* even though we have not *seen* (1 Peter 1:8). And for this, Jesus says that we are blessed (John 20:29).

Does this mean then that God the Father is far away from us, discreetly hiding in some corner of the universe waiting for our telescopes and cosmic receivers to pick up some faint glimmer of His existence? Does this mean that in seeking the sacred we engage in a completely useless pursuit of Someone whom we will never discover anyway, except through the written facts of Scripture? Does this mean that we really *are* all alone, and God is nowhere to *be* discovered, and that communion with Him is purely an exercise of one's spiritual imagination?

The answer to these questions requires that we recognize God's "presence" in two different contexts. When we talk about "seeking the sacred," we are really talking about *seeking an ever-deepening fellowship with the Sacred God of Heaven.* This concept of fellowship necessarily implies *communion* with God, which itself has several different levels. A person is in communion with God as soon as he rises from the water of his baptism. One who spends his life zealously and reverently enveloping himself in God's grace discovers an even deeper communion (Ephesians 3:14-19). In this way, just as we have been "born again" by water and the Spirit (cf. John 3:3-5), we are also being renewed daily by dwelling in the presence of the Lord. This is not something we are able to do alone, but is made possible only through Jesus Christ (Hebrews 13:20-21).

Having said this, we must recognize a second context by which the Scriptures refer to the presence of God, which bears directly upon our understanding of God Himself. In previous chapters, we have spent a fair amount of time examining what God "looks" like; now we must begin to discover where God *is.* And He is much closer to us than we might have first imagined.

The Uncontainable Omnipresence of God

Searching for God is like searching for oxygen: if you knew what you were looking for, and if you had the right instrument to detect it, you would quickly discover that it is everywhere. I don't mean to imply that we need a certain mechanical "instrument" to detect God's presence, for the human soul is a far more powerful, sophisticated, and sensitive instrument than anything we have assembled here on earth. It is perfectly adequate for sensing the otherworldly presence of its Creator. After all, inasmuch as God is the Source of all life, He has also given all living souls a link back to Him.

Just because God is invisible to us does not mean He is nowhere near us. We cannot measure God's presence with spatial, voluminous, or dimensional criteria. "God is spirit" (John 4:24), and therefore He cannot be bound by physical limitations. God is not "big," like we think of bigness; He is not "tall," or "heavy"; He does not occupy a certain amount of space in the physical universe. On the contrary, the physical universe exists only within the midst of God's presence. In other words, we have it all backwards. God is not in our world; rather, it is God's world and we are just living in it.

Let's think about this conceptually. God's presence cannot be contained by anything physical since He Himself is a spiritual, omnipresent Being. Therefore, if we can learn to appreciate how vast this physical universe is, we would begin to appreciate how limitless and incalculable God's presence is. We will not appreciate the vastness of the universe until we recognize how "small" *we* are. The world we live in is huge when compared to the amount of space we actually occupy. Someone has calculated that we could presently fit the entire world's population—over six billion people— in the expanse of the Grand Canyon. Even if we needed *two* Grand Canyons, it would still be just a blip on the global radar map. We just don't occupy much space. Our homes, transportation systems, infrastructure, and other accommodations take up considerably more space than do our own physical bodies. The earth is nearly 8,000 miles in diameter, and yet we live only on the very surface of it; the entire biosphere is wafer-thin compared to the earth's mass. Proportionately, we live on the outermost skin of an onion, nothing more.

This begs a question: if we occupy so little space, then why is this physical world so large? After all, if God wanted to He could have easily put us upon a much smaller, very flat *terra firma* instead of giving us all of this seemingly wasted material, most of which we will never see or use. To accommodate this, He could have easily spoken into existence different laws of physics and gravity than those which presently govern our world.

This question also transcends the scope of this earth. Consider the tremendous amount of space and unused material in the observable universe and ask yourself: Did God really have to make the sun so incredibly large? Couldn't He have made a much smaller sun (but one just as hot as ours)? Jupiter and Saturn, as far as our own earth is concerned, are *immense*— and yet their existence does not seem to contribute to *our* existence at all. Astronomers have since discovered distant planets that make Jupiter look like a cue ball sitting next to the Epcot Center. Beyond our solar system are other cosmic behemoths, silently twirling and coasting through the frozen blackness of space, waiting thousands of years to even be discovered by us, their visible light already ancient and obsolete by the time we observe it. It is fascinating to think that God has created things so wonderful as, say, the Horsehead Nebula, some 1,500 light years distant from us, knowing full well that it would take men thousands of years to create a mechanical device powerful enough to see it. This makes us wonder what else is "out there," silently and patiently waiting to be discovered by some succeeding generation with instruments and devices much more powerful than ours.

What of space itself? Consider just how incomprehensibly *vast* outer space really is. Our own galaxy, the Milky Way, is estimated to be some 100,000 light years across. In linear miles, that is (roughly) the number 6 with 22 zeros after it. That is just *one* galaxy, yet our astronomers are confident that there may be *billions* of galaxies out there. And that refers only to the ones they can account for. We ask, with reverent wonder: Did God really need to make the universe so enormous that it could hold billions of immense galaxies?

There seems to be much material excess and wasted space in the universe ("excess" and "wasted" are, of course, used both subjectively and rhetorically). Practically-speaking, it is not clear that we *need* a universe of this size in order to exist. Secular scientists also are of no help here since they have no good explanation for the immensity of the universe. The best that they can do is to say that, given the laws of statistics and probabilities, there needed to be a tremendous amount of raw materials to work with so that life could evolve into existence. But this assumes evolution and does not prove it; therefore it assumes that all this "material excess" and "wasted space" leads to human life, but it does not explain why human life is in the midst of all this material and space.

The Bible declares God to be the Maker of all that we observe in the universe (Genesis 1:1; John 1:1-3, et al). Secular scientists scoff at this, of course, and counter with "Big Bang" theories and the mindless luck of "natural selection" that apparently has led to human intelligence and spiritual consciousness. Nonetheless, the very concept of a supernatural, omnipotent, divine Being having spoken everything into existence is far superior to the unproved theories of men. The simple answer to our conundrums then is that we do not have to know why things are the way they are except that God saw fit to make them this way. As Creator, God has the prerogative to make whatever He wants, and He does not have to explain Himself to us.

While that answer is both accurate and simple, it sidesteps some of the advantages in examining such observations more closely. First of all, as mentioned earlier, the One who *made* all these things is at least as vast and infinite as our universe appears to be. Secondly, this Creator is not limited in material resources, intellectual capacity, or space in which to demonstrate His handiwork. It is entirely plausible that God created such an oversized earth ("oversized" in comparison to our immediate needs, since so much of the world remains largely uninhabited and unused) simply to provide us with a glimpse of just how powerful and limitless He is. As if that were not enough, He filled the cosmos with beauty, wonder, and massive celestial sights just so that we would further appreciate the supernatural power and glory which God seems to be able to effortlessly expend. If *that* were not enough, He also made the microscopic world just as fascinating, complex, and (seemingly) vast as the cosmos itself.

Bigger Than Life as We Know It

However, there is something else here worthy of consideration. What we call "space" simply refers to the absence of physical, material substance. In reality, it may not be nothingness: it may be filled with that which is invisible but real all the same. This is certainly not a new thought, but it bears upon our present discussion. Think about the common theme in following passages from Scripture [emphases and bracketed words mine]:

- Acts 17:27-28, "He [God] is not far from each one of us; for **in Him we live and move and exist.…**"
- 1 Corinthians 8:6, "…there is but one God, the Father, **from whom are all things and we exist for Him**; and one Lord, Jesus Christ, **by whom are all things, and we exist through Him.**"
- Ephesians 1:22-23, "And He put all things in subjection under His feet, and gave Him as head over all things to the church, which is His body, **the fullness of Him who fills all in all.**"
- Ephesians 4:6, "[There is] one God and Father of all **who is over all and through all and in all.**"
- Colossians 1:16-17, "For by Him [Christ as God—MY WORDS] all things were created, both in the heavens and on earth, visible and invisible, whether thrones or dominions or rulers or authorities— all things have been created through Him and for Him. He is before all things, and in Him **all things hold together.**"
- Hebrews 2:10, "For it was fitting for Him, for whom are all things, and **through whom are all things,** in bringing many sons to glory.…"

These passages all converge upon a single point: God's presence is not hiding somewhere in a distant quadrant of the universe. He is *right here* in our own midst—indeed, He is *everywhere* amidst His creation. While our physical bodies take up a negligible amount of space on earth, the entire universe cannot contain the presence of God. If the universe is filled with God, then it most certainly is not empty, for there is no empty space in God. Rather than us thinking that we need to draw God into our little world, as though He were otherwise floating somewhere in the cosmos, untethered and surreal, once again it is we who are living in *God's* world.

When we think of God's presence filling the universe, we probably tend to imagine God as an incomprehensibly huge entity in whose literal body is contained the entirety of the physical creation. Immediately this seems incomprehensible, if not outright absurd. Yet if we recognize that God's *power* and *authority* permeate all that exists, the meaning becomes inescapably clear as to what the above Bible passages are talking about:

Wherever there is life, there is God. The Law of Biogenesis states that life comes from life, and nothing comes from nothing. Nothing that is alive has willed *itself* into existence, nor can living things procreate apart from the system of reproduction that has been imposed upon them. Beyond this, there is something mysterious about *all* of life that defies all physical, biological, or scientific explanations and can only be attributed to supernatural intervention. Not only has Someone of transcendent power set all life in motion, but He continues to contribute to the existence of every living thing. Put another way: God has not merely made life possible, but He is *personally involved* in giving and sustaining all forms of life.

Wherever there is *energy*, there is God. The presence of all the energy in the universe (electromagnetic, nuclear, chemical, etc.) begs the question: where did this *come* from? The First Law of Thermodynamics dictates that energy can change form but cannot be created or destroyed (within the context of the physical universe). However, to assume that energy is *eternal* in nature—which demands that the context of energy (i.e., the universe) is also eternal—is a different situation altogether. To assume that the forms, physics, properties, and functions of energy have *always been* deifies energy itself: it attributes god-like qualities to energy without authority or purpose. The Bible offers a logical, explanative rebuttal to this: "In the *beginning*, God *created* the heavens and the earth" (Genesis 1:1, emphasis mine)—the Eternal God is the Source and Manager of all energy that exists. Whenever we observe the various forms of natural energy, we witness the effects of a Divine Creator—testaments of His invisible omnipresence in our visible world.

Wherever there is *light*, there is God. Visible light is an expression of energy that did not will itself into existence; it is not a mere by-product of a so-called accidental universe. While we would not say that the universe is "filled" with light, since it seems predominated by darkness, nonetheless visible light is everywhere to be seen in the cosmos.[5] Light can be measured while darkness cannot. Furthermore, the fact that light *exists* implies One's authority over darkness since darkness by itself cannot produce anything. Thus "The Light shines in the darkness, and the darkness did not comprehend it" (John 1:5).

Wherever there is *matter*, there is God. Albert Einstein proved that all matter (mass) is essentially a static form of energy. But raw energy cannot form itself into anything on its own without the intervention and manipulation of Someone more powerful than energy itself. Furthermore, energy cannot manipulate itself into anything which effectively or efficiently *uses* energy for any productive purpose—such as the support of human life. The fact that *anything* exists in a tangible, material form requires nothing short of a supernatural, all-powerful God.

Wherever there is *design*, there is God. An unintelligent, impersonal force called "Nature" cannot be responsible for all the interdependent systems that we observe on earth and in the universe. "Blind forces of nature" cannot make a human eye, much less a human brain—even less, a human conscience. Furthermore, blind chance cannot make a human eye *compatible* with a human brain, nor can a physical brain will a spiritual conscience into existence. But an omniscient, benevolent Creator most certainly *can* be responsible for all such complexities. Whether we consider (for example) the human cardiopulmonary system, procreation, photosynthesis, the ecosystem, the meteorological system, or the gravitational relationship between suns and planets, *Someone* far beyond our comprehension is responsible for having designed and implemented these things.

Wherever there is *law*, there is God. Absolute chaos, which is what the universe would be (assuming it could exist at all) apart from a Higher Being imposing His will upon it, cannot make laws to govern itself. Unintelligent, non-living physical elements cannot exceed their own properties and limitations. They cannot organize themselves, make decisions, create law and order, or invent that which exceeds their own abilities. While seemingly random chaos *does* seem to manifest itself in the world (e.g., the path of a tornado, an atomic explosion, or a "black hole" in space), there are still laws and forces that govern the parameters and limitations of such actions. Furthermore, these things do not alter or bring to an end the physical laws which govern the entire universe. An exploding star, for example, certainly wreaks havoc within its own galaxy, but the galaxy itself still remains, as do the laws that govern the universe, and the God who *made* the galaxy remains undisturbed and retains sovereign authority. Wherever we *observe* such stability and control—which permeates the entire universe—demands the supernatural existence of One who is above all the elements and forces *in* the universe.

Wherever there is *morality*, there is God. Worldly people loathe any connection between "morality" and God: they want to separate the two, so that they can accept the one (morality) and reject the other (God—or, at least, personal accountability *to* God). Morality—a law that governs the spiritual existence of man—cannot will itself into existence any more than can a rock, tree, or monkey. "Right" and "wrong" necessarily require absolute standards: there must be an *absolute right* and anything less than this is *wrong*. Likewise, in order for "evil" to exist, "good" must already exist in an absolute form. Some believe that society simply legislates morality into existence, yet this wrongly assumes the *pre*-existence of absolute truth, human intuition (concerning right and wrong), and human spirituality (which immediately implies moral *accountability*). Right, wrong, good, evil, justice, fairness, love, hate, human decency, etc. are meaningless unless an Absolutely Good Creator first *revealed* these things to us (Romans 1:18-20). Thus, our world is filled with either the *influence* of God (righteousness, goodness, love, kindness, etc.) or the *rejection* of that influence (wickedness, sin, hate, malice, etc.).

God is not an impersonal, collective "force" of the universe (as New Age philosophy teaches). He is not a super-colossal, morally-vacant, impersonal "Energy Field." We dare not rob the Living God of the divine nature which He has disclosed to us in His revealed Word. At the same time, we cannot reduce God's existence to mere physical forms, human levels of understanding, or perceived conditions. Jesus Himself said, "God is spirit"

(John 4:24), which means that God's nature, form, divine presence, etc. cannot be gauged or measured by human or physical standards. God—as a supernatural, spiritual, heavenly Being—fills the universe in ways which cannot be grasped by human understanding. We are told that "All things came into being through Him [Christ as God], and apart from Him nothing came into being that has come into being" (John 1:3, bracketed words mine). Whatever does exist, Christ (God) is the creative, active, and life-sustaining force behind it. It is *His* world, and we are just living in it—we do not own it, we are not its master, and we cannot change what He has given to us. We are simply required to *accept* this fact, and then respond *rightly* to its spiritual implications. We cannot be seekers of the sacred if we fail to acknowledge the omnipresence of the Sacred God.

Body, Soul, and God's Presence

While you and I live in God's world, we see only our *human perception* of it. We are not seeing everything that is happening; we are not *able* to see all such things. It is impossible for us to view this world exactly as God does, just as it is impossible for us to see God as He really is. Try as we might, there is an insuperable barrier between our three-dimensional vision and the supernatural, omni-dimensional realm of the sacred which prevents us from seeing the raw and unfiltered *reality* of our existence.

You and I cannot create something that does not exist; we can only reformat, reassemble, or disassemble that which already exists. Our world is composed of physical elements—raw materials which we did not create—which contribute to physical and biological processes that we did not set in motion and we cannot prevent from occurring. Everything we experience through our five senses actually could, if we had the power to do so, be reduced to microscopic molecular structures which themselves could be reduced to molecular, atomic, and subatomic particles.[6]

Look at the details of your surroundings. Look at the forms—solid wood, concrete, metal, brick, or gypsum—that compose the structure of your home. Look at the shapes, textures, colors, gloss (or flatness) of the paint on the walls, and the artificial lighting fixtures that may be all around you at this present moment. Artisans and craftsmen manipulated raw materials into these present forms, but they did not create the raw materials themselves. Even the *intelligence* to manipulate those raw materials did not originate with them.

As pleasing as our man-made surroundings may be to the human eye, they may actually be unattractive and unrecognizable on a microscopic level. Have you ever seen pictures of smooth or well-machined objects under extreme magnification, such as with an electron microscope? Suddenly those things which we thought were aesthetically-pleasing and familiar to us become foreign and even hostile-looking. A polished billiard ball becomes rough and cratered; a fine human hair turns into a barbed or serrated medieval weapon. Things only look "right" to us as we see them because we only can see things from a human perspective.

Now let's pull back on that perspective a bit. Consider the natural realms and formations that may be beyond your present view: valleys, canyons, rivers, forests of evergreens, arctic tundra, sweltering deserts, crests of mountain ranges, spans of savannah grasslands and prairie fields, great expanses of ocean and all that is contained in them. At the most basic level, these things are diversely, creatively, and intelligently arranged atomic and molecular constructions that, when composed on a massive scale, appear as beautiful, scenic, and "natural" features of our physical world. This is because we see them only as God has created us to see them—really, as He has *allowed* us to see them. If we were to see them as they really existed, from a supernatural perspective, we would have an entirely different view—and opinion—of the physical world. This doesn't mean God's perspective sees everything as ugly; rather, He sees everything *differently* than we do because He sees all things as they really *are*.

Let's apply this thinking to one's own physical makeup. From an earthly perspective, a human being has a tangible body, literally composed of some of the same elements as the natural world in which it exists. These elements were diversely, creatively, and intelligently assembled to produce a composite whole, a human form. None of us created the process of this assemblage, nor did we control the assemblage itself, nor the energy required to perform this. Our parents participated in (but did not create) the natural process that was required to bring each of us into a physical existence, but they cannot be credited for designing our bodies or giving us our characteristic features. The eleven different systems within the human body—nervous, pulmonary, endocrine, muscular, skeletal, etc.—were not created through our parents' genius any more than we are able to assemble our own children's bodies.

So you are, essentially, a highly complex and intelligently-integrated collection of molecular and cellular configurations. When put together in a certain way and programmed by certain genetic codes (which themselves are highly sophisticated arrangements of specialized proteins), these molecules and cells form what we call a "human being"—at least, this addresses the "being" part. "Human being" is just a specie designation, a classification of living creatures, a tangible interruption of allegedly empty space. We haven't even really touched on the "human" part. We do not just "exist" (like a plant or animal), but we are specifically a *human* being, which by definition implies a spiritual consciousness that transcends a mere physical presence in this world. We are not mere spasmodic masses of physical flesh and organs; we exist as intelligent life forms capable of rational thought, intelligent communication, abstract feelings and emotions, domination over all other living things, utilitarian manipulation of natural resources, and even spiritual insight.

Where did all that *come* from? What did you or I ever do to make that *happen*, much less *sustain* it? What kind of energy fuels our "human being-ness" so as to exist as living souls? Since our souls are not composed of molecular structures, proteins, tissues, or any other organic material, there is something immediately otherworldly about us. Take away this invisible spirit, and the body is lifeless and inanimate. Just as God's presence fills the cosmos through the supernaturally-imposed features discussed above, so His presence is evident within *us* by virtue of the fact that we are living, intelligent, and spiritually-conscious creatures (Romans 1:18-20). Just as God's Spirit gives life to the human soul (John 6:63), so the human soul gives animation to the human body (James 2:26).

The soul's existence cannot be detected in the physical world without a physical body; however, one's soul will survive even the destruction of the physical world. The apostle John wrote, "The world is passing away, and also its lusts; but the one who does the will of God lives forever" (1 John 2:17). The soul is eternal, just as the Father who gives us our soul is eternal. God never intended for the physical world to last forever; He had *every* intention, however, for the souls of men to be with Him forever. With this in mind, we are supposed to direct our attention "not at the things which are seen, but at the things which are not seen; for the things which are seen are temporal, but the things which are not seen are eternal" (2 Corinthians 4:18). While the physical world is continually deteriorating and growing colder, the soul of man is supposed to be *growing* and *flourishing* as it draws closer to God.

Growing in God's World

This concept of *growth* deserves further attention. Growth is one of those natural processes that we often take for granted. We do not sit around wondering *why* something grows—we just assume that it will, or that it should, or we think of what we will do when it does. But in the present discussion—God's omnipresence in His Creation—we would sidestep a valuable opportunity to enhance our appreciation for God if we did not expound upon this idea. After all, seekers of the sacred are to "press on to maturity" (Hebrews 6:1) instead of simply rehashing the same elementary concepts that we first learned when we came to Christ.

Life and growth are inseparable concepts. Whatever is physically alive necessarily exhibits characteristics of growth; whatever is non-living (inorganic) cannot grow. For example, a granite boulder cannot grow into something other than what it is because it is not alive. That rock could be melted down, reshaped, added to, broken apart, etc., but only because of external forces acting upon it. It cannot "grow" in the sense of being able to expand in size all on its own through its own internal processes. Even an increase in size and mere accumulation of mass do not by themselves indicate *living* growth. For example, a star "grows" in size, but it is not alive. Its expansion is not an organic or instinctive process; its increase in size is simply the result of physics (i.e., assimilation of outside materials, nuclear reactions, heat, gravitational forces, etc.) and nothing more.

The same God who created boulders and stars also created all living things, Man being the *highest order* of all Creation (Genesis 1). While even inanimate objects carry the imprint of God's supernatural power, living things that *grow* manifest His glory in an inexpressibly fascinating way. When we speak of *life* in this world, we necessarily mean *deliberate growth*—that is, whatever is alive is *supposed* to grow. Things that *deliberately* expand in size, complexity, and maturity are understood to be "growing"; they were *meant* to grow and are *programmed* to increase.[7] More specific characteristics of growth include cellular division (both mitosis and meiosis), metabolism, respiration (of one form or another), reproduction, etc. Inasmuch as these processes are all functions of *life,* they are all functions of *growth.*

We should recognize the difference between artificial growth (man-made) and natural growth (independent of human intervention). A computer, for example, may appear to "grow" in knowledge or capability, or a car may have certain characteristics of growth (such as metabolism, respiration, etc.), but these things are produced and programmed by men. They are not *natural* since they are inventions of *human* design. On the other hand, all *natural* life has a divine, otherworldly, non-human source, and that source is God.

Spiritual Growth

We know that human beings are alive, but what about the human soul—is it "alive"? Most certainly we would agree that it is, but does it "grow"? If it does *not* grow, then it cannot be alive; in order to *be* alive, it must have the capacity for growth. We should not assume earthly processes like physical reproduction or metabolism here, for these are irrelevant to a spiritual entity. When a tree grows, for example, it gets taller, wider in circumference, and *bigger*. It also (usually) manifests certain features in maturity that it could not manifest as a younger living organism. It stands to reason, however, that a soul does not grow in order to increase in size, as though to occupy more "space." Physical space, as we have already observed, is not applicable to the spiritual world.

The Scriptures make it clear that the soul—like the body of Christ (His church), which is spiritual in nature—is *designed* to grow. Consider the following passages, for example [emphases mine]:

• 1 Corinthians 3:6-7, "I [Paul] planted, Apollos watered, but **God was causing the growth**. So then neither the one who plants nor the one who waters is anything, but **God who causes the growth**."

• Ephesians 2:19-22, "So then you are no longer strangers and aliens, but you are fellow citizens with the saints, and are of God's household, having been built on the foundation of the apostles and prophets, Christ Jesus Himself being the corner stone, in whom the whole building, being fitted together, **is growing into a holy temple in the Lord**, in whom you also are being built together into a dwelling of God in the Spirit."

• Ephesians 4:15-16, "but speaking the truth in love, **we are to grow up in all aspects into Him who is the head**, even Christ, from whom the whole body, being fitted and held together by what every joint supplies, according to the proper working of each individual part, **causes the growth of the body for the building up of itself in love**."

• Colossians 2:19, "…[Hold] fast to the head, from whom the entire body, being supplied and held together by the joints and ligaments, **grows with a growth which is from God**."

• 1 Peter 2:2, "like newborn babies, long for the pure milk of the word, so that by **it you may grow in respect to salvation**,"

• 2 Peter 1:5-8, "Now for this very reason also, applying all diligence, in your faith supply moral excellence, and in your moral excellence, knowledge, and in your knowledge, self-control, and in your self-control, perseverance, and in your perseverance, godliness, and in your godliness, brotherly kindness, and in your brotherly kindness, love. **For if these qualities are yours and are increasing** [which necessarily implies growth], they render you neither useless nor unfruitful in the true knowledge of our Lord Jesus Christ."

• 2 Peter 3:17-18, "You therefore, beloved, knowing this beforehand, be on your guard so that you are not carried away by the error of unprincipled men and fall from your own steadfastness, but **grow in the grace and knowledge** of our Lord and Savior Jesus Christ...."

These passages reveal several important facts. First, what we call "spiritual growth" comes from God. Human effort alone cannot achieve the growth described here. Just as plants cannot grow without light and heat from the sun, so our souls cannot grow apart from the warmth and illumination of God's grace. Similarly, just as a plant may survive for a little while even if it is cut off from its energy source, so the souls of men can "survive" for a little while (but no longer than a human lifespan) before succumbing to spiritual death. Indeed, the soul that is not being nourished by God's Spirit is *already* "dead" (Ephesians 2:1). The ultimate and literal experience of that death is represented by the biblical concept of hell.

Second, the *purpose* of spiritual growth is for fellowship with God, not mere survival. Being *saved* (as in Romans 10:13) means far more than merely continuing to exist; it means to dwell forever in the visible presence of God. God's grace does not merely extend the duration of the soul's existence; rather, saving grace is given so that we might be forever immersed in joyful *communion* with God. The one who is "saved" is not only spared an eternity of endless *dying*, but he also looks forward to an endless *life* with the Giver of life.

Third, while it is God's energy that makes spiritual growth possible, He does not force growth to occur apart from one's own consent. As 2 Peter 1:5-8 necessarily implies, we are to *receive* what God supplies to *increase* our faith which *leads* to spiritual growth. He provides the resources as well as the opportunity for applying them, but *we* are to make the actual applications. In a simple analogy, God provides the food, puts it on the table, provides the proper environment in which to dine, and encourages us to eat, but *we* must first come to the table, *we* must put the food into our mouths, and *we* must consume it. We cannot acquire this food on our own, but neither does God stuff it down our throats against our will. Our failure to participate in the process of spiritual growth leads to the starvation—and death—of our souls.

Fourth, *what* our soul grows into (or increases in) is as important as the fact that it grows at all. A person may grow in knowledge of the occult, amass a great deal of criminal information, increase his ability to manipulate people, or make great strides in pursuing his own self-centered ambitions. Such "growth" is useless, since it is artificial, man-made, and the result of only human decisions and efforts. The nature of such growth is not desirable to God, will not improve that man's soul, and cannot transcend the world in which it was experienced.

In order for one's soul to grow successfully, that person must conform to and comply with the necessary means by which spiritual growth is accomplished. God's Spirit must be the source of energy for *our* spirits: "It is the Spirit who gives life; the flesh profits nothing; the words that I have spoken to you are spirit and are life" (John 6:63). This requires us to "[fix] our hope on the living God, who is the Savior of all men, especially of believers" (1 Timothy 4:10). If a man feeds his soul with useless information, abandons his Lord, loses sight of his heavenly objective, or chooses to pursue a path of self-destruction, then his soul will most certainly die. Like any vicious parasite, sin eventually kills its host.

On the other hand, God is not a parasite; He does not suck the life out of us in order for Him to survive. On the contrary, when God is directly and actively involved in our spiritual lives, we most certainly will *grow* in the Lord (1 Corinthians 3:7). We are completely dependent upon His absolute power in order for our souls to survive, but *we* are not parasites either. We are His *children*, having been adopted into His *family* (Romans 8:14-15). Drawing near to Him is a completely wholesome and mutually beneficial arrangement.

Perhaps someone has already thought (cleverly), "If something has to grow in order to be alive, then God Himself would not be alive since He does not grow!" But a *Divine* Being cannot be defined by qualities or characteristics that can only be applied to a *created* being or any earthly life form. God has never "grown" into being God; He has never been anything less than what He is right now or what He will always be. God is perfect, flawless, irreducible, and immutable. He cannot *change* in any way because He can neither be diminished nor improved. The absolute nature of God, upon which all other absolutes are based and maintained, cannot be altered. If God ever became anything less than absolute perfection, then all life—and all creation—would implode and immediately and permanently cease to exist.

Thus God—the Father, Son, and Holy Spirit—cannot "grow" because He is [They are] the *object* of all growth in the universe He has created. As Paul revealed through the Spirit, "For by Him [Christ] all things were created, both in the heavens and on earth, visible and invisible, whether thrones or dominions or rulers or authorities—all things have been created through Him and *for* Him" (Colossians 1:16, emphasis mine). All things *have been* created in order to exalt the Creator Himself; all things *continue to grow* toward the Creator as a testament to His Glory and Sovereignty. Just as flowers adoringly follow the sun as it moves through the sky, all of nature grows *toward* God in tribute to and adoration of His glory.

The Purpose of Growth

God has created the natural world to *grow* as an example of what He expects from us in a spiritual context. Since we live in God's world, our souls are *expected* to grow toward God in honor of His glory—in gratitude toward the Giver of life. The natural world has no choice but to obey God's innate laws and instincts and (thus) to *grow*. In the spiritual context, however, man is given a *choice* as to whether or not he is going to grow. Biological processes cannot be suppressed at will; but man *can* suppress the increase and improvement of his soul.

God did not create us to snub Him; He created us to *exalt* Him. He also created us with the freedom to choose between these two responses. This is a characteristic unique to man, to *choose* to exalt God (or not). In God's world, everything grows toward Him; in man's proud, self-centered, and self-serving world, all things grow toward *himself*. In all of God's physical creation, man is the only one capable of such defiance.[8] Indeed, of all of the earthly creatures God has made, we are the only ones who have questioned our Source of Life. We are the ones who deliberately followed a deviant path as we shook our fists in defiance at the Sacred God. We are the ones who choose, according to our own self-serving, twisted logic, to worship the *creature* rather than the *Creator* (cf. Romans 1:21-23). Whoever refuses God also forfeits his life (soul) in the end; no one will be able to "rob God" of His deserved glory without incurring a wretched curse (cf. Malachi 3:8-9).

Everything in the natural world adheres to a certain *cycle* of growth which includes decline and death. (In a sense, death itself is a paradoxical objective: all earthly life "grows" toward death.) On a macro level, this is still part of "growth," since death and decomposition actually perpetuate the God-given biological processes of the organic world. While there are similarities to this cycle in the spiritual person, there are distinct differences as well. We are to "die" in order to be made alive to God in a *new* relationship—i.e., to be "born again" as a "new creature" (John 3:5; 2 Corinthians 5:17). We are also to "put to death" the "deeds of the body" that oppose the Spirit (Romans 8:13; Galatians 5:19-21). One's spiritual life depends upon this process; one who refuses to put such things to death will eventually be *overcome* by them. God will not allow one's soul to live that chooses to embrace ungodliness; He will not have fellowship with a contradiction to His holy nature. We are to take up our cross daily and carry it—in a sense we walk to our "death" everyday (Luke 9:23). Such death is necessary in order for life with God to be possible. In the natural world, something (or someone) else dies so that we might live; in the spiritual world, *we ourselves* must "die"[9] in order that *we* might live to God. The paradox of this situation is very characteristic of a gospel which defies conformity to all human expectations.

We know that the earth undergoes a continuous cycle of life, death, and rebirth, not only in its seasons but in other contexts as well. All living things on earth are subject to this cycle; even the "lifespan" of non-living things (clouds, glaciers, mountains, etc.) can be explained through a similar process. This will all continue without ceasing (Genesis 8:22) until God calls the entire process to a close—which He has promised to do (2 Peter 3:7). However, the soul which grows toward God lives in His world *never* to die again. Listen to what Jesus and Paul have said [bracketed words mine]:

- Matthew 16:25, "For whoever wishes to save his life will lose it [i.e., will die forever]; but whoever loses his life for My sake will find it [i.e., will live forever]."

- John 11:25-26, "Jesus said to her [Martha], 'I am the resurrection and the life; he who believes in Me will live [spiritually] even if he dies [physically], and everyone who lives and believes in Me will never die. Do you believe this?'"

- Romans 14:7-8, "For not one of us lives for himself, and not one dies for himself; for if we live, we live for the Lord, or if we die, we die for the Lord; therefore whether we live or die, we are the Lord's."

- 1 Corinthians 15:36, "You fool [i.e., who gauges spiritual things by physical limitations]! That which you sow does not come to life unless it dies;"

Seeds can "die" to what they *are* (i.e., seeds), but contain within them the germ of life to become something else (i.e., a mature plant). It is, however, impossible for things that are truly dead to *live again* (i.e., be regenerated) in the natural world. Picture a dead tree branch lying on the ground, for example, having broken off from a tree in a storm years before. The branch was once alive; now it is dead; it will never be alive again. Furthermore, *everything* that lives in the natural world dies eventually.

But God never *intended* for the soul of man to die; eternal life is what He created man to *pursue*. Thus there is nothing wrong with God expecting us to die to the *world* so that we might grow toward *Him*. Even though we had once chosen to defy God, we can still be reconciled to Him through the life-giving blood of His Son (Colossians 1:19-23). His saving grace has made it possible for us to regain the life which we forfeited when we sinned against Him. Even though the righteous laws of God "killed" us when we disobeyed them (Romans 7:9-12), nonetheless we can be "born again" through the same supernatural power that raised Christ from His own physical death (1 Peter 1:3). Because of His "great love with which He loved us" (Ephesians 2:4-5), God gave us the greatest gift we could ever receive: the opportunity to be *restored* to fellowship with Him forever.

What This Requires of You

Seeking the sacred does not mean we will literally see God while in our present existence. Likewise, just as we have never seen Jesus in the flesh, so we never will: that particular part of His ministry is over and will not be recreated for us. While we are in this world, we are bound by its physical restrictions and human limitations.

Seeking the sacred does not require us to literally see God here, for we *know* that we will see Him in due time (1 John 3:2). We do not have to put our hands in the nail wounds of the Savior's hands to know He was crucified for us, for we *know* that we are redeemed by His blood, as the Holy Spirit has testified (Colossians 1:19-20). We did not have to see His resurrection from the dead in order to believe that it occurred, for we *know* that He sits in glory at the right hand of the Father (Acts 2:33). "These things have been written to you who believe in the name of the Son of God, so that you may *know* that you have eternal life" (1 John 5:13, emphasis mine). The same Scripture which affirms the core truths of our salvation *also* testifies of the omnipresence of God (Christ): all Creation is filled with His energy; He holds together all things; He has filled this world with His glory.

God has created this immense, beautiful, diverse, and incredibly complex world for us not only to enjoy, but to inspire us to search for the One who made it (cf. Romans 1:18-20). The fact that most choose not to do this does not make His evidence any less compelling or His glory any less appreciable. Someday, after everything has run its full course, when "days" and "time" have disappeared, God's presence will be obscured to us no longer. Then we will see Him as He really is, and we will realize just how close He has been to us all along.

Meanwhile, God sits in the center of His creation while all life bows in veneration toward and admiration of the Giver of life, the Source of all energy. All creation grows toward Him, the Cause and Energy of all that *does* grow, gratefully showering Him with praise and worship. This is what seekers of the sacred anticipate above all else: basking in the supernatural brilliance of God's real and visible presence. This is where the search for the sacred ultimately leads us.

Endnotes

5 The universe seems rather filled with darkness than light, although that is only how things are presently. God lives in "unapproachable light" (1 Timothy 6:16), and those who live in fellowship with Him are filled with this light (see Luke 11:34-36, where the meaning is immediately spiritual, but also implies that the presence of light demands the presence of God). The present physical darkness of the universe seems intentional, so as to subdue the glory of its spiritual Creator until all things have run their course. Given the unlimited expression of an omnipotent God, it is not at all inconceivable to accept that, when God finally reveals Himself to His Creation (Colossians 3:4; 2 Thessalonians 1:7), the darkened universe will be overwhelmed with His glory.

6 I'm referring to what we experience, not the thoughts, memories, or emotions that are evoked through the experience. These latter things are spiritual in nature, and therefore cannot be reduced to physical properties.

7 Of course our bodies die; anything that lives in this world has a finite lifespan; it cannot grow perpetually. Our perspective here takes into account what the person (or organism) achieves at any time in its existence, not its ultimate demise. In other words, as part of its existence, it grows—even though, in the end, it dies.

8 We know angels and Satan himself have defied God as well, but they are purely spiritual beings and therefore belong to a different discussion altogether.

CHAPTER SEVEN

In the Middle of Everything

This is good and acceptable in the sight of God our Savior, who desires all men to be saved and to come to the knowledge of the truth. For there is one God, and one mediator also between God and men, the man Christ Jesus, who gave Himself as a ransom for all, the testimony given at the proper time.
1 Timothy 2:3-6

Sometimes we use the expression, "I need to take in my surroundings." We are referring to spending time to carefully observe the environment around us, whether it is a room, house, tract of land, city, or (on a more conceptual level) the season of one's life or the particulars of one's circumstances.

Seekers of the sacred should learn to take in their surroundings. Instead of simply rushing from one day to the next in breathless pursuit of one thing or another, we should pause for reflection and meditation on the world which God has made. By reflecting upon the world that our God has made, we will gain a greater appreciation for the Maker Himself. In other words, we are not only interested in who God *is* and where He can be *found*, we are also interested in what He has *done*.

If you take the time to look, what you will immediately discover in both the physical and spiritual world—in matters of earthly as well as spiritual survival—is that God pays great attention to design, symmetry, versatility, and *details*. When we look closely—with our eyes *and* our hearts—at the physical creations of God, we see an impressive and meticulous attention to little things, the hallmark of a master craftsman. Whether we examine plants or animals, birds or fish, quartz crystals or massive constellations, the details continue to impress and amaze us. God has not just *made* things; He has *fashioned* everything He makes into something worthy of our attention, inspiring closer scrutiny.

The psalmist said, "I will give thanks to You, for I am fearfully and wonderfully made" (Psalm 139:14). This is so true: regardless of how others view our physical or social attractiveness, there is no doubt that each of us, as an independent, systematized, organic machine, is meticulously designed and wonderfully created. No wonder the apostle Paul wrote that we are *all* "without excuse" who deny the intelligent design of our physiological composition (Romans 1:20). And we haven't even *begun* (in this discussion, anyway) to address the profundity of our spiritual existence.

"Location, location, location!"

The Chinese believe there is a "spiritual" connection to the placement and arrangement of fixtures and furniture. According to this belief (called *feng shui* or "wind-water"), things have to be positioned a certain way—energy has to "flow" in a certain direction—in order for you to be in harmony with your environment (and vice versa). The location of your furnishings and the context of your living space are of great importance—if indeed you want to maximize your positive energy and be at peace with nature.

Certainly there is something to be said concerning aestheticism and the virtues of a positive living environment. Much more important than the placement of furniture and fixtures is *God's* placement of things. This refers to both the orientation of things as well as the proximity of one thing to another. You've heard entrepreneurs talk about the three most important factors in achieving a successful business: "Location, location, location!" Well, God has not only known about these conditions from the beginning, but has been teaching us this important detail all along.

Consider again the human body: It is fascinating enough that God came up with the idea for a liver or kidney or heart—organs whose design and functionality continue to amaze even those who spend their entire careers studying them—but God went one step further and ideally *positioned* them in the human body as well. The human heart, for example, is where it is because it is *perfectly suited* for that location. God created not only the heart itself, but also the environment in which it was to be placed. Not only is the heart properly oriented to the rest of the body, but in that position it operates at maximum efficiency, is kept at an ideal temperature, and is sufficiently protected on all sides.

The same observation can be made with regard to our planet: Earth is ideally placed in the solar system for the optimum conditions for life to exist and flourish. Its distance from the sun, the speed of its orbit and revolutions, the tilt of its axis, the proximity of its moon, etc.—all these factors can *never* be attributed to happenstance or coincidence but are the sovereign decisions of a supremely intelligent God. Earth did not just fall into place over millions and billions of years but was strategically and deliberately *positioned*. Just as a new house does not just "appear" over time on a surveyed lot in perfect orientation to its residential street, so the earth did not just accidentally slip into a perfect spot in the solar system and then begin accidentally sprouting systematic, intelligent life.

God not only knows what to make, He also knows how it is to be *designed* (down to the microscopic, even subatomic detail) and where it is supposed to be *placed*. God does not create life to exist on its own, as though in a vacuum; rather, He provides an environment—a "package deal" if you will—for that organism to survive optimally. God situates things exactly where they need to be: only an omnipotent, omniscient God is able to do this.

Man is certainly the crowning achievement of Creation. God did not just create a generic "man" as an austere, featureless, organic blob of different chemicals, proteins, and plasma. Instead, He created man (and certainly woman!) as an attractive, symmetric, and fully functional living being who exhibits attributes and characteristics of God Himself. Before God created man, however, He first created the physical world in which man was to live. This world is as diverse, complex, and wonderful as the physical body of man himself. It is filled with all the evidence of supernatural planning and organizing, remarkable efficiency and capable engineering, breathtaking beauty, and incredible dimensions (on both micro and macro levels). "For thus says the LORD, who created the heavens (He is the God who formed the earth and made it, He established it and did not create it a waste place, but formed it to be inhabited), 'I am the LORD, and there is none else'" (Isaiah 45:18). God created this "package" *exclusively* for man; God made the world for no other reason. Man was not an afterthought, nor the topping on the cake; he *is* the cake, and everything else is the cake's icing, and the platter upon which it sits. God made man perfectly and ideally suited for his environment, but everything in man's environment is perfectly positioned, most effectively located, and ideally situated for man's overall success.

"Then the LORD God took the man and put him into the garden of Eden to cultivate it and keep it" (Genesis 2:15). Take a moment to savor this sacred thought. God created this incredible, beautiful, and functional world, and then put this incredible, beautiful, and functional being called Adam ("Man") into it. ("Man" was the name He gave to both man *and* woman, Genesis 5:2.) Specifically, God made a wonderful garden called Eden, then placed man in the middle of it—in the midst of all the trees, foliage, flowers, and animals. In the *middle* of the earth, God placed the crowning glory of all that He had created. This was no accident; this was not a matter of circumstances. It was God's deliberate and purposeful decision to put man geographically and logistically where He did. God put His Garden in the middle of the world, and then put man himself in the middle of His Garden.

In the Middle of the World

Let's pause in our observance of man in the Garden of Eden for a moment to first pursue a related thought. (We will return to the Garden shortly.) If God favors one position for the placement of His most important creations, it is the *middle*. Scripture, and our own scrutiny of the physical world, verifies this absolutely. (Things do not have to be *directly* centered in order to be in the middle. "Middle" is used as a figure of speech to denote the general placement of things in proximity to their larger surroundings.)

Consider the tabernacle of God, for example, which was designed by God and then situated in the midst of Israel. The outer sanctuary of the tabernacle was a perfect square, in the middle of which was the sevenfold lamp stand (*menorah*), golden altar of incense, and table of showbread. Imagine you are the high priest of Israel, walking into this sanctuary. Once you are inside this elaborate tent, you find yourself in the midst of precious, gold-plated, ornate objects which signify God's holy presence. There are even better things yet to see, for if you were to continue walking forward, you would find yourself passing through the heavy, cherub-embossed curtain (veil) which leads you into the most sacred chamber: the Holy of Holies. This innermost sanctuary represents the middle—the heart, in a sense—of Israel. In a very real sense, it serves as the throne room of God in the midst of Israel.

In the middle of this sacred room, you can see the ark of the covenant, an elaborately engraved, gold-plated chest, radiating with heavenly glory. It is overshadowed with cherubic creatures with wings, the tips of which touch each other as they bow toward the space above the ark (Exodus 37:7-9). In the middle of this space—above the ark's lid, which is known as the mercy seat—and below the angels' wings, there is *nothing*. There is no idol of God, no molten or graven image, no bust of God's head, no bejeweled crown or decorated icon of any kind. There is only a seemingly empty expanse of open space. But it is understood that that space is occupied (not literally, but symbolically) by Jehovah Himself, since it is He who is the rightful King over all Israel.[10] It was above the mercy seat, in this most holy place, that God would "meet" Israel through the intercession of Moses and the high priest (Exodus 30:6; Leviticus 16:2; Numbers 7:89).

We would do well to dwell for a moment on what has just been described. Inside—in the middle—of the ark of the covenant was contained the written Law of Moses and other proofs of God's gracious dealings with Israel (Hebrews 9:3-4). In the middle of the space between the mercy seat and the cherubim was the holy presence of God in the midst of His throne room. This room, the Holy of Holies, was in the middle (heart) of the tabernacle, which itself was situated in the middle of all the tribes of Israel as they wandered for forty years through the wildernesses of Sinai, Paran, Kadesh Barnea, and elsewhere. Ultimately, the tabernacle would be placed permanently in the middle of the Promised Land, in Jerusalem, completely surrounded by the northern and southern tribes. Israel itself would be located in the middle of major north-south highways, trade routes, and

Gentile nations. In a very real sense, Israel would be placed (through no planning of its own, but by God's divine will) in the middle of the ancient world, purposely and strategically orientated in such a way so as to maximize its monotheistic influence on all the polytheistic nations. Ultimately, this would also serve for the benefit of all the families of the earth (cf. Genesis 12:3; Acts 3:25).

Seekers of the sacred should appreciate the importance of this observation. God does not want His church placed in some cave somewhere in the desert, like the ascetic Essenes of Jesus' day, as though it were a sacred yet inaccessible monastery, disconnected from and even unconcerned with the world. No, but the church—God's people—are supposed to be in the middle of the world, as a beacon of hope for the lost, as a brilliant representation of God's mercy to those who live in darkness. As Jesus Himself said (Matthew 5:14-16),

> You are the light of the world. A city set on a hill cannot be hidden; nor does anyone light a lamp and put it under a basket, but on the lampstand, and it gives light to all who are in the house. Let your light shine before men in such a way that they may see your good works, and glorify your Father who is in heaven.

The point is: whenever we see certain recurring themes in the Bible being illustrated by God in a physical way, we must be perceptive of their spiritual applications. Indeed, this is why God has preserved the holy writings of the Old Testament so that we can learn from them and gain hope for ourselves *because* of what we learn (Romans 15:4).

The positioning and placement of God's holy things—and yes, His holy people—are obviously extremely important to *Him*; therefore these must be extremely important to *us*. Nowhere is this as powerfully illustrated as in the example of Christ Himself.

In the Middle of Man

To understand the centrality (or in the present discussion, the "middleness") of Christ with proximity to man, we must first appreciate something about the human condition itself. Let's return now to Adam in the Garden of Eden, for that is really where our discussion—and our first knowledge of our human condition—actually begins. In the middle of the earth, God placed this beautiful garden; in the middle of the garden, two trees. Then God placed Adam in the middle of the two trees, in the sense that he apparently had equal access to either one. There was no prohibition against the first tree, the "tree of life." We might wonder about that: why no warning or caution concerning *that* tree? Yet Adam already *had* life; to eat of that tree would not seem to have offered any particular advantage; therefore it presented no particular temptation. We are not tempted by what we *have*, but we crave what is not yet ours.

The other tree, "the tree of the knowledge of good and evil," was a different subject altogether. This tree seemed rather intriguing and mysterious, which meant that it naturally appealed to the human appetites of curiosity and desire. Notice that man's prohibition from God was not, "Do not go too *far away*"—for God never gave any caution against leaving the Garden—but was, in essence, "Do not get too *close*." Temptation, after all, does not really exist when we are too distant from its effects; only when we are close (or in proximity) to its allurement does temptation have its strongest attraction.

Both life *and* death resided, in a sense, in the middle of the Garden. Of one, Adam derived his existence, since the tree of life represented the Giver of Life. Who else could provide life but the One who planted this tree and designed its fruit? But of the other tree, Adam was warned of his death: "The LORD God commanded the man, saying, 'From any tree of the garden you may eat freely; but from the tree of the knowledge of good and evil you shall not eat, for in the day that you eat from it you will surely die'" (Genesis 2:16-17). It wasn't that the fruit from this tree was itself lethal or poisonous; rather, it was the act of *eating* from the tree that made it deadly. By tasting of this tree's fruit, Adam would have defied God's decree *not* to eat of it. In doing so, Adam would have made a bold yet foolish attempt to actually exalt himself *above* his Creator and God. (We will soon examine this more closely.)

Meanwhile, God was not yet finished with providing Adam with everything he needed for his success. From the rib of man God formed "woman"—that is, from the very heart of man's body, from the very *middle* of man, God formed and then breathed life into Adam's perfect counterpart. This woman, whom Adam named Eve, was given to man—she was a gift, not a requisition—as an act of divine grace (1 Corinthians 11:8-9). (Grace is, after all, whatever God does to bring man to completion despite his inherent inadequacies.) She was indeed a part of him in the most profound and intimate sense. Eve was a part of Adam in a way that no woman would ever again be a part of any man; Adam was a part of Eve in a way that no man would ever again be a part of any woman. Yet every one of a man's children from that point forward would come into the world through the womb of a woman (1 Corinthians 11:12; 1 Timothy 2:15).

Thus from the middle of man, God formed a woman; from the middle of woman, God would form, through the natural process that He Himself designed and spoke into existence, every man thereafter. Every child, being born in the middle of woman, would be joined *to* its mother in the middle; in a profound sense, all humanity would be joined in the middle. The umbilical cord symbolizes a biological lifeline with several spiritual implications. For now, this one implication will suffice: every child that comes into the world must be severed from the middle of its mother, just as ultimately every person who becomes a "man" (i.e., an adult) will sever himself from his God in his own Adam-like act of defiance (Romans 5:12). Every person ultimately tries to be like God—in essence, usurps God's rightful authority over him—and thus "all fall short of the glory of God" in a futile attempt to achieve our *own* glory (Romans 3:23).

I have not forgotten about our discussion concerning the two trees, or of man's proximity to them. Adam and Eve were given a pristine existence in the midst of the Garden, to tend it and eat from it, but never to succumb to its only temptation. For all we know, Adam and Eve stayed clear away from the tree of the knowledge of good and evil. As intriguing as it was, they respected God's decree even while they did not fully understand the *implications* of the decree. Satan knew the implications all too well, however. He knew that God's warning was not merely an exercise in human discipline; rather, he knew there was something in man—indeed, in the *middle* of man—that would draw him to the tree like a bear is drawn to the scent of salmon in a stream. Satan knew something about man that man did not know about himself, and he exploited that knowledge in order to destroy, if possible, the crowning glory of God's creation.

With this agenda, Satan then appeared in the form of a serpent, or possessed an actual serpent—the means is irrelevant, for the conclusion is the same—in order to tempt Eve. His real target was not Adam *or* Eve; rather, it was God Himself. Man was simply God's "Achilles' heel," as he saw it, the most vulnerable access to God's power and control. Thus Adam was the weakness of God, and Eve was the weakness of Adam. By corrupting Man, Satan would bring God to His knees and cause His death, if possible, so that he himself might reign instead.

Notice that Satan did not tempt Eve from outside the Garden, but from within—from the *middle* of the Garden. There the forbidden tree quietly yet conspicuously stood like a lone sentry, guarding the entrance to knowledge and liberation—that's how Satan would package his temptation, anyway. He would convince Eve that God was not merely putting a restriction upon her and Adam, but that He was *hiding* something from them, as though God was afraid that man might become a god himself. While Satan did not know man's literal thoughts, he well understood the desire and exhilarating quest for self-exaltation and control that dwells in the middle of man. Somewhere in an eternity before man was ever created Satan himself had indulged in these same desires, proudly pursued them, and had given birth to them. Somewhere in Satan's past he himself had tasted of his own forbidden fruit, sucked the dripping nectar from its juicy flesh, felt the intoxicating rush from having done what he was warned never to do. In having given life to his monstrous pride, Satan brought upon himself a most awful death. With the knowledge that he himself had gained through his own self-exalting, God-defying experience, he knew that he would die— but he would not die alone. Perhaps if the One who was to put him to death would Himself be subdued, then Satan would not have to die at all. In the middle of this seemingly benign conversation—benign to Eve, not to Satan or the Lord—was a plot to destroy man, and in the middle of that, a plot to overthrow God.

Eve, of course, was oblivious to the implications; we assume Adam was too. Satan, having full advantage and no scruples, spoke smoothly and convincingly to Eve: "Indeed, has God said, 'You shall not eat from any tree of the garden'?" This was a taunt and a trap, not an innocent question; Satan knew full well the answer already. And at first, Eve responded both obediently and beautifully. "The woman said to the serpent, 'From the fruit of the trees of the garden we may eat; but from the fruit of the tree which is in the middle of the garden, God has said, 'You shall not eat from it or touch it, or you will die'" (Genesis 3:1-3). The tree was in the middle of the Garden, but Satan knew that the seeds of Eve's destruction lay in the middle of her own soul.

So it is with each one of us: the seeds of our own destruction are internal, not external. The temptations which threaten to destroy us are really not from the outside but from the inside, just as we are later told: "But each one is tempted when he is carried away and enticed by his own lust" (James 1:14). This "lust" of ours is not kept somewhere on the periphery of one's consciousness or in some distant sanctuary of one's being, disconnected from day-to-day life. Instead, it is kept somewhere very close to us, in the very depths of our soul, right in the middle of our invisible existence. While the *seeds* are there, they cannot produce any fruit until they are conceived, no more than a woman's egg (ovum) can produce a child by itself. Yet once that seed (temptation) is fertilized with a catalyst (desire), sin is conceived. Paradoxically, the only thing sin can give "life" to is *death* (Romans 6:23; James 1:13-15). So sin brings forth, in a sense, not just a stillborn child of death, but even worse: it brings forth something unholy, unnatural, and demonic (cf. James 3:14-16). Everything God has created—the heavens and the earth, and all that is upon the earth, including man himself—is "very good." On the contrary, man created sin, which is patently evil and can only give birth to death. God did not create death, Eve did, Adam did—in fact, *every one of us* did, all of us who have sinned against God.

Satan laid the trap; Eve, despite her seeming disadvantage, should have known better. (Indeed, we *all* should know better. Sin is never something that accidentally happens *to* us, but is something we *choose* to do.) In answer to her defense of God's instructions concerning the forbidden tree, Satan chided mockingly, "You surely will not die! For God knows that in the day you eat from it your eyes will be opened, and you will be like God, knowing good and evil" (Genesis 3:4-5). This was partly true: Eve *would* have her eyes opened; indeed, she *would* know good and evil. The lie, which was planted in the middle of these truths, was that she would really become "like God" in the process. God is all-knowing and has the perfect ability to govern His own thoughts and behavior. With such perfect knowledge, He knows all the flaws and fallacies of temptation, how sin always leads to death. We might even conclude that if God Himself ever *were* to sin, He would die—and so would everything else. This is impossible, of course, since God would never violate His own perfect, absolute nature. God would never do this, but Eve allowed the thought to germinate in her head while the serpent spoke to her. She considered these words themselves as being enlightening, enticing, even . . . exciting. My eyes opened? she relished. The ability to be like God? Knowing good and evil? The allurement and opportunity was a thrilling rush, an intoxicating chance of a lifetime.

Then Eve did what we all do once we finally crack the door just enough for Satan to stab his ugly foot upon the threshold: she began to rationalize just how *profitable* this action really might be. "When the woman saw that the tree was good for food, and that it was a delight to the eyes, and that the tree was desirable to make one wise, she took from its fruit and ate...." (Genesis 3:6). The fruit appeared to be *good* (even though God said it was wrong to eat of it). It was a *delight to the eyes* (even though God said that it was forbidden). It was *desirable* for wisdom (even though God promised that such wisdom would prove fatal). In essence, the decision was already made; it was now just a matter of justifying it. Once that was complete, Eve took hold of the fruit and ate. Ingesting the fruit was, by itself, not the sin; partaking of *anything* which God had already prohibited was and most certainly is sinful. Adam, who was even more responsible in this situation than Eve since God had instructed him *first*, also succumbed to the same seductive process and ate of the fruit. Even though Cain was the first *child* born to Adam and Eve, their first real creation was a putrid monster called sin, which offered them nothing but death and misery. There, in the middle of the world, in the middle of the Garden, in the middle of man, sin was conceived and death was its unholy offspring.

The Nature of Human Desire

Someone asks, "Why did God put the tree of knowledge of good and evil in the Garden at all? Doesn't this make Him responsible for what happened?" Perhaps we have all wondered this. Perhaps we have all imagined a Garden without such a tree, therefore without such a temptation, so that sin might never have even had an opportunity to come into the world. But remember, God did not bring sin into the world, *man* did—thus we *all* did. By placing the tree in the middle of the Garden, and our own human desires in the middle of man, God forced man to be *responsible*. In order for him to independently seek after God, man *had* to be responsible for his own life. Responsibility is impossible to achieve without allowing man to make his own choices and decisions, moral or otherwise. A man without moral responsibility might as well be a vegetable or a stone or a robot; he would have no means by which to honor God other than merely being in existence. What better way to honor God than to *choose* to honor Him versus being programmed to do so—or worse, to have no such opportunity at all? Man was made in God's image; just as God chose to give of His life to man, so man must choose to give his life to God.

Ironically, while God put in the middle of man the desires of his heart, human desire is not inherently evil. Evil is the *absence* of God's holy influence, not the product of it; it is a *rejection* of God, not His imposition. The desire to serve God and pursue fellowship with *Him* can be just as powerful as those corrupted desires with which we serve *ourselves*. One can have a hunger and thirst for righteousness just as he can nurture an appetite—an illicit hunger and an unholy thirst—for that which is selfish and demonic (Matthew 5:6; James 3:13-18). Each person has the freedom to make decisions concerning his relationship with God; He sets up the conditions, but does not force one's hand. No one can make us sin; "The devil made me do it!" is literally an impossible defense.

God, by giving us these desires and choices, has indeed given us *freedom*, not oppression. The only oppression we ever endure, spiritually-speaking, is that which we bring upon ourselves when we sin against Him. Once we have given life to sin, spawning something which God never intended to be created, we become slaves to sin, prisoners of Satan, inmates

125

sitting on death row awaiting a perpetual execution (cf. John 8:31-36). Once this is done, the truth shall indeed make us free from that enslavement—but only *if* we choose to abide by it (Him).

Notice that we do not have to go very far (in distance or thought) to give life to evil. We need to make no great excursions, no distant treks across the world, no perilous sailing across the ocean. No, but God has placed *in the middle of us all* the potential to either serve Him or serve ourselves. To each of us, He has said, in essence, "From all these good things (the fruit of the Spirit) I have given you, you may eat all you want; there is no law which constrains you concerning these. There are some things (forbidden fruit) which you may never eat. In the day in which you eat of these other fruits, you shall surely die" (see Galatians 5:19-23). What He demands then is that we master what is going on inside of us—in the middle of our spiritual existence. Often we have this backward: we make strenuous efforts to master what is on the *outside*, trying to change or affect the exterior life while ignoring what is going on in the middle of man. Adam and Eve did not have to contend with what was going on outside the Garden; their struggle was in the middle of the Garden. Indeed, their *real* struggle was in the middle of themselves. So it is with us: the conflict really is not *without*, but *within*.

Left to themselves, Adam and Eve were without hope after having been seduced by Satan. Without the grace of God providing for their deficiencies and inadequacies, they would have been lost forever. It is no different for us since we are all too similar to them: we have all lost a battle of wits in the middle of our souls, wherein Satan promised life but made us prisoners of death instead. In doing so, we lost our innocence and our child-like existence with God. The umbilical cord was severed and we were given a life independent of God, *separated* from God, banished to a godless and cursed world. With such grim and hopeless prospects, what would we have to look forward to? Without the grace of God, there would be no hope, no release from captivity, no salvation from our own self-inflicted demise.

Instead of beating us over the head with our own condemnation, God has unveiled an amazing plan—it was central to all His plans all along—which provides a way of escape from the sin to which we have given birth and the death which we have chosen. Where did God place this salvation, this Savior? Exactly where He needed to be: right in the middle of humanity—indeed, right in the middle of everything.

Jesus Christ, the Mediator

"In the beginning was the Word, and the Word was with God, and the Word was God" (John 1:1). The Word (Christ), as He has existed for eternity past, stood face to face with the Father.[11] While we know very little of Christ's identity prior to His incarnation, we know that He (the Word) was in the very center of the Godhead. Just as we speak words from our hearts, so also Christ, having forever existed in the "heart" of God, is the embodiment of God's spoken (revealed) word to man. Thus, this verse means, in the real sense of His proximity to and fellowship with the Father, Christ came *from the middle of God.*

It is no surprise to any student of the Bible that Christ is the central character, theme, and purpose behind all that God has revealed to us in His Word. He is indeed the "summing up of all things...things in heaven and things on the earth" (Ephesians 1:9-10). Even while God was laying out the consequences for Adam and Eve, banishing them forever from the Garden of Eden, He already looked ahead to the Savior who would redeem all that had just been lost through their sin. In Genesis 3:15, God spoke of a "seed" (Galatians 3:16) which would come from the woman and which would ultimately crush the "seed" of the serpent. The language is purposely vague and nearly indecipherable if not for the full revelation of the gospel. It means that Satan (symbolized by the serpent) would injure Christ, but could not destroy Him; Christ, however, would inflict a mortal injury to Satan (symbolized by a head wound) by robbing him of his power, leading to his complete destruction.

Since Adam's banishment from the Garden, God worked to bring this Savior into a human existence. "But when the fullness of time came, God sent forth His Son, born of a woman, born under the Law" (Galatians 4:4). In the middle of all humanity—not at one end or the other, but *right in the middle*, where we most needed Him—Christ left the spiritual realm of God and entered into our dark, pathetic, hopeless world. He was indeed born "under the Law," that is, as One subject to the Law of Moses, but He also seemed to straddle two systems of reconciliation as well. This point needs to be very clear: Christ lived and died as a Jew who served the Law of Moses perfectly; He did not change a single word of it, according to His own promise (Matthew 5:17). He did, however, stand on the very cusp of that Law, and also touched—in anticipation and prophecy, anyway—the gospel to come. (Think of the language of, say, John 4:23, "But an hour is coming, and now is....") Thus Christ was, in a very real sense, in the middle of both worlds. He ushered in the end of one and was Himself the inauguration of another. He *fulfilled* the one in order to *become* the other.

So Christ, the Word of the Father who had always been in the middle of God, came into this world from the very middle of a woman, from within her physical womb. Just as the rest of men have been joined together in the middle of their own mothers, so Christ takes His appropriate place there as well. It was fitting that He should identify with us in this way. Certainly He was much *more* than any of us, given His supernatural conception; but this—the fact of His dual identity as both man *and* God—was critical to His role as an appeasement of God's wrath toward the sins of men (cf. Romans 5:8-9).

In the middle of His life (had He lived a natural life expectancy), Jesus Christ began His ministry in the midst of His own countrymen. During that ministry, He taught two unprecedented revelations. First, He spoke of what is in the *heart* of God, and thus revealed what the Father had always wanted man to know about Him. "For God so loved the world"— and Christ explained, in so many words, *just how profound* this "love" is—"He gave His only begotten Son"—God was not willing to hold back anything in His power to save man from his wretched demise. God *gave* His Son to man as a gift; He did not just loan Him to us for a time. Those who receive the Son of God receive Him *forever*, never having to relinquish such a tremendous gift nor to have it confiscated. This act of selfless love (cf. 1 John 4:9-10) permeated the entirety of Jesus' preaching. In the middle of God, this desire to express His love had been burning and demanding release from all eternity. Indeed, the very reason for which God had *created* man was so that He might *give* such love to those who would appreciate it in a way that no angel or other "living being" could. No angel had ever been in *need* of

God in the way man needs Him, since the angels in heaven already *behold* God and serve in His presence. Yet man—at least *some* men and women— would choose to appreciate the gift and would give up everything they have on earth to receive the ultimate *expression* of that gift: eternal life with the One from whence the gift had come.

In the middle of God is everything that man's soul truly craves: love, light, peace, purity, completion, perfection, all knowledge, and all power. Jesus shared these things with men in such a way that they had never heard before and would never hear again from another human being. Even more than this, He *lived* these things: from the middle of Christ's own heart poured forth a river of living water, eager to quench the thirst of men's souls, able to supply every need of man's God-given spirit. "If anyone is thirsty," He implored, "let him come to Me and drink. He who believes in Me, as the Scripture said, 'From his innermost being will flow rivers of living water'" (John 7:37-38). From man's innermost being—from the middle of man—he would find his true contentment, having been supplied by Him who comes from the middle of God.

While the first revelation of Christ's teaching concerned what is in the middle of *God*, the second concerned what is in the middle of *man*. Some of this information was new to us, while other parts of it only confirmed what we had already thought to be true; however, *all* of it has always been known to Christ. Thus, "...Jesus, on His part, was not entrusting Himself to them, for He knew all men, and because He did not need anyone to testify concerning man, for He Himself knew what was in man" (John 2:24-25). This means that Jesus did not rely upon the testimony of men to confirm for *Him* who He was or to validate what He was doing. It also means that Jesus knows man better than man even knows (or in many cases wants to know) himself.

This makes perfect sense. We are unable to see our true nature clearly or objectively, left to ourselves. We are, after all, imprisoned by the same finite perspective that imprisons every other man and woman upon the face of the earth, since none of us can really see ourselves from *outside* of ourselves. Jesus, however, came from a world beyond our own—a world *superior* to our own in every way—and was thus able to explain our situation like no one else could. "You are from below," He declared, "I am from above; you are of this world, I am not of this world" (John 8:23). This was no idle claim, no empty boast: He proved His otherworldly existence through the irrefutable miracles which He performed. Thus He rightly argued, "...the works that I do in My Father's name, these testify of Me" (John 10:25). So we have this Person who came to dwell among us, in the flesh—in the likeness of *our* flesh (John 1:14; Romans 8:3)—who has declared to us the true nature of our humanity. Put another way: our physical existence, from Christ's perspective, is in the middle of two eternities, in the very center of an otherwise unbroken continuum of a higher form of life than we have ever known. This supernatural Being, this Divine Creator, revealed Himself as one of *us* in order to enlighten us to the reality of our condition. Jesus put Himself in the middle of all humanity in order to identify—and save us from—what was in the middle of man himself.

When we imitate the Father and conform to His Son, we are impressive creatures. When we love unconditionally, forgive uninhibitedly, give liberally, and live righteously, we emulate the very virtues and values which God has placed within our hearts; we shine with the brilliance of heaven. All such actions only magnify the fact that we are indeed endowed with the potential to partake of the Divine Nature, His Sacred Life (cf. 2 Peter 1:3-4). When we choose to be, we can be godlike in character and conduct. Others can "see" God in *us* even though they cannot literally see God Himself (the essential meaning of 1 John 4:12).

Unfortunately, we have all chosen at some point—and many times thereafter—to be more like the "father of lies" (John 8:44) rather than the Father of spirits (Hebrews 12:9). Jesus knew this; it was His objective and obligation to tell us. We all have the capacity to alienate ourselves from God and choose death over life; indeed, we all have done this (Romans 3:23). This is what is in the middle of us; this is what corrupts everything else "good" about us. We think that we are alive, but Christ tells us that without Him we are dead (Ephesians 2:1-2; John 8:24; Revelation 3:1). Outside of God's grace we are all rotting from the inside out, having been despoiled from within, from the very middle of our soul. We are, when left to ourselves, selfish, greedy, and self-destructive. We are also, left to ourselves, most pitiful and hopeless creatures.

This picture is grim, yet Jesus knew all this from the beginning and told us about it. It is not the outward, external things which corrupt and destroy us: it is that which comes from within, from a man's heart. These are the things which "defile" us (Matthew 15:11, 15-20). Jesus did not come to us "in the flesh" merely to impart knowledge *about* our predicament; however, He came to save us *from* our predicament. His entrance into the world was unlike anything we would have expected from a great King; His ministry was unlike anything man had ever seen. For awhile He enjoyed relative popularity and success. He was the center of all attention, having cast Himself in the middle of a troubled, volatile people who were desperate for change but largely unable and/or unwilling to accommodate it. Nonetheless, Jesus spoke of the heart of God as well as the heart of man. He illustrated the love of God as He exposed the ugliness of man. He spoke of the grace of God and also highlighted the resistance men often have toward that grace. In the middle of God is light and love; in the middle of man is fear and darkness.

In the middle of His ministry, Jesus ascended a mountain somewhere near Caesarea Philippi and was transfigured before the eyes of Peter, James, and John (Matthew 17:1-8). In the middle of nowhere, He stood illuminated in the midst of God's presence, knowing that what had gone so terribly wrong in the middle of man would require Him to step in the gap between man and God. Until this point, His ministry had enjoyed great popularity, but He knew this would not last. The fickle support of the people would evaporate; the hostility of the Jewish priests and elders would escalate; the nature of His preaching would take on a much darker tone and perspective. Physically, He descended downward from the mountain, away from the powerful and dynamic scene upon its peak. Spiritually, He would descend even lower than the lowest valleys below the mountain: He would descend downward into the very bowels of humanity where all the ugliness and hatred against God was most vivid and intense. He would not merely feel the ripple effects of man's hostility toward Him but would cast Himself into the churning, venomous, mockery-spewing cauldron of man's heart. He did this purposely, deliberately, and fearlessly.

Jesus knew what had to be done. He knew what He Himself had to do. He predicted, "And I, if I am lifted up from the earth, will draw all men to Myself" (John 12:32). In order to draw all men to Himself, He would have to be thrust in the middle of all men. Jesus put Himself in the center in order to most effectively reach—figuratively and spiritually—all those in need of His grace, which, of course, are all who have committed sacrilege against the Sacred (cf. Romans 3:23). As Paul would later remark, "[God] desires all men to be saved and to come to the knowledge of the truth. For there is one God, and one mediator also between God and men, the man Christ Jesus, who gave Himself as a ransom for all, the testimony given at the proper time" (1 Timothy 2:4-5). God needed a Man to stand in the gap (cf. Ezekiel 22:30), to mediate between Himself and His highest creation. Jesus did what for anyone else would have been the impossible: He stood in the middle of everything.

When "the proper time" came to make the ultimate sacrifice, Jesus continued to press into that middle, refusing to stay anywhere on the periphery. In the middle of all the wonder, amazement, controversy, and hatred which centered upon Him, Jesus was crucified between two thieves, in the middle of two men (Luke 23:39-43). This was no accident or coincidence; it fits perfectly and beautifully with God's theme of proximity and orientation. It also fulfills a 700-year-old prophecy concerning the Christ: "...He Himself bore the sin of many, And interceded [lit., was made to be the middle] for the transgressors" (Isaiah 53:12). God's Son was not to die in some remote location by Himself; He was to die in the optimum proximity to those who needed Him the most. Symbolically, those two men on the cross portray the whole of humanity: having sinned against God, we are all under a similar condemnation.

Jesus did not give up His life quickly; He immersed Himself in the sacrifice for sin, the agony of suffering, and the pain of death (cf. Mark 10:38). For hours He endured His own cross in the middle of two other crosses, in the middle of all humanity, in the middle of the Law of Moses and the gospel of Christ. Jesus was suspended between heaven and earth—not really in one or the other, but in the timeless and indefinable realm linking the two— in an ideal position to serve as Mediator between the God of heaven and the people of this earth. In His hearing were hecklers and scoffers, mockers and conspirers, those who either hated Jesus or hated the Jews in general, men who hurled insinuations, accusations, and condemnations. Others simply watched Him as He suffered, laboring for every breath, wincing with every fiery spasm of pain from His wounded feet and wrists, encrusted with blood, perspiration, and the spittle of unholy men.

Indeed, *we* should stare at Christ in awe of His great sacrifice. We should consider the awful injustice: the innocent Lamb of God was not delicately made to bleed through a surgical swipe at the throat with a knife, but was tortured to the point of disfigurement and bludgeoned with the fists of men. We should look with wonder upon the incredible paradox: the Sacred Word of God portrayed as a vulgar profanity, a kind of effigy of man's own sacrilege. We should take a moment to appreciate *what it takes to be put in the middle* of such a wretched situation. We quickly ought to realize that being in the middle may be the optimum position as far as God is concerned, but it is certainly not the safest or easiest. Thankfully, Jesus did not dwell upon the pain and suffering but focused intensely upon "the joy set before Him" (Hebrews 12:2). For the joy of obedience, for the joy of redemption, and for the joy of doing what no one else could do but what needed to be done, Jesus put Himself in the middle of everything. No wonder God is so proud of His Son; no wonder we who are redeemed by Him are so proud of Him as well.

When the end finally came, Jesus, the Passover Lamb, gave up His life at a time which, from a Jewish perspective, nearly defies being a "time" at all. The Passover, from its ancient beginnings, was to begin at twilight of the 14th day of the (Jewish) religious month of Nisan (Exodus 12:6; Leviticus 23:5). The word "twilight" in the Hebrew literally means, "between the two evenings." Rabbinical exposition on this subject differs; some believe this means somewhere between when the sun touches the earth and finally disappears beneath the horizon; others believe it to last until total darkness. In either case, it is a limited and very special duration of time. In the middle of two days—in the midst of the transition from one day to the next (since Jews count days from sundown to sundown)—the Passover lambs were to be sacrificed. Likewise, in the middle of two days, while He hung in the middle of two men—one angry and defiant, the other broken and contrite—Jesus willfully and deliberately gave up His spirit (life) to God. In a nearly timeless, undefined, and incalculable moment in history, Jesus offered His life in place of all those who throughout human existence had ever offended the very One who had created them. The veil in the Temple was torn in two (Matthew 27:51)—ripped in half in the very middle of its fabric—symbolizing that access to God was no longer an impossible, remote, or even limited thing, but that "whoever will call on the name of the Lord will be saved" (Romans 10:13). The sanctuary of God was now open to all—still conditional, as salvation always is, but entirely *possible* and *accessible*—because of the Man who died in the middle of all history (Ephesians 2:14).

Jesus' body was placed in the middle of a rich man's tomb, just as Isaiah had prophesied (53:9). There His body lay for three days and three nights, just as Jesus promised it would (Matthew 12:40). Somewhere in another nearly timeless, imperceptible moment—at some undefined moment between the end of one week and the beginning of another—Jesus rose from the dead. While Satan had once stood in-between God and every sinner, accusing the sinner of *being* a sinner and God of being a *God* of sinners, Jesus bound the "strong man" and plundered his house (Matthew 12:29). Jesus then "led captive a host of captives" to freedom, having overpowered not only Satan but also death itself (Ephesians 4:8; Hebrews 2:14-15).

This same Jesus, in His last appearance on earth, stood in the middle of His disciples and blessed them. Then as they looked on, He lifted up from their midst and disappeared into the middle of the sky, being swallowed up by the clouds, and then translated into the spiritual realm of the Father Himself (Acts 1:9). There He now reigns as King of kings and Lord of lords, sitting at the right hand of God (Acts 2:33). There too He serves forever as our High Priest who as our Friend and legal Advocate stands between God and man on our behalf (Romans 8:34; 1 John 2:1-2).

In the Middle of Two Eternities

Now we too stand in the middle of two eternities where decisions must be made and loyalties must be chosen. God entreats us through His gospel to stand in the gap between Him and all others so that not only will we be blessed but that we might also be a blessing to others in contributing to their salvation. We cannot dwell in the heart of Christ until we first master what is in the middle of our own hearts: our lusts, desires, and personal ambitions. Christ does not ask us to master that which is going on in the world or even the circumstances surrounding us; these are beyond our ability to control. Instead, He wants us to give *Him* mastery over what is in the very center of our heart, in the very middle of our soul.

This is what it means to be a seeker of the sacred. And look what God has done to make our search not only possible but entirely successful! God has taken great care to position everything *in* His creation for optimum performance, to the maximum benefit *for* His creation. Likewise, Christ has also placed Himself accordingly: in the very middle of everything. His throne sits in the center of the universe, ideally and symmetrically surrounded by life and beauty, in the midst of all praise and glory. Heaven and earth bow in deference, angels sing songs of seven-fold praise, all the "living beings" of heaven kneel before Him and cast their crowns at His feet. From the middle of His throne pours forth an endless river of life which courses through the middle of trees of life, laden with fruit that is to be forever shared and enjoyed by all the redeemed. The picture is symbolic but the truths it illustrates are real, powerful, and—despite whatever faithlessness or cynicism persists in this world—undiminished.

One day, those who are seekers of the sacred will stand before this Almighty God and join the praise of all the hosts of heaven. One day—if we continue to put our search for the sacred above all other pursuits—we will stand with Christ in the middle of this fantastic and inexpressible scene. One day—if indeed we do not compromise or abandon our search—we will be ushered into glory by the angels.

On that endless, timeless, perfect day, we will not be taken to some faraway excursion on the furthest reaches of heaven, but Christ will bring us into the very midst of fellowship with Him, in the middle of His own heart.

"…and so we shall always be with the Lord" (1 Thessalonians 4:17).

Endnotes

9 In essence, we are united in the likeness of Christ's own death. Christ physically died for us so that we might live to God; but we must also deliberately choose to "die" to this world and our own human will in order to make fellowship with God a reality. Christ's death saves no one who does not himself choose to follow Him through death to the Living God. As He raised Himself from the dead, Christ "resurrects" our souls from spiritual death (divine condemnation) so that we might walk "in newness of life" (Romans 6:3-11).

10 This foreshadows an expression of Christ: "You have made Him [Christ] for a little while lower than the angels..." (Hebrews 2:7). Indeed, Jehovah God had Himself, for a little while, condescended to the primitive understanding of the ancients so they could comprehend Him at all. The "mercy seat" serves as a physical form of the future Christ, who Himself is rightly referred to as our Mercy Seat. (See Leviticus 16:14 and Hebrews 9:1-7, but also Romans 3:25, where the word "propitiation" [appeasement or satisfaction] is translated from the exact same Greek word which is also translated "mercy seat.")

11 This is the literal meaning of the original Greek text, per A. T. Robertson, Word Pictures in the New Testament, vol. V (Grand Rapids: Baker Book House [no date]), 4.

CHAPTER EIGHT

Drawing Near to God

The former priests, on the one hand, existed in greater numbers because they were prevented by death from continuing, but Jesus, on the other hand, because He continues forever, holds His priesthood permanently. Therefore He is able also to save forever those who draw near to God through Him, since He always lives to make intercession for them.
Hebrews 7:23-25

One aspect of seeking the sacred that is often misunderstood or is overlooked altogether is that of *sacrifice.* It is not uncommon to find someone wanting to "follow God"; it is quite another thing to find one who will make necessary sacrifices in order to accomplish this. In order to draw near to God, one must be prepared to make sacrifices. Before discussing what exactly those sacrifices might be (and how they might vary from one person to the next), it is critical that one first have a good grasp of the *concept* of sacrifice.

Several years ago I read a true story that will serve to introduce this most important subject. A young Native Alaskan boy—about ten years old—fell into a swift river while fishing in the Bush with his family. His uncle jumped in after the boy and managed to grab hold of him. The two of them clung desperately to a log near the bank, the current being too swift for them to do anything more. Family members ran down the bank and were able to reach the boy, but as soon as the uncle let go of the child, he no longer had the strength to hang on. Exhausted by the exertion expended in saving his nephew, he let go of the log and the current immediately swept him down the river. This man drowned, but his nephew lived; this man made the ultimate sacrifice while the boy was saved as a result of this.

There are several important points to consider in this story. First, this man did not *have* to jump in after his nephew. He made a conscious decision to do so; nobody asked him to save the boy; nobody pushed him into the water. Sacrifice, ideally, is a conscious decision, not an accident or a coerced action.

Second, this man had an objective in mind, but did not have the time to weigh all the costs and requirements involved in achieving that objective. His foremost objective—*save the boy*—was important and urgent enough to demand a response on his part without taking time to deliberate over its consequences. Sacrifice always seeks a higher objective than one's own personal comforts, considerations, or conveniences; its purpose for acting transcends all these other things.

Third, in order to save the boy, this man had to give up something of himself. He likely did not know that it would be his life, but at the very least we can say that he put his life on hold for the sake of this boy. Whatever was going on in his life, whatever he was doing, whatever he was working toward—even if it was just a good catch of fish—was immediately set aside in order to focus entirely upon the rescue of this child. The rescue was not free; even if he had survived the rescue, it would not have been free, not for him. Sacrifice requires a giving up of oneself in order to respond to a cause more noble than one's own self-preservation.

There are some limitations to these lessons too that are as profound as the lessons themselves. First, this man's sacrifice was of human origin. As noble and valiant as I believe his efforts were, this man still made the decision to jump into the water *himself*—that is, God never told him to do this. Even though I don't believe he did anything *wrong* in his decision, it is still an important point to acknowledge. Certainly God teaches us that life is sacred, even our own, but He has not told us explicitly the lengths to which we are to go—or the means we are to employ—to *save* a life.

Second, while this man valiantly saved his nephew's life, he could not do anything to save the boy's soul. While a ten-year-old boy's soul hardly needs saving, since he is still an innocent child in the sight of God, he will grow up to be a man and will thus be held accountable as an adult for the sins he *will* commit (cf. Romans 3:23). His uncle's sacrifice could not contribute anything directly toward that boy's spiritual salvation. His death could not redeem the boy-turned-man's soul from the condemnation of sin. His death could not transcend this life to provide a worthy sacrifice toward the boy's soul in the life to come.

Third, this man's sacrifice could not even atone for his *own* sins. His act, though noble and altruistic, still fell short of what God considers a *redemptive* sacrifice. Whatever sins this man had committed would not be remitted simply because of his own sacrifice; they must be taken care of by a sacrifice more worthy than he was able to offer.

Let's summarize what has been said thus far:
• Sacrifice, by definition, must be voluntary and not forced.
• Sacrifice responds to a higher (transcendent) objective than the immediate context.
• Sacrifice requires the giving of *oneself* (up to but not always including martyrdom).
• Not all sacrifices are equally worthy (in God's sight).
• Not all sacrifices are direct responses to divine requests.
• Human sacrifices may save a life, but cannot save a soul.
• One's own sacrifice is not worthy of saving (or redeeming) his *own* corrupted soul, but must appeal to the perfect sacrifice of an uncorrupted soul for this.

The point is: there is a lot more to the concept and nature of *sacrifice* than one might initially realize. Furthermore, if one is going to be a seeker of the sacred, he is going to have to make some very *serious* sacrifices. One who is unwilling to make such sacrifices cannot draw near to God. While our sacrifices cannot begin to equate to those made *for* us by Christ, ours must be *like* His, modeled on those which He provided on our behalf. Seeking the sacred is a sacrificial life, just as Christ's own life was a sacrificial one (Mark 10:45).

A Necessary Loss

Making a sacrifice, in the truest sense of the expression, is to purposely incur a loss with the full assurance that ultimately one will gain *more* than what was given up. It is not gambling, since gambling offers no guarantee of superior gain. A person may think he has "sacrificed" much in order to gamble, but this *kind* of loss falls into a different context than what God would consider. If one sacrifices himself for God, there is a guaranteed return (2 Timothy 1:12); he does not gamble his soul, or his eternity, but God ensures his salvation. This is what the "pledge" of the Holy Spirit is all about: a guarantee of more to come *if* one continues in his commitment to the Lord (2 Corinthians 1:21-22; Ephesians 1:13-14, et al).

Genuine sacrifice is not the result of chance, ignorance, or poor decisions. In a chess game, for example, a person may play poorly and have his queen captured. He did not *sacrifice* his queen, but he simply *lost* it, since he never intended for that outcome. However, in a different chess game a player may *purposely* allow his queen to be captured in order to capture the opponent's *king* and win the game. In this case, the loss (of his queen) was intentional, purposeful, and productive, inasmuch as he won more than he lost as a direct result of his sacrifice.

It is this latter *kind* of loss that the Bible refers to as a "sacrifice." This is not the *only* meaning of sacrifice (as I will discuss shortly), but it is most certainly a primary meaning. Thus, "by faith Abel offered a better sacrifice than Cain" (Hebrews 11:4), which is to say (at least) that he suffered a greater loss than did Cain in making an offering to the Lord—i.e., he gave a living animal rather than mere vegetables (Genesis 4:3-4). Likewise David would not sacrifice to God that which cost him nothing, since the absence of any loss to himself negated the very act of sacrifice (2 Samuel 24:24). Likewise also Christ "loved [us] and gave Himself up for us, an offering and a sacrifice to God as a fragrant aroma" (Ephesians 5:2). Christ gave *Himself* up in order to gain something better than what He had before: *us*.

Again, a sacrifice must be deliberate in order to *be* a sacrifice; otherwise it is simply a loss (or a waste). For example, say a man's house burned to the ground through no fault or intention of his own: an electrical short caused the fire. Everything he owned was destroyed in the process. Has he incurred a tremendous loss? Most definitely he has, whether or not he has insurance. Was that loss a *sacrifice*? Not according to the nature of sacrifice as defined in Scripture and demonstrated by Christ. This man suffered loss, but gained nothing better in the process; it was not purposeful or deliberate; he did not "offer" it for any reason.

Now let's change the scenario a bit. Say a man is converted to Christ in a part of the world that holds God and the Christian faith in contempt. The locals converge upon his lawn one afternoon and demand that he recant his faith, or else suffer the consequences. The man refuses, not because he is stubborn and defiant, but because he loves the Lord more than he loves his safety. The locals further threaten him, even more menacingly than before; the man politely but resolutely refuses. That night while he is dining out with his family, local thugs torch his home and burn it to the ground. It is a total loss. Is it now a sacrifice? Absolutely, due to the reasons for which the loss was incurred. He *chose* the loss of his house over the loss of his fellowship with God.

Thus, two men suffer the same physical calamity, but to one man it is a *loss* while to the other it is a *sacrifice*. The tangible loss is the same in both cases, but the *kind* of loss is completely different. A genuine sacrifice must always *cost* the giver of that sacrifice *something*. To sacrifice *to* God, one must give up something *for* (or because of) God. The spiritual application of this concept in Christian life goes far beyond mere physical losses.

Critics of Christians have construed this to be a very selfish sort of "sacrifice," since the person only appears to offer it in order to benefit himself. By itself, this would be true: if a person offers a "sacrifice" *primarily* to benefit himself, this manifests an improper (i.e., self-serving) motive and corrupts the purity and genuineness of the sacrifice itself. Yet the one who sincerely pursues God—he who is seeking the sacred—does not put his own interests first. He sacrifices out of respect and admiration for the One who receives the offering. In his heart, his offering is presented not upon a literal altar nor put into a collection plate, but it is humbly presented before the Lord Himself. It is as though he lays his gift at the feet of the One who *most certainly deserves it.* His primary objective is to pay homage to the One who is higher and greater than himself.

In this way, the offering itself symbolizes the allegiance and devotion of the offerer to the Father. Such sacrifice is an expression of sincere respect and adoration; as a response to what is expected by believers, it is also an expression of obedience. God is always pleased with willful obedience. It was because of Christ's obedience that "God highly exalted Him, and bestowed on Him the name which is above every name" (Philippians 2:8-9). Likewise, our personal obedience to God rises up to Him as did the "fragrant aroma" of an appropriately-offered animal sacrifice (Leviticus 3:5, for example). It wasn't the actual smoke of the offering that pleased the Lord but the *humble and grateful heart* that put the animal on that altar in the first place. So it is with our offerings: it is not the thing being done itself but the *heart which does it* that means so much to Him. So it was with Christ, who put *Himself* upon the altar, so to speak, and therefore offered up a "fragrant aroma" to God in His obedience (Ephesians 5:1-2).

The Giving of Oneself

By putting God first in one's heart, that person is blessed by God beyond whatever his human effort alone could ever achieve. Whatever God does for us that we cannot do for ourselves (with regard to salvation) is called *grace.* By giving freely to the Father, the offerer receives divine grace beyond measure. This is one of those spiritual paradoxes that make our relationship with God so intriguing: we gain more by *making* sacrifices than we do by *withholding* them.

Regardless of how small, seemingly insignificant, or visibly obscure the offering itself might be, God sees the *heart* of the one who offers it and responds accordingly. Jesus underscores this idea in Matthew 10:42: "And whoever in the name of a disciple gives to one of these little ones even a cup of cold water to drink, truly I say to you, he shall not lose his reward." The "cup of cold water" is literally given to a person, but it is presented as an *offering* before the Lord. God recognizes the offering and thus blesses the offerer. No such sacrifice goes unnoticed by the Sovereign God who sees all things and knows every heart. As Paul said, "Therefore, my beloved brethren, be steadfast, immovable, always abounding in the work of the Lord, knowing that your toil is not in vain in the Lord" (1 Corinthians 15:58). In other words, the Corinthians' sacrifices—their perseverance and toil—were being remembered and recorded by God even if the recipients of their efforts did not notice the loss they incurred to provide such efforts.

Someone protests, "What 'loss' is incurred through providing a cup of cold water?!" On the surface, the loss may seem negligible. The loss itself depends upon the attitude and circumstances of the one who suffers it. The Macedonian Christians gave generously to Paul's ministry even though they were in "deep poverty." The *dollar amount* was never the point; the attitude of their heart was what made their contribution such a meaningful *sacrifice* (2 Corinthians 8:1-5). A rich man who hands a $20 bill to an out-of-work widower with two hungry children has hardly suffered much loss; his sacrifice was indeed small, if indeed it can be characterized as a sacrifice at all. (Often such "sacrifices" are more about appeasing one's guilty conscience than any heartfelt devotion to the Lord.) Another man who himself is struggling financially who also gives $20 to the same widower may do so *as an act of homage to God* rather than a begrudging or trite response to guilt or peer pressure. He has incurred a deliberate loss in anticipation of a greater, guaranteed gain; he has offered a sacrifice indeed. So it was with the Macedonian Christians: before ever giving a single shekel to Paul, "they first gave themselves to the Lord and to us by the will of God." Think about that: *they first gave themselves*. This is the first and most important sacrifice a person must ever make to God. No one can be a seeker of the sacred who refuses to give himself *first* to the Lord.

Some men, in sharp contrast, refuse to give themselves to God but are wholly bent upon serving their own pride. Jesus describes such a person as one who gives to the poor and "sounds a trumpet" to let everyone know of his seemingly pious act (Matthew 6:1-4). He calls this person a hypocrite, since the primary reason for his having given anything at all is to receive attention and applause of men, not to render a humble offering to God. Certainly this is something common to men: seeking the praise of *other* men rather than seeking the sacred. Many of the Jewish leaders of Jesus' day refused to believe in Him simply because "they loved the approval of men rather than the approval of God" (John 12:42-43). Men cannot make genuine sacrifices to God if they are unwilling to suffer the loss of what is most important to them—in the present example, public approval. Proud people have nothing to offer the Father since they already serve another god.

The genuine Christian, however, has already committed his life and heart to God in having *become* a Christian. Making sacrifices—for the sake of God and His kingdom—is what discipleship is all about. The Christian's losses are only temporary since God will return to him (both now and in the hereafter) "many times as much" as he has given up or left behind (Luke 18:29-30). Once again, if a person will not give *himself* to God, then it does not matter what else he offers to God. Such loveless offerings are not genuine sacrifices, but are complete *wastes* of time and effort. In the end, he gains nothing for the losses he has incurred; even God Himself is deprived of the fellowship of that man's soul.

The Seeker's Personal Sacrifices

Every act of Christian duty, when properly carried out, involves some sort of personal sacrifice. Love, for example, *always* incurs personal loss on behalf of the object of that love. Love is meaningless if little or nothing is given up to *express* that love. God loves us with an immeasurable love; accordingly, He has expressed this love with immeasurable sacrifice (1 John 4:9-10). In love, God suffers such losses (for now) in order that people might come to their senses and repent (2 Peter 3:9).

All other Christian virtues or objectives require sacrifice as well. For example, in order to gain fellowship with God, a man must sacrifice his pride: he must demonstrate through obedience that God's fellowship is more important than gratifying his own ego. Likewise, every act of forgiveness, compassion, grace, patience, kindness, hospitality, etc.—as long as it is "for the sake of righteousness" (cf. Matthew 5:10)—requires a sacrifice of one's time, energy, resources, and personal (earthly) advancement. A person cannot practice forgiveness, for example, without suffering the loss of the punishment that the one who sinned against him truly deserves. He must absorb that loss in himself; he must sacrifice *to God* his rightful appeal to justice. He does so, however, knowing that God will *be* his justice in the end, just as Jesus "kept entrusting Himself to Him who judges righteously" (1 Peter 2:23). That person believes in God to the extent that he is willing to sacrifice his vengeance and face-saving vindication—in essence, his pride—in order to gain a life with God in the future.

Once again, having faith in a future reward *and* justice is not like gambling on the Stock Market or buying a Lottery ticket. We cannot cross our fingers and hold our breath, hoping (against all odds) that we will "win" something when it is almost certain that we will lose our entire investment. Faith is not what a person practices when he has nothing else to believe in; faith is what a person practices when he has been given a *reason* to believe and has chosen *to believe* because of that reason. "Now faith is the assurance of things hoped for, the conviction of things not seen. ...without faith it is impossible to please Him, for he who comes to God must believe that He is and that He is a rewarder of those who seek Him" (Hebrews 11:1, 6). No one should sacrifice to God who does not believe in Him; likewise, no one should believe in God who is unwilling to sacrifice to Him.

The Sacrificial System

When students of the Bible begin talking about sacrifice, invariably the discussion circles around two main bodies of thought: first, the animal sacrifices required by the Law of Moses; second, the sacrifice of Christ. Often what is concluded is this: the one (Christ's) was a fulfillment of the other (Law). It doesn't take a seminary degree to make the connection, after all: it is clear, logical, and even fascinating. Still, there is so much more to consider in all of this than the mere *connection* of the two ideas. This subject is worth at least a brief examination with regard to seeking the sacred. Indeed, the more we understand *of* sacrifice, the better we will be able to *participate* in the sacrificial life to which God has called us. One cannot actively be seeking the sacred without making sacrifices *toward* the sacred.

The sacrifices required under the Law of Moses—specifically, those defined in Leviticus—might seem foreign to and disconnected from us at first. After all, we are not offering up sheep and goats and bulls upon an altar as a part of our worship to God. At that time, the kinds of sacrifices which Israel was commanded to make were ideal under the circumstances. While we might look upon the process as a tedious, bloody, even unpleasant system of worship, the Israelites had a much deeper insight to this (at least those who took it seriously did).

In Leviticus 1:2-3, God told Moses:

> Speak to the sons of Israel and say to them, "When any man of you brings an offering to the LORD, you shall bring your offering of animals from the herd or the flock. If his offering is a burnt offering from the herd, he shall offer it, a male without defect; he shall offer it at the doorway of the tent of meeting, that he may be accepted before the LORD."

The idea of a burnt offering went well beyond just bringing a gift to God, although that idea too is embedded in the concept of sacrifice. It was a common practice in the ancient Near East to bring a gift whenever presenting oneself before the king (1 Samuel 16:19-20, e.g.). How much more important is Jehovah God than any earthly king! Therefore, in Exodus 23:14-17, when God instructed Israelite males (age 20 years and older) to appear before Him three times a year, He explicitly said, "…And none shall appear before Me empty-handed" (verse 15). Participation in the festivals included bringing a gift—a personal sacrifice—to God.

The primary emphasis there was not in the gift itself. The word "offering" (in the phrase "burnt offering") is translated from the Hebrew word *qorban*. (This is transliterated in Mark 7:11 as "Corban.") The word is difficult to translate easily or succinctly into English. In essence, it means "to draw near (the altar) with (something)." Thus, *qorban* is a word (really, an expression) that conveys the idea of *drawing near to God* through the process or action of offering up a (certain) sacrifice. As the Israelite brought his sacrificial animal to the courtyard of the tabernacle, he understood that this animal's life was the divinely-prescribed means by which he could *draw near in worship to God*. It was not enough, in other words, that this man professed belief in Jehovah; it was not enough that he was circumcised, having been born into a national covenant relationship with God. His personal presence before the tabernacle was also insufficient by itself. To appear before Almighty Jehovah (at His tabernacle) was understood to be such a profound, important, and intensely *sacred* experience that a *life* was required of all who stood before Him. The idea was: this Awesome God would spare the Israelite's life as long as he brought a *qorban*—in this case, a *sacrificial* life offered on behalf of his own.

We should *never* interpret this to mean that God purposely made it difficult to approach Him, for it is *impossible* to approach Him otherwise. Thus, the picture is just the opposite: God *wanted* the Israelite to draw near to Him and thus provided *opportunity* for him to do so through the Levitical sacrificial system. The purpose of *qorban* was "that he [the offerer] may be accepted before the LORD." This is what God wants: to *accept* people, not destroy them. While the picture in Leviticus seems primitive and crude, it is not because God could not think of a better system at the time. It was an *ideal* system for the people of that time, per that culture, for the purpose of leading them to something better (cf. Galatians 3:23-24). In order to appreciate a sacrifice to end all other such sacrifices (i.e., Christ; Hebrews 10:1-14), Israel first had to understand and appreciate the very nature of sacrifice itself.

The Burnt Offering

Now consider the different categories of sacrifices which God required of the Israelite under the Law of Moses (hereafter, simply "Law.") There were three major kinds of sacrifices: sin offerings, burnt offerings, and freewill offerings. This is not the order in which they are first presented to us in Leviticus, but this *is* the order in which they were to be offered. The first kind of offering mentioned was the burnt offering. It was called "burnt" because the entire animal (except the hide; Leviticus 7:8) was entirely consumed in the altar fire. None of its meat was given to the priests (as in a sin offering) or to the offerer himself (as in a freewill offering).

Now "burnt offering" may not sound particularly appealing to us at first, given our modern perception toward anything "burnt." The connotation may be rather negative. When someone burns dinner in the kitchen, for example, it is hardly a time for rejoicing; rather, it is time to open windows, turn on exhaust fans, and disable smoke alarms. In the context of religious sacrificial offerings, however, a burnt offering indicates the *full dedication of one's heart* to God, as illustrated through the total consumption of the sacrificial animal by the flames of the altar. God *wants* people to draw near to Him; He *seeks* those who will worship Him in spirit and truth (John 4:23-24). Therefore, there is nothing negative about this procedure, unless of course it is done wrongly or insincerely.

Put yourself in the sandals of an ancient Israelite for a moment. Picture yourself bringing your animal before the priest for inspection, since only approved, unblemished offerings of the highest quality are acceptable. As you lay your hands on this animal and then slit its throat (allowing for a quick and quiet death), you realize that *this* animal's life represents the essence of your *own* life. As the animal is skinned and prepared, you realize that there is a certain process and procedure that is acceptable to God, thereby invalidating all other procedures, regardless of how well-intentioned they might seem to be. As you watch this animal's body be consumed by the fire, you consider your own life as being consumed—in a positive sense— by your zeal for God (cf. John 2:17).

The highest objective an ancient Israelite could strive for was to be consecrated to God. Such consecration—the act of being holily dedicated to the service of Jehovah—surpassed all other pursuits in terms of one's personal relationship with God. While the overall emphasis in the Old Testament seems to focus on Israel's national relationship with God, the personal aspect is embedded in the Law through such sacrifices such as the burnt offering.[12] This is why the instructions for the burnt offering are the first to be listed in Leviticus. It is not the first sacrifice of *necessity*, but it is the ultimate sacrifice in terms of *drawing near to God*.

The Sin Offering

No matter how earnestly one desires to be consecrated to God, he cannot do so without first dealing with his sins. Atonement—the expiation or removal of sins through whatever process God requires—is absolutely necessary in seeking the sacred: it is the first step in the process. Thus, while burnt offerings spoke to the higher nature of sacrifice *in importance* (i.e., drawing near to God), sin offerings had to be offered first *in sequence*.

While it is true that a certain aspect of burnt offerings also dealt with atonement (in that the blood of those animals was poured out at the base of the altar for this reason), their main purpose was *consecration*. Sin offerings dealt specifically with *sin*; that was their sole purpose. Certainly the Law identified different kinds or classifications of sins (as expressed in Leviticus 4–6), but in the end sin is sin and it must be dealt with via sacrificial offerings. In making a sin offering, the offerer presented his sacrificial animal before the priest and had it slain outside the courtyard of the tabernacle. The blood was brought near the tabernacle, however, and was smeared on the horns of the altar and (the remainder was) poured out at the base of that altar.

The fat portions of the animal were offered up "in smoke," that is, completely consumed on the altar. As long as the sin offering was not made for the priest himself or the entire congregation of Israel, the priest received a certain meat portion of that animal for himself. This was part of his payment for services rendered, since he was the one who officiated over the sacrifice *and* pronounced the sinner's atonement. (If the offering was for the priest's own sin, however, he received no portion of it. No one was allowed to profit from his own sin.) The rest of the animal, however, was taken outside the camp of Israel and burned entirely. Since the body of that animal represented sin, it could not remain in God's presence (i.e., before the tabernacle).

This pronouncement of atonement (as in Leviticus 4:26, "Thus the priest shall make atonement for him in regard to his sin, and he will be forgiven") was *impossible* without an animal's life given on behalf of the sinner.[13] An Israelite could not draw near to God while contaminated with sin, and he could not have those sins removed (atoned for) without a blood sacrifice. Blood is *essential* in any offerings of purification; "without shedding of blood there is no forgiveness" (Hebrews 9:22; see also Leviticus 17:10-11). Once again the sin offering represented the sinner himself: inasmuch as he had transgressed the law of Jehovah, so he stood condemned and deserved to die. Furthermore, the word "burn"[14] (symbolically) indicates fire that *comes down* from heaven as a pronouncement of condemnation. The word "burn" in regard to a burnt offering[15] indicates smoke which *rises up* to heaven as pleasing to God through the willingness and obedience of the sacrifice itself.

The Freewill Offering

Sin offerings atoned for one's offenses *against* God. Burnt offerings symbolized one's consecration *to* God. Freewill offerings indicated one's appreciation *of* God. This last grouping of offerings, which included peace, thank, and votive (vow) offerings expressed gratitude to God for His having allowed the Israelite fellowship at all. Inasmuch as all men have sinned (Romans 3:23), so every Israelite was unable to stand before God on his own merit. One was to respond to the profound privilege of being able to draw near the Sacred God with his expressed gratitude.

By offering a freewill sacrifice, the Israelite implied that he *was* at peace with God; he found his completion in *God*; God completed *him*.[16] This implied, of course, that apart from God he was incomplete and his soul was in turmoil. Fellowship and peace are mutually dependent states of being: one cannot have fellowship with God without being at peace with Him; likewise, one cannot be at peace with God without enjoying His fellowship. In acknowledgment of this, the Israelite offered his freewill offering in *honor* of God and with *thanks* for his participation. The transaction between man and God is never complete without man's *thankfulness* and God's *reception* of that thanks.[17]

Freewill offerings were just that: offerings made of one's own free will. The Law did not command such offerings but only regulated their format. Gratitude is not something God can command, no more than He can command love, forgiveness, compassion, or joy. These are expressions of one's heart, not prescribed responses to a codified law. Laws can express what is *expected* of believers (as is the case with freewill offerings), but cannot force the heart to act against its own will. Thus, a "freewill" offering implied that a person's will had deliberately chosen to worship God without compulsion. Such a person was not blindly or mechanically responding to law, under threat of punishment if he did not, but made his sacrifice in adoration of God, as a means of *seeking after Him*. While having never *seen* God, he actively demonstrated his faith *in* God through the substance of his offering.

A unique aspect of the freewill offering was that the one who offered it was also allowed to partake of it. Burnt offerings were wholly consumed upon the altar; sin offerings were offered up "in smoke" upon the altar, except for the priests' allotted portions. Peace offerings were shared with several different parties—even those who were not directly involved in the sacrifice.[18] For each offering of this kind, God received His part (the fat portions), the priest received his portion (the breast and right thigh, Leviticus 7:30-34), and the offerer received the remainder of the animal. This latter portion, along with an accompanying grain offering (Numbers 15:2ff), was to be shared with his family, his servants, "the Levite who is within your gates" (Deuteronomy 12:10-12), and the poor and needy (implied; cf. Deuteronomy 15:7-8). This meal had to be eaten in the courtyard of the tabernacle, since it was considered a *fellowship meal* with Jehovah Himself (Deuteronomy 12:17-18). In a sense, God served as the Host of this meal, since it was His tabernacle, altar, mercy, and grace that made the worshiper's completion even possible. No one who was unclean— i.e., ritually contaminated or guilty of transgression—could partake of this meal, however, because he was *not* complete before God (Leviticus 7:20). Such hypocritical participation was a deep offense against the purity and sacredness of the occasion for the offering in the first place.

*   *   *

What must not be forgotten is that *all* these various offerings had *one* ultimate objective: to draw near to God. Drawing near to God is equivalent to seeking the sacred: to do the one is to pursue the other. Each sacrifice provided a different yet essential aspect of the offerer's desire and ability to draw near to God. This, of course, was impossible without *God's* desire and ability to make this possible in the first place. If not for such divine grace and mercy, the Israelite had no hope of drawing near to God no matter how much he desired to do so. Thus, God did not just tell the Israelites (in so many words) to seek the sacred; He made it possible for them to do so, and then told them how this was to be accomplished.

The Christian's Sacrifice

While we are not asked to offer animals on an altar anymore, the concept of sacrifice as presented in the Law carries over into our covenant with Christ. Unfortunately, Christians today are very disconnected from the reality of sacrifice since we do not participate in it as actively and graphically as did the ancient Israelite. We do not commit a living animal to its death on our behalf; we do not see its blood (life) draining from its body; we do not skin its body and put its flesh upon an altar; we do not see its body being swallowed up in fire. Therefore, we do not often associate the full surrender of our own lives when God asks *us* to sacrifice *ourselves* (cf. Romans 12:1-2). Instead, we have been conditioned to the rituals and formalities of Bible classes and "worship services." We may reduce sacrifice to a mere concept or sermon topic, but we often fail to relate to its necessary implications. Certainly God does not need gifts from His people—He already owns the entire world (Isaiah 66:1-2)—but He requests these only so that we might learn the importance *of* sacrifice in drawing near to Him. Indeed, the genuine seeker of the sacred must see himself upon the altar, so to speak, his life completely "emptied" for the sake of the One to whom he is drawing near (cf. Philippians 2:7).

While our sacrifices may be similar in *kind* to His, Christ has done what is *impossible for us to fulfill or perform*. Such is the grace of God: He does for us what we cannot do for ourselves. On the other hand, grace *never* operates in the absence of faith; as powerful as divine grace is, it will not help the one who refuses to put his trust in the God who provides it. Thus, Paul declared: "For by grace you have been saved through faith; and that not of yourselves, it is the gift of God" (Ephesians 2:8). By God's grace *and* through your faith is the only process by which your soul can become a partaker of the divine nature (cf. 2 Peter 1:3-4).

What this means first of all is that you must personally and actively draw near to God. Think of the several times the New Testament uses this expression, whether literally or implicitly [bracketed words or phrases mine]:

- Matthew 6:33, "But seek first [i.e., draw near to] His kingdom and His righteousness, and all these things will be added to you."
- Colossians 3:1, "Therefore if you have been raised up with Christ, keep seeking [i.e., draw near to] the things above,

where Christ is, seated at the right hand of God."

• Hebrews 4:14-16, "Therefore, since we have a great high priest who has passed through the heavens, Jesus the Son of God, let us hold fast our confession. For we do not have a high priest who cannot sympathize with our weaknesses, but One who has been tempted in all things as we are, yet without sin. Therefore let us draw near with confidence to the throne of grace, so that we may receive mercy and find grace to help in time of need."

• Hebrews 7:18-19, "For, on the one hand, there is a setting aside of a former commandment [i.e., the Law of Moses] because of its weakness and uselessness (for the Law made nothing perfect), and on the other hand there is a bringing in of a better hope, through which we draw near to God."

•Hebrews 7:25, "Therefore He [Christ] is able also to save forever those who draw near to God through Him, since He always lives to make intercession for them."

• Hebrews 10:1, "For the Law [of Moses], since it has only a shadow of the good things to come and not the very form of things, can never, by the same sacrifices which they offer continually year by year, make perfect those who draw near."

• Hebrews 10:21-22, "...since we have a great priest over the house of God, let us draw near with a sincere heart in full assurance of faith, having our hearts sprinkled clean from an evil conscience and our bodies washed with pure water."

• James 4:8-10, "Draw near to God and He will draw near to you. Cleanse your hands, you sinners; and purify your hearts, you double-minded. Be miserable and mourn and weep; let your laughter be turned into mourning and your joy to gloom. Humble yourselves in the presence of the Lord, and He will exalt you."

• 1 Peter 2:4-5, "And coming [i.e., drawing near] to Him as to a living stone which has been rejected by men, but is choice and precious in the sight of God, you also, as living stones, are being built up as a spiritual house for a holy priesthood, to offer up spiritual sacrifices acceptable to God through Jesus Christ."

When God uses the expression, "draw near to Me" or, "seek after Me," He is in essence saying, "Bring your *sacrifice* to Me." This is because no one can approach the Father without bringing an appropriate sacrifice (the principle in Deuteronomy 16:16: "...and they [the men of Israel] shall not appear before the LORD empty-handed"). The losses sustained in these sacrifices are made acceptable in view of the supremacy of what is gained: eternal fellowship with God.

Our sacrifices are no longer in the form of animals, handfuls of grain, or jars of oil. They are instead expressions of one's devotion to God and offerings of the heart. Our love, forgiveness, kindness, compassion, hospitality, and stewardship all serve as forms of sacrifices which we lay upon the altar, so to speak, and pay homage to the Lord. Our prayers, praise, and songs—"fruit of lips" (Hebrews 13:15)—are acceptable offerings which we present to the Lord in honor of Him. Likewise, our "doing good and sharing"—especially with the brotherhood of Christ, but also with all people (Galatians 6:9-10; Hebrews 13:16)—are heart-rendered offerings which ascend to God as a fragrant aroma and a sweet savor (cf. Ephesians 5:1-2).

God does not always decide for us *exactly* what we will give to Him, but He does define what an *appropriate* offering is and what we are *expected* to give to Him. The quality and quantity of the offering to Him is left up to each one of us (cf. 2 Corinthians 9:6ff, for example). He cannot wrest from our heart its love, devotion, and allegiance; He can only tell us what such love, devotion, and allegiance *looks* like, how *appropriate* it is that we give it to Him, and how it is in our *best interest* to sacrifice to Him.[19] Thus, our freewill offerings are particularly pleasing to God in the very fact that *we have chosen to give them to Him*, having complied with His specific instructions as to how they are to be offered. If not for that decision on our part, He would not have received anything from us, and we could not receive eternal life from Him.

A seeker's sacrifice really consists of two major groupings: those things which we choose to *give* (out of gratitude and adoration) and those things which we choose to *give up* (out of allegiance and obedience). While these offerings are virtually simultaneous, it is nonetheless important to see them as separate actions. A person cannot *give* his love and praise to God before he *gives up* his pride and self-will for the Lord's sake. No expression of adoration will be acceptable to God in the absence of self-surrender and the relinquishment of one's self-serving claim to this world. The action of drawing *away* must precede the action of drawing *near*. Thus, when God says, "Draw near to Me," He requires that we *draw away from that which we once served and trusted.* "No one can serve two masters," Jesus taught us, "for either he will hate the one and love the other, or he will be devoted to one and despise the other..." (Matthew 6:24). We cannot serve two Lords anymore than we can go both north and south all at once.

The Reconciliation of Christ

"Well, I'm not sure that I can give Christ *everything*," someone might say. "I mean, I want to, but I struggle with the full extent of what is being asked of me." To struggle with these things is extremely *human*. If you are not struggling at all, someone might want to check your pulse: you might not be alive any longer!

The reality is—and we cannot downplay this—God is not asking for *part* of you to draw near to Him, but the *whole* of you. He is not asking you to select which small part of your life is to be given to Him (while you control the rest), but demands nothing less than *the entire offering.* When Abraham was asked to sacrifice Isaac, for example (Genesis 22:1-13), he did not ask God, "Which part?" He understood that the offering up of Isaac necessarily implied the *entire life* of Isaac. Thus, the entire body of Isaac was laid upon the altar, not merely an arm or a leg. Likewise, when one is baptized into Christ, it is not only a part of him that gets wet, but he is *completely immersed*—this is what "baptism" literally means. One's baptism symbolizes his death to the world and re-birth in Christ. How can a person partially die, or partially be buried, or partially raise to walk "in newness of life" with Him (cf. Romans 6:3-7)?

God wants from us no single act of allegiance or incidental gesture of gratitude. He wants *our entire self* to be given to Him, since this is what He (through Christ) has given to us. He wants *our entire attention* to be devoted to Him, since His full attention is given to our souls. He wants *a full surrender of our will* to be laid upon the altar of self-sacrifice, since Christ emptied Himself and surrendered everything He had to provide for our salvation. We are told to present to Him nothing less than *everything we have*, including our own physical bodies, as "a living and holy sacrifice, acceptable to God, which is your spiritual service of worship" (Romans 12:1). Only this *kind* of offering is acceptable; only this *magnitude* of sacrifice is appropriate. If we deliberately and selfishly hold anything back, then we forfeit all we had sought to gain *and* jeopardize all that has been given. The story of Ananias and Sapphira (Acts 5:1-11) reveals what God thinks of people who give partial sacrifices while claiming to have given the full requirement. We must do our best not to imitate them.

No matter how great our offerings of gratitude and adoration may be, or our expressions of obedience and allegiance, they still cannot *compare* to Christ's. You and I have never had to *give up* what He gave up; we have never had to *give* what He gave; we will never *suffer* what He suffered. Christ not only "emptied Himself" of His heavenly glory, He died a gruesome, excruciating death as though the lowest of all mortal beings. He deliberately took upon Himself the curse destined for one who truly had sinned, even though He Himself was innocent (Galatians 3:13; 1 Peter 2:21-24). While *we* may limit His suffering to the physical and psychological torture of the cross, we cannot even comprehend the mental and spiritual agony—the weight of all the sins of the world—which He bore.

What about all the bodies and blood of those animals once sacrificed under the Law of Moses? Were these for naught? It is true that *no law* (by itself) can deal with men's sins. Law can only do one of two things: it can either justify a perfect *law-keeper* or condemn a *law-breaker*. It can do nothing else. The purpose of the Law was not to make sinners whole again, but to show the *need for divine intervention* in order to do this. By magnifying the sacredness of God, the Law also magnified the weakness and moral depravity of men. It also showed that man was unable to reconcile himself to God on his own (Romans 3:19-24). God illustrated through Law not only the *need* for such reconciliation but also the *process* by which it must be accomplished—i.e., through blood sacrifice.

The system of animal sacrifices was only a *type* of that process. This was to lead men *to* the ideal remedy, but was not to *be* that remedy. After all, "…the Law, since it has only a shadow of the good things to come and not the very form of things, can never, by the same sacrifices which they offer continually year by year, make perfect those who draw near" (Hebrews 10:1); furthermore, "it is impossible for the blood of bulls and goats to take away sins" (verse 4). Physical offerings cannot absolutely rectify spiritual deficiencies. Nothing of this earth can remedy the problem created by man's spiritual fall from God's glory.

Christ who is of *heaven* is able to do what we cannot; not only this, but in the giving of His body and blood, He has fulfilled all that the Law foreshadowed. This was necessary in order to prove the righteousness of God, in that He *knew* of our problem all along and brought about its *solution* "in the fullness of time" through His Son, Jesus Christ (cf. Galatians 4:4). The Law, including all its sacrifices and rituals, served as a grand prophecy of He who was to come. Everything in the Law pointed forward to the One who would *personally embody* each of the sacrifices required for man's reconciliation to God. That Christ *is* our reconciliation is irrefutable (Romans 5:10-11; 2 Corinthians 5:18-21; Ephesians 2:14-18; and Colossians 1:19-23); *how* He is our reconciliation is illustrated through the concept of physical sacrifice. *Without* His sacrifice, we could not draw near to God; we could not be seekers of the sacred.

The Sacrifice of Sacrifices

In drawing near to God, one must appreciate the magnitude and infinite worth of Christ's sacrifice that makes this even possible. God did not merely throw another lamb or bull on a fiery altar—not even a million sheep can remove the stain of a single human sin. God did not ask any ordinary man to be sacrificed for all other men, for no man's offering can redeem even a single soul. Likewise, God never asked an angel—regardless of how wonderful that entity is in comparison to our humble nature—to be given on our behalf, since angels cannot identify with the human condition (and vice versa). Instead, God gave us the very best *of* heaven in order to give us access *to* heaven: His only begotten Son (John 3:16). No other offering would do; no other Person would be appropriate; no other body or blood would be acceptable.

Christ did not merely offer a better sacrifice than whatever we could produce; He offered the very best that *could* be offered. It is impossible to surpass the flawless offering of both a perfect man *and* God Himself *all in one Person.* This is not only unprecedented; it cannot be duplicated or superseded. We are "…not redeemed with perishable things like silver or gold…, but with precious blood, as of a lamb unblemished and spotless, the blood of Christ" (1 Peter 1:18-19). Christ has entered not a physical tabernacle with the blood of a bull or goat to merely symbolize the atonement of men's sins. He has entered the true Holy of Holies—the very heart of all that is sacred, the very presence of God Himself—with His own body and blood.[20] No Levitical priest was ever able to do this; no other man before or since has been able to do this. But Christ—He who is God in the flesh (John 1:14)— *did this.*

With this thought, consider again the three types of offerings required by the Law and how Christ fulfilled them in His one supreme sacrifice. First, Christ became our burnt offering in that He was wholly and completely offered up to God in a way that no man or animal *could* be offered up. An animal does not offer up itself as a sacrifice but is offered up by someone who chooses it; Christ, however, chose *Himself* and offered up *Himself* as a perfect, flawless "whole" offering. Likewise, even if a man were to offer up himself on an altar, his offering would be tainted by the fact that he has sinned *and* that his sacrifice could not be greater than the price of the offense itself—i.e., human life.[21] In the present case, man has defrauded God of a perfect human life but cannot offer up anything beyond that life in compensation. Christ, however, *can* offer up something beyond human life: *the life of a Divine Person.* Thus, Christ was offered up completely upon the cross, having emptied Himself of all the privileges of divine glory, and provided "a fragrant aroma" by which God was both honored and pleased (compare Leviticus 1:1-13 [especially verse 13] with Ephesians 5:1-2).

Christ also became our sin offering when no animal would suffice for what was required for atonement of the human soul. God allowed men to offer animals for a time, but now He recognizes only *one* sin offering: that of His Son. According to the Law, the sin offering had to be physically pure, unblemished, and taken in the prime of its life. Fat portions of the sin offering were offered "in smoke" on the altar, while the rest of the animal was burned "outside the camp," away from the holy tabernacle. In like manner, Christ was physically intact *and* morally pure (perfect), and was offered up in the prime of His life. His *heart and passion*—the "fat portions" or health of His life—were given to God in the course of His ministry to Israel; His physical body was taken "outside the camp" (i.e., Jerusalem) and executed (Hebrews 13:11-13). His blood was poured out not on the bronze altar in the courtyard of the Temple, but upon a new and superior altar: His cross. His blood was not brought into the physical "Holy of Holies," like the sin offering made for the nation of Israel under Law (Leviticus 16:5ff), but was instead presented before the *heavenly* Holy of Holies, "that which the Lord pitched, not man" (Hebrews 8:2). Thus, Christ took the elements of Levitical sacrifice to a much higher, spiritual plane.[22]

Christ *also* fulfilled all the forms and symbolism of the peace offering. For one, Jesus represents our peace to God, inasmuch as we are unable to *have* peace apart from Him (Romans 5:1-2; see also Philippians 4:7, paying special attention to the expression "in Christ Jesus"). In having secured peace for us, Christ has provided our *access* to the Father (Ephesians 2:14-18), which is to say that He has made *fellowship* with the Father possible. The presence of peace (between God and man) implies the presence of fellowship; one cannot exist without the other. Thus, inasmuch as Christ is our Prince of Peace (cf. Isaiah 9:6), He is the substance and embodiment of our fellowship with God. His offering of Himself upon the cross does not merely symbolize such peace; His body and blood are the *reality* of that peace (Colossians 1:19-22). Just as an Israelite could not offer an imaginary or (purely) symbolic peace offering, so the Christian cannot refer to an imaginary or merely conceptual offering. It is absolutely necessary that we have a real, bodily offering in which blood is shed, just as the Law foreshadowed. Sinful man is incapable of providing his own peace (thus, fellowship) with God through his own body or blood; he must defer to that which is superior to him (Hebrews 8:6).

Recall that a special aspect of the peace offerings is the fact that all parties participated in the sacrifice: the Father, the priest, the offerer himself, and those who were also in fellowship with both God *and* the offerer. We can easily see this carried out in Christ through the communion (sharing) of the Lord's Supper. The Father has received His share of the sacrifice: the "fat portions"—the health and best part—of His Son's life. Christ also has received His part of the sacrifice: He reclaimed His physical body upon being resurrected from the dead.[23] Likewise, the believer partakes of the unleavened bread and "fruit of the vine" of this memorial, which symbolize the body and blood of Christ: to the believer, they *are* His body and blood.[24] Not only this, but this memorial is shared with *all believers* (see 1 Corinthians 10:16-18, and notice the allusion to the sharing of a literal peace offering). No one who is "unclean"—that is, no one who is still in his sins—is allowed to partake of this offering; one who does so brings judgment to himself (compare Leviticus 7:20 with 1 Corinthians 11:27-28). However, it is equally offensive to *refuse* to partake of the Lord's Supper, just as it was offensive to let the peace offering go uneaten (cf. Leviticus 7:15). To refuse to observe the Lord's Supper is to disregard the sacrifice that was made to provide for our peace in the first place. A person cannot celebrate his fellowship with God on the one hand and neglect the ritual observance *of* that fellowship on the other.

We could say more since Christ also fulfilled the offering of the scapegoat, the grain offering, the offering of "first fruits," all the offerings of cleansing and purification, etc. The main point is this: Christ is the Sacrifice of all sacrifices. His ministerial work *as* the Christ *and* the Son of God (cf. Matthew 16:16; John 20:31) cannot be described by any one offering, since He is the fulfillment of *all* necessary offerings by which man is able to draw near to God. He is the "summing up of all things," whatever is required on earth as well as in heaven (Ephesians 1:9-10).

Furthermore, Christ has not just offered a *token replica* of each sacrifice, but has offered the *absolute essence* of *every* sacrifice that God required. (We are speaking of those sacrifices which man is *unable* to offer—thus, we are speaking of divine grace—and not of those sacrifices every believer is *expected* to give by faith.) What this means is: every sacrifice that Christ has fulfilled is brought to a full and complete closure; not a single one will have to be re-offered or re-sacrificed. If any *would* need to be offered again, it would necessarily imply that Christ did not really fulfill what was required. In contrast, animal sacrifices according to the Law had to be offered year by year, indicating that they were inherently incomplete and unfulfilling; they "could never...make perfect those who draw near" to God through them (Hebrews 10:1-4). God *allowed* those under the Law to draw near to Him by faith, but ultimately the substance of what the Law's sacrifices represented would have to be offered. Christ, however, was offered "once for all" (Hebrews 10:9-12). No wonder Paul exclaimed, "Thanks be to God for His indescribable gift!" (2 Corinthians 9:15).

Seeking the Sacred through Sacrifice

Since what was necessary for us to draw near to God has been accomplished, "...let us draw near with confidence to the throne of grace, so that we may receive mercy and find grace to help in time of need" (Hebrews 4:16). There are sacrifices that we still need to offer, but they are those which we are *able* to offer. That which is beyond us—and has always *been* beyond us—has been offered by Christ. Thus, seeking the sacred is not a hopeless endeavor; it is something God expects us to do. He has done everything necessary to make this possible.

The point of this entire chapter has been to emphasize the desperate need we have for a Savior. We cannot be seekers of the sacred simply by engaging in a life of religious epiphany or protocol. We cannot draw near to God simply because we feel spiritually moved to do so. We cannot offer to God sacrifices to atone for our sins, consecrate us to His service, or establish peace with Him. In being seekers of the sacred, we must not only humbly realize our limitations; we must also pay special homage to the One who has transcended our limitations so that we might also be where He is now.

I hope the information in this chapter has been very helpful in appreciating the concept of sacrifice *and* how we cannot draw near to God apart from sacrifice. Next we will focus our attention on how we *are* to draw near to God, that is, how we are to worship God in spirit and truth. This is where our discussion naturally leads us.

Endnotes

12 It is true that the burnt offering sacrifice was used in conjunction with the entire nation's drawing near to God as well, as in the Day of Atonement offering; Leviticus 16:5. The nation of Israel was often viewed symbolically and for the purpose of illustration as "one man" anyway, just as the church is viewed as "one man" or "one body" of Christ (1 Corinthians 12:12-13; Ephesians 2:15-16).

13 This expression, "he will be forgiven," is not to be taken lightly. Those who claim that God never actually offered forgiveness under the Law but instead "rolled men's sins forward" until Christ's death must ignore passages such as this (Leviticus 4:26). God did forgive those people's sins, based upon their faithful participation in God's remediation for sin (Romans 1:17). Of course He did so in anticipation of Christ's perfect offering, but it is a misrepresentation to think that He withheld forgiveness of the sins of faithful believers until that time. When God declares a person forgiven—and the Levitical priests, as long as they were in agreement with the Law, served as His spokesmen—he is forgiven in fact, not with strings attached or by any other halfway measure.

14 In Hebrew, this is *qatar*, "to burn (into smoke)," from which we get "cauterize." The emphasis here is on the fire itself, symbolic of the fire of divine judgment that is used throughout Scripture.

15 In Hebrew, this is *olah*, "(smoke) of ascension." The emphasis here is on the upward direction of the smoke, as in a "fragrant (or pleasing) aroma."

16 The freewill offerings (Leviticus 3) are literally rendered "offerings of completion" in Hebrew.

17 Grain offerings were a blend of burnt and peace offerings. Rightly, then, their description is found between the two (Leviticus 2). Being bloodless offerings, they have nothing to do with atonement, but their having been offered at all necessarily implies both consecration and thankfulness. Such offerings corresponded with the "first fruit" offerings of Leviticus 23:10ff, but also included the grain offerings that accompanied the daily (morning and evening) sacrifices (Exodus 29:38-42).

18 Ultimately, the determination as to who could eat what was made by the disposition of the blood of an offering. When blood was brought into the tabernacle itself, that offering was dedicated to God alone. Offerings whose blood was literally daubed upon the horns of the altar and poured out at its base were shared with the priests. Offerings whose blood was merely sprinkled upon the altar were shared with all parties involved.

19 Let no one construe from this that, since our offerings are voluntary, therefore they are not necessary. They are voluntary in the sense that we choose to give them; but they are necessary in that we cannot have fellowship with God without such decisions. The idea of discipleship without sacrifice is completely foreign to the gospel.

20   I mean this in the same way Hebrews 9:11-14 means this: not literally, as though literally appearing before God in the flesh (as some have assumed), but with reference to the historical event of His sacrifice on the cross. The heavenly kingdom has nothing to do with "flesh and blood" (1 Corinthians 15:50-53; see also 2 Corinthians 5:16); rather, Christ has glorified Himself with a glory commensurate to that which is spiritual and heavenly (Philippians 3:20-21).

21   The Law indicated that man's guilt requires a restitution of that which was defrauded God and a one-fifth fine; see Leviticus 5:14 – 6:7. In the case of one's sinful soul, this is something that man cannot provide, since he cannot give anything better than himself

22   Christ could not have literally applied His blood in the exact same method as prescribed by Law for the high priest (on the Day of Atonement; cf. Leviticus 16) since He was not of that (Levitical) priesthood and therefore could not have performed the ministry of such priests (see Hebrews 7:11-14; 8:4-6). His self-sacrifice fulfilled what was required by the Law and in doing so established a new and eternal priesthood (Hebrews 7:23-28) and inaugurated a new law (i.e., the gospel).

23   This is the difference between "resurrection" and the so-called "reincarnation": resurrection is the raising up of the same body that had died; reincarnation claims that a different body is raised, yet the spirit is that of one who had died. Resurrection has, through Christ especially, historical and biblical precedent; reincarnation is nothing more than the fancy of mystic religions.

24   The elements of the Lord's Supper always remain literally what they are: unleavened bread and grape juice. There is no mysterious change from these into the literal flesh and blood of Christ in the stomach of the one who partakes of them (a.k.a. transubstantiation); such a teaching is not only unbiblical, it profanes the very sacredness of Christ's body and blood. Nonetheless, Christ did say, "This is My body" and "This is My blood," but in the context (Matthew 26:26-29, et al) He meant, "Let these elements serve as My body and blood; remember the reality of My sacrifice through these vicarious symbols; as you partake of the one, so you spiritually remember and proclaim the other" (see also 1 Corinthians 11:24-26).

CHAPTER NINE

Worshiping in Spirit and Truth

But an hour is coming, and now is, when the true worshipers will worship the Father in spirit and truth; for such people the Father seeks to be His worshipers. God is spirit, and those who worship Him must worship in spirit and truth.
John 4:23-24

In the community where I live are a number of churches, most of which are of various denominations. Within those groups are different flavors *of* denominations. Then there are the (what I call) "fringe element" churches which cater to niche cultures, specific ethnic groups, or personal preferences. So far I'm just talking about the so-called "Christian" religions—those centered, more or less, on a biblical appeal to Jesus Christ. (I'm not even going to take time to address groups which bear no semblance to Christianity.)

The reason I mention any of this is due to the part of seeking the sacred which necessarily involves *worship*. I am certain, especially if you live in the United States, your community is not so very different from mine. You too probably see different churches with different names and different attitudes toward the Bible, religion, and, yes, *worship*. You will probably also notice, as I have, a popular innovation: the separation of churches based on their "worship" format. I am referring to "traditional worship" and "contemporary (or mainstream) worship" designations. These two groups allegedly comprise the same church, but meet at different times, sing (and listen to) different music, hear different sermons, and usually appeal to different age groups.

One is made to wonder: are they all worshiping the same *God*? More directly, is the worship of God left to individual or collective discretion, or does He have something to say on the matter? Are we allowed to worship God in whatever manner we *feel* is appropriate (for us *or* Him), and then present it to Him with a "This-is-our-worship-and-you-will-like-it!" attitude?

This subject is not one that can be lightly regarded. If there really are as many legitimate faiths as there are denominations (and the self-proclaimed "non-denominations"), then certainly we must have authority for such diversity. Put another way: if whatever people do in the name of Christian religion is supported by *God*, then we must be able to know this for certain through an examination of His *Word*, the Bible. If we do not have biblical authority for who we are through the *Word* of God, then we have no right to do anything in the *name* of God (Matthew 7:21-23; 1 Timothy 4:6; 6:3-5; Titus 1:9; 2 Peter 3:1-2; et al).

At the same time, it is not my intent to inundate you with an involved theological dissertation on this subject. Such examination takes us beyond the tone and thesis of this book. However, it is extremely worthwhile—even enlightening—for us to at least survey some of the critical questions dealing with *seeking the sacred*. It is entirely inappropriate to talk about the "sacred" or the search for it (Him) without discussing "worship." Seeking the sacred requires legitimate worship of the God of all that *is* sacred.

So then, with that stated premise, let us begin.

Defining Worship

Ancient concepts of worship were considerably more involved than the contemporary, Americanized understanding of the word. For most of humankind, religious worship and social life were inextricably woven together: to be a citizen of a given community meant embracing and honoring its god(s). Similarly, to achieve political power over a given people meant invoking the name and power of whatever patron god(s) that oversaw them (see Acts 14:11-18, for example). Of course, such worship (and polytheism in general) was meant to both appease and petition the various nature gods that these people believed did exist. When the gods were happy, everyone benefited; when the gods were angry, everyone suffered—or so it was believed. Worship and sacrifice were invariably bound to *virility* (male sexual potency) and *fertility* (female reproductive potency). Both homage and blood sacrifices were offered as a means to achieve these, both for the people's successful procreation as well as that of their crops, flocks, and herds. In extreme cases (as among certain Canaanites and the Aztecs, for example), priests of antiquity offered human sacrifices to achieve such potency. (Human sacrifice was linked to survival even in the New Testament era. Consider John 11:50, for example: "...it is expedient...that one man die for the people, and that the whole nation not perish.")

Christian worship does not require sexual or procreative connotations. The reason for worship of Christ is not to enhance sexual dominance (of men) or increase fertility (either of women or the land), but to bring homage to God and fulfill individual and collective obligations. The modern "church" experience and its generally staid, measured liturgy were virtually unknown in the ancient world. "Religion" (as in Egyptian life under the Pharaohs, for example) was an unknown concept: one's religious life was completely assimilated into his daily social life. The ancients did not "go to church"; they participated daily in *worship*, often actively and passionately, albeit primitively and ignorantly. Granted, such participation (depending on the time and peoples involved) may have included bizarre rituals—self-mutilation, drinking (or being doused with) animal blood, sexual intercourse with temple prostitutes, etc.—but these were performed as acts of homage to their god(s). Our "worship" today is bland and uneventful by comparison, but it ought not to be *intentionally* so. There should be nothing bland about worshiping the Almighty God of heaven, even though it can easily descend to this when people lose respect for Him (as in Malachi 1:7-13).

Whenever we talk about "worship" today we tend to think only of "worship services." The phrase is foreign to the New Testament, but the practice expedites carrying out our collective expressions of devotion to God and mutual fellowship with each other. The New Testament defines these merely as "assemblies" rather than worship services, but the assemblies are for the purpose *of* worship. While the exact format (i.e., order or structure of such services) and venue (i.e., buildings or cathedrals) of "church services" are man-made, the functions carried out are supposed to be authorized by Scripture. While these functions are intended to glorify God, the immediate objective is clearly to *prepare* and *instruct* people to worship God (as seen in Colossians 3:16 and 1 Timothy 4:13, 16, for example). Knowing *how* to worship God properly and reverently is as important as the specific acts of worship themselves.

However, a "worship service" is hardly the only occasion for worship. In fact, if this *is* the only worship we offer God, then we admit that we do not rightly understand the subject. The word "worship" in the New Testament is most often derived from (Greek) *proskuneo*, which literally means "to kiss toward [one's master]." In essence, it is what people offer to an entity that they perceive (rightly or wrongly) is more powerful than themselves. Especially, it is the response of mortal, earthbound man when he comes into contact with the eternal, heavenly God (as was Jacob's experience; Genesis 28:16-17). It is one thing to consider the sacred abstractly or conceptually, as in a discussion about God; it is another thing to be suddenly confronted *with* the sacred. We do not need to have God literally manifested to us in order to be confronted with Him; it is enough to realize that His majesty and presence is everywhere and ever-present (Ephesians 4:6). This is cause enough, for those who have any respect *for* the sacred, to bend the knees and humble the heart in worship.

"Worship" itself always involves three major concepts: reverence, service, and sacrifice. Reverence is the healthy respect and appropriate attitude one has toward God (Isaiah 66:2; Hebrews 12:28). Such reverence is often called "fear," which is fitting since an appropriate response to God is always mingled with a certain fear of what God is capable of doing to those who *refuse* such response (as implied in Luke 12:5; see also Hebrews 10:26-27). "The fear of the LORD is the beginning of knowledge; fools despise wisdom and instruction" (Proverbs 1:7). Logically, we ought to have a healthy respect for *anyone* who is more powerful and intelligent than man since there is nothing *on earth* with such capability. (There is much more to say on the subject of reverence, but I will save such comments for later in this chapter.)

Worship without service is like an ocean without water, faith without trust, and love without expression: it just doesn't make sense. God never described in Scripture *how* He was to be worshiped without men *doing something* to express and fulfill that worship. Such activity was structured, purposeful, and spiritually-significant. The book of Leviticus, which is filled with sacrifices, ceremonies, and festivals to be observed by Israel, exemplifies this very point. No Israelite could worship God who did not conform to the various prescriptions for these occasions; but by following these prescriptions, the Israelite enjoyed a right relationship with God that translated into his physical prosperity.

Serving one's fellow man, and especially one's brother in the Lord, is an expression of sincere worship to God. This thought begins in Leviticus[25] and is continued in the New Testament through the teachings of Christ and His apostles. Jesus said in Matthew 25:40, "...to the extent that you did it [i.e., showed kindness—MY WORDS] to one of these brothers of Mine, even the least of them, you did it to Me." Jesus Himself "went about doing good" (Acts 10:38) but His "doing good" to others was always done as an act of worship to the Father (John 8:29; 17:4). By focusing on "worship services," as we may be prone to do, we focus only on protocol and procedure, often forgetting the reason for our having assembled together in the first place. By focusing instead on *service worship* (as Jesus taught), our service will remain dynamic, focused, and purposeful. We will then worship God *through* our service to Him rather than trying to worship Him only *during* an official "service."[26]

The third aspect of worship is sacrifice of which I spoke in great detail in a previous chapter ("Drawing Near to God"). Suffice it to say here that sacrifice always involves a personal loss of some kind *as* a dedication to an entity that one regards as more important than oneself. Something offered to God begrudgingly or regretfully is not a sacrifice but a waste—a loss without purpose. Likewise, something that incurs a loss to the giver but fails to properly honor the one for whom the sacrifice is made is really no sacrifice at all; it too is wasted. Paul summed it up best: "Now this I say, he who sows sparingly will also reap sparingly, and he who sows bountifully will also reap bountifully. Each one must do just as he has purposed in his heart, not grudgingly or under compulsion, for God loves a cheerful giver" (2 Corinthians 9:6-7). The context of this passage concerns monetary contributions, but the principle certainly applies to all kinds of sacrifices, tangible or otherwise.

These three things—reverence, service, and sacrifice—work together, never separately, since any one of them (if offered properly) becomes a part of the other. For example, one's sacrifice is also part of his service, which must be offered up in reverence; one's reverence must be manifested by his service, which will always cost him something (sacrifice). This cooperative process breaks down, of course, when a person refuses any one (or more) of these aspects in his ministry to God. Some men are so bold as to manifest *none* of these aspects yet still claim to offer "worship" to God.

Just because someone deems his actions *as* "worship" does not mean that God *receives* it as such. One's worship may be misplaced, as when one worships men (Acts 10:25-26) or angels (Revelation 19:10; 22:8-9). It can be carried out in misunderstanding, as in the case of the Samaritans (John 4:22) or in sheer ignorance, as in the case of the Athenians who worshiped gods they did not even know (Acts 17:23). The Jews of Jesus' day worshiped "in vain" when they put their own doctrines and teachings on par with God's Law (Matthew 15:9). Certainly all of these scenarios are repeated today— men worship men, men worship angels, men worship in misunderstanding or sheer ignorance, and men marry together their own doctrines with God's—and yet many appear to be oblivious to the offense (see 1 Timothy 4:1-3; 2 Timothy 4:3-4).

The Gospel of the Bible

Worship is based on faith. No one worships anything without having faith in it, and no one will have faith in something in which he sees no profit. For example, a man will not worship his 401k account, new car, or beautiful wife without having faith that such things (or people) will be of some advantage to him. Likewise, no one worships God without first having an appropriate *faith* in Him, which requires that he also see some *advantage* for having such faith. Faith itself must be based upon something substantive; otherwise it is nothing more than someone's personal opinion about something rather than an intelligent *reason to believe* in it. For example, we are not to have faith in the gospel for no reason, but only because God has given us a *reason* to believe in it.

Obviously, these concepts and their practices—worship, faith, and the gospel—are not disconnected, independent subjects. Any one of them falls without the other; they are mutually dependent. Consider, for example, John 8:31-32: "So Jesus was saying to those Jews who had believed Him, 'If you continue in My word, then you are truly disciples of Mine; and you will know the truth, and the truth will make you free.'" Involved in this tightly-woven tapestry of doctrinal assertions are several essentials to man's relationship with God:

- **"Jesus was saying…"**: This implies an authoritative and legitimate *source* for what follows. Jesus, through the miracles He wrought, and especially the resurrection itself, has given us sufficient *reason to believe* in Him (Acts 17:30-31; Hebrews 2:4). Thus, what Jesus *says to us* is paramount to what *we believe* concerning our salvation.
- **"to those…who had believed in Him"**: "Believing" here is not a passive or incidental acceptance of something; it is not mere cerebral acknowledgment. When Jesus asks us to *believe* in Him, He is not asking us to merely admit His existence, nod in approval of His actions, or give Him an occasional gesture of appreciation. To *believe* in Him requires obedience (compare John 3:16 with 3:36, for example); obedience requires the *demonstration* of one's belief (John 14:15; James 2:21-24).
- **"If you continue in My word"**: This begins a conditional ("if… then") clause. *If* one continues in His word (i.e., teaching, instruction, authority), only *then* is he Christ's disciple; if he does *not* so continue, then he *cannot* be His disciple. Everything having to do with our relationship *with* Christ is ultimately conditioned by our faith *in* Christ (Colossians 1:22-23).
- **"then you are truly disciples of Mine"**: Again, one does not become a disciple (follower, pupil, supporter) of Christ without meeting His prerequisites *for* discipleship. Such conditions include, besides belief in Him: repentance, sacrifice (Luke 14:27), self denial (Matthew 16:24-25), symbolic ritual (i.e., baptism; Matthew 28:19), and confession of His name (Matthew 10:32-33). Notice the "truly" in Jesus' statement, as if to say, "You are My disciples *indeed*, genuinely, without question." A person cannot be a seeker of the sacred if he refuses the terms and conditions of discipleship which is necessary for sacred worship.
- **"and you will know the truth"**: This indicates that "truth" is

not something everyone knows intuitively or automatically; it has to be first *learned* and then *internalized*. Faith for the purpose of spiritual salvation is based upon spiritual knowledge; otherwise it is blind (John 9:41) or dead (James 2:26). Such knowledge ultimately comes *from* Christ (Romans 10:17) and leads *to* Christ (Romans 10:2-4). The purpose of such knowledge (truth or doctrine) is succinctly summed up on Colossians 1:9-10 (bracketed words mine):

- To "walk in a manner worthy of the Lord";
- To "please Him in all respects";
- To "[bear] fruit in every good work";
- To "[increase] in knowledge of God" (i.e., knowledge ought to lead to further knowledge);
- To be "strengthened with all power" (i.e., endowed with grace); and
- To "joyously [give] thanks to the Father."

- **"and the truth will make you free":** The "freedom" here is spiritual in nature, that is, it is freedom from condemnation for having sinned against God (Romans 6:3-7, 8:1-2)[27] The source of *freedom* is truth; the source of *truth* is Christ. One who worships God must do so in spirit and truth (John 4:24); there is no other appropriate or acceptable way *to* worship Him. Worshipers must conform to the standard which God (Christ) has established. It is not—and never has been—left to mortal men to determine how to worship the Eternal God.

According to Christ then, how many acceptable "faiths" are there? ("Faith" here refers to a body of core beliefs and teachings, as used in 1 Corinthians 16:13 or Jude 3.) Christ only spoke of one; He called it the "gospel." Paul underscored this: "There is one body and one Spirit, just as also you were called in one hope of your calling; one Lord, **one faith** [gospel], one baptism, one God and Father of all who is over all and through all and in all" (Ephesians 4:4-6, emphasis and bracketed words mine). Paul also necessarily implied that the gospel he preached was the only gospel (see Romans 1:1-4, 16-17; 16:25-27; 1 Corinthians 15:1-2; Galatians 1:11-12; Ephesians 1:13-14; et al). Christ never varied His gospel to accommodate the fickle or preferential tastes of men; He preached the only gospel given to Him by the Father, that which fulfills God's "eternal purpose" (Ephesians 3:11). One has to wonder: if Jesus appeared today, who would He say was actually preaching *His* gospel? Or as Jesus Himself posed the question, "When the Son of Man comes, will He find faith on the earth?" (Luke 18:8).[28]

There are significant and necessary implications involved in the singularity of God's gospel. The most obvious is: if God only recognizes one gospel, then He recognizes no other. When Jesus said, "I am the way, and the truth, and the life" (John 14:6), He Himself excluded all other ways, alleged truths, and appeals to life. He is not "a" way, as if there were other equally-valid ways, but *the* way. All salvation—thus all faith, truth, and worship—is predicated on sole and unequivocal allegiance to the Son (John 3:16). In fact, a curse is laid upon anyone who would preach a gospel that differs from the one authorized by Christ and preached by His apostles (Galatians 1:6-8).

That is pretty serious language, to be sure, but it tells us how serious Christ's *gospel* is to Him. How important then should it be to those who claim to be seekers of the sacred? How important is one's faith *in* that gospel and the worship which that gospel defines? You can see where this is going. A person cannot claim to be a disciple of Christ while choosing to worship in a manner that suits *him* [the person] but violates Christ's *gospel*. This is not only unbiblical, it is illogical. It would be like a person who has just become a naturalized citizen saying, "I've become an American according to the laws of the land, but now I am going to serve my country in direct violation of all those laws *as an expression of my patriotism!*" Patriotism, like worship, cannot violate the very entity (or God) that the patriot seeks to honor.

Since there is only one Christ who authorizes only one gospel, there can be only one kind of personal faith: that which is predicated upon Christ's gospel. (If a person's faith is based upon something *other* than Christ and His gospel, then he still may have faith, but it is not in Him or His message. This also means that it will ultimately be of no advantage to that person.) Likewise, since there is but one gospel, there can be but one appropriate form of worship. The singularity of the gospel makes other implications as well:

- **We cannot even explain "the sacred" satisfactorily; far be it from us to determine sacred *worship* on our own.** Men do not have the ability or authority to define absolute truth (by themselves), especially in the realm of things invisible or transcendent. The realm of the Eternal Father is most certainly above us in every respect; we are unable to dictate the manner of worship He expects, apart from what He has revealed to and prescribed for us.

• **The gospel was given by God to men; men did not give the gospel to God.** This is a fundamental but important acknowledgment. The source of truth is from heaven, not earth; therefore the source of the one true gospel is from heaven, not from men. We did not write God's gospel; God wrote His gospel to us through the agency of Spirit-inspired men (Galatians 1:11-12; 2 Peter 1:16-21; et al). Since we cannot claim authorship of the gospel, we cannot authorize changes to, amend, or customize it either. (This is not to say that men have *not* done this; it means men have no *authority* or *permission* to do it.) Therefore, whatever the gospel says about worshiping God is final and binding.

• **Worship (of God) is not something man defines for God, but something God defines for man.** This is merely the next logical step: Since the gospel of truth did not originate with man but God, therefore whatever man is supposed to do *in response to* this truth is also from God. In other words, God did not just toss us a gospel to use (or not) only at our discretion; He did not provide heavenly truth without any direction as to what to *do* with or how to *live* by such truth. Many well-intentioned people misunderstand this: they think the *worship* of God is something separate from the *gospel* of God, as if men could divorce the two.

• **God's truth is not united by man, but man is united by God's truth.** Men are divided within themselves and amongst themselves by selfishness, jealousy, and greed (James 3:15-16). Anything men attempt to do, or however men attempt to coalesce, will ultimately be compromised by these corruptive vices. Men's hearts are divided and contradictory; therefore, whatever "truth" we come up with on our own will be likewise tainted. God's truth, however, is completely unified; it has no inconsistency or contradiction. Since His truth is united, those who are united by His truth are also united with God *and* each other (John 17:17-21; 1 John 1:3). This solid basis for fellowship makes both individual and collective worship possible.

- **God's Spirit is not given to anyone who does not abide by God's gospel.** This is a logical statement as well as a scriptural one: since the gospel is given to men through the agency of the Spirit (1 Corinthians 2:1-5,9-16; Ephesians 2:3-4; 1 Thessalonians 1:5, et al), it stands to reason that the *content* of this gospel will be in perfect agreement with the Spirit Himself. Those who agree to this gospel are thus in agreement with the Spirit who gave it; thus they are recipients not only *of* the gospel but also of the *Spirit* of the gospel (Acts 5:32; Romans 8:4-9; 2 Corinthians 1:21-22; Ephesians 1:13-14; et al). Indeed, men are invited ("called") into fellowship with God by the Spirit *through* the gospel (2 Thessalonians 2:13-14).

*   *   *

Certainly more could be said on this subject, but hopefully this provides the groundwork for what will be said from here forward. Men can choose to worship God according to their preferences, but it is erroneous and foolish to think that God is somehow obligated to accept whatever men decide to serve up. God only accepts one *kind* of worship—that which is done "in spirit and truth" (John 4:24). These two conditions—spirit and truth—are coexistent: together they define the *context* and *attitude* of those who approach God. While we will examine these ideas ("spirit and truth") separately for clarification, neither one is more important than the other.

Worshiping in Spirit

When Jesus said, "God is spirit, and those who worship Him must worship in spirit and truth," the Bible translators have given "spirit" a lower-case designation. This is interesting, since "spirit" (in lower case) comes from the same Greek word [*pneuma*] from which "Spirit" (upper case) is translated.[29] In this passage (John 4:24), Jesus is *not* saying, "God is [the Holy] Spirit," for this is not His intention, given the dialogue. Jesus said these words in the midst of a discussion concerning *how to approach God*, not one in which God is personally defined. Thus, the translators are correct: "God is spirit," which is to say, *the context of God's existence and nature is spiritual*, not of this earth. Men may worship God *from* an earthly context, but they cannot reduce God or the worship of God to the confines of this (physical) world. Men may worship God from a variety of geographical locations, but this is irrelevant to the *manner* and *type* of worship that God requires.

Since God is spirit, He does not conform to man-made conventions. What God expects from men is not always what men want to give to God; likewise, what men choose to give to God is not always what God expects. We cannot impose mere earthly desires upon a spiritual God who leads us with His own Holy Spirit; these lead in two opposite directions (Galatians 5:16-17). In order to seek after the sacred (which means seeking a spiritual God) we must subject ourselves to the standards and desires of the sacred world. The sacred, after all, does not adapt to us, but we must comply with the sacred. One of the inherent qualities of sacredness or holiness is the separation from that which is *not* sacred. This world is unsacred, as are those who conform to it; to worship God according to the spirit of man (which is of the world) is *sacrilege*.

"God is spirit" means that God is not *us*. "Even though we have known Christ according to the flesh, yet now we know Him in this way no longer" (2 Corinthians 5:16) since He also is "spirit." We are still "flesh and blood," which means we are of this world and not (yet) in God's spiritual world (1 Corinthians 15:50). We are striving to be like Him, but He is not striving to be like us; we are "born" of Him, but He is not born of us (John 1:12-13). Consider this then when we speak of "worshiping" God according to the philosophies and practices that *we* prefer regardless of what God has said. We cannot bring God down to *our* level to worship *Him*. This is not only offensive to His holiness; it does not even make sense. We are supposed to set our minds on His world, not force Him to endure our self-determined, man-made religions (cf. Colossians 3:2). Since God is spirit: we cannot worship Him in selfishness; we cannot mask our self-gratifying desires for *self-exaltation* with a pretense of humility and submission to Him; we cannot impose upon Him our earthbound conventions; we must *worship* Him "in spirit."

People sometimes confuse "spirituality" with "worshiping God in spirit." Human beings are "spiritual" by nature, that is, we all have a consciousness of, capacity for, and inclination toward that aspect of us which is real but unseen. We are not merely of the flesh; we are also spiritual. Inasmuch as we recognize our *own* spirituality, we are able to relate to spiritual beings or entities beyond ourselves. (This does not mean we will fully comprehend those beings or entities, but that we can appreciate the fact of their *existence*.) Some people assume, however, that because we have this "spiritual nature" in common, we can *communicate* and even *honor* such beings according to what makes *us* feel good. Since we are a spirit (with a human body), just like God *is* spirit, therefore whatever makes *us* feel good will make *God* feel good. Then we call our expression of feel-goodness "spirituality."

Did you see the huge leap there? We find something in common with God and then put ourselves *on par* with God through that one common characteristic. This is the substance of the lie that Satan fed to Adam and Eve: if you have something in common with God—such as the knowledge of good and evil—then "you will be <u>like</u> God" (Genesis 3:5, emphasis mine). Satan is an expert at contorting the facts in order to soothe the human appetite for pleasure and so-called "spiritual" gratification. If we really think that we (or our decisions) are as good as God's, then it is hardly "worship" we are offering Him anymore, is it?

Worshiping in Truth

People often equate what *they* know to be true with what God has *declared* to be true. However, there is a difference between what is "true" to *you* and God's truth. For example, someone might say, "I prefer to go to church in my faded Levi jeans and Birkenstocks, while listening to a professionally-trained choir accompanied by live band music, as I'm sipping on a caramel frappuccino that I got from the coffee kiosk in the church lobby." Well, that is all *true* to that person: that is what he prefers; that is what he wants to call "worship"; that is how his church perceives "worship." Regardless, that is not what *God* calls worship. Such self-gratification and self-indulgence is hardly reverent, servile, or sacrificial. What is true to this person does not mean God agrees with it, even though the "truth" offered is purported to be in the context of spiritual "worship." This is another fallacy people perpetuate either through ignorance or selfishness, that is, the idea that whatever *we* put into a spiritual or religious context (such as a church building) automatically becomes acceptable to *God.*

We have biblical injunctions and precedent to the contrary. Nadab and Abihu, newly-ordained priests of God under a just-inaugurated Law (of Moses), were instructed as to their duties and prescribed functions. During Israel's very first sacrificial offering under the new priesthood, however, these men did something they were not told to do: they put fire on their own censers and offered this to God. God's response to this seemingly innocent and sincere gesture of religious spontaneity?—*He executed them on the spot.* Some people are quick to judge God as being a bit hasty, over-reactive, or outright *unjust* in the matter. Such people obviously know more about the situation than God did since they see nothing improper with judging *Him* with wrongdoing. But it was Nadab and Abihu who had sinned, not God. Their sin was *at least* irreverence in failing to follow the pattern which God had prescribed for *worshiping Him.* God, in righteous—and justified—indignation, has every right to respond in such a way that protects His holiness. As Moses told Aaron (the men's father) in response, "It is what the LORD spoke, saying, 'By those who come near Me I will be treated as holy, And before all the people I will be honored.' So Aaron, therefore, kept silent" (Leviticus 10:1-3).

How are we to treat the Lord as holy while imposing upon Him what *we* declare to be "holy"? If it is holy to you, does that make it holy to God? Or isn't it supposed to be the other way around? God Himself has said, "You shall be holy, for I am holy" (1 Peter 1:16). Remember, holiness is not something that comes from earth, but is given to (or bestowed upon) us from heaven. The failure to respect that which is holy—and especially, the failure to respect *Who* is holy—is irreverence. Regardless of how important reverence is to the man who sips syrupy coffee concoctions in a state-of-the-art church building while he taps his foot to the rhythm of the church band, reverence is a serious matter of life or death to those who approach God wrongly. Nadab and Abihu were not killed because they merely offered fire at an inappropriate time; they were killed because they were *irreverent.* Likewise, the man who was executed for gathering firewood on the holy Sabbath (Numbers 15:32ff) was not killed because he picked up a few sticks but for *irreverence.* Uzzah (2 Samuel 6:6-7) was not struck dead by God because he merely touched the holy ark of the covenant but for *irreverence*. The man (in the parable) who was invited to the king's wedding feast but refused to dress appropriately for the occasion (Matthew 22:1-14) was not cast into "outer darkness" because of mere disagreement over attire but because of his *irreverence* to the king.

Violating what *God* has said is true is an act of irreverence. It is antagonistic and hostile to God's holiness; it is an attempt to profane God's holy nature. While something may be reverent to *you*, it does not mean that it is reverent to *God*; just because something is true to *you* does not mean that God is obligated to agree and abide by that "truth." I have my personal "truths"; you have yours; every person has his or her own. Our truths are self-chosen, subjective, often fickle and emotionally-based, and will not transcend this life into the life to come. God's truth, however, is divinely decreed, entirely objective, never changes, and is based upon what is absolutely real. Furthermore, God's truth most certainly *will* transcend this life into the life to come. Unfortunately, many, many people will only acknowledge this after it is too late for them to do anything about it.

It is not as though God's truth has been hidden. The basic message of Christ is known everywhere, even among those who are avowed opponents of the gospel. (I have heard, for example, so-called atheists and other non-believers speak more accurately of the Scriptures than some who have been Christians for years.) Even though *The X-Files* has informed us that "The truth is out there," the fact is that the truth is *right inside of your Bible*. We do not have to send someone up to heaven to find it; God has sent His Son *from* heaven to disclose it (John 1:17-18). We do not have to descend into the grave to search for it; God has raised His Son from the dead to reveal it to us (Acts 17:30-31). The "word of faith"—synonymous with the "message of truth, the gospel of your salvation" (Ephesians 1:13)—"is near you..., that is, the word of faith which we [the apostles—MY WORDS] are preaching" (Romans 10:5-8). In other words, if you want the *truth*—God's truth—about what is to be believed and how He is to be worshiped, then open your Bible and read what He has revealed to you.

The "word of faith" implies that we must believe in something that we cannot see or touch. That is what "faith" is all about (Hebrews 11:1). The *message* is real as are the *truths* declared therein; but we have not yet *seen* reality. We cannot seek after God in faith (Hebrews 11:6) while simultaneously imposing upon God *our* so-called "reality"; otherwise, we immediately cease to be sincere toward whomever we claim to be worshiping *in faith*. For example, some men justify spending Sundays fishing or hunting out there in "God's country." They claim to feel more comfortable worshiping God in the middle of a salmon-filled creek than in a stuffy church building. Well, I'm certainly not going to defend stuffy church buildings, but I have to ask the obvious question: who or what exactly are these men really worshiping? Are they really seeking the sacred, or are they simply justifying what they want to do by labeling it "worship"? What these men really want to do is fish or hunt; they choose this over the work of the kingdom and the needs of fellow believers; "worship" really has nothing to do with it. Yet it is amazing to hear people say something to the effect of, "This is how *our* church worships God" or "This is how *I* choose to worship God." People may mean well in what they say, but this alone does not equate to *reverence to God*: "those who worship Him [God] <u>must</u> worship in spirit and truth" (John 4:24, emphasis mine).

Acceptable Worship

God is not interested in people who are merely "spiritual" or "religious." He is seeking people who are seeking *Him*, people who are "acceptable" to *Him*. (This, of course, *can* be any person who comes to Him on His terms.) Being "acceptable," or "approved by God," is a major theme throughout the Bible. Sacrifices (under the Law of Moses) would not be accepted *by* God if they were not prepared *for* or offered according *to* God (Leviticus 22:17-33, for example). Offerings not acceptable to God's Law were not acceptable to God Himself (as in Jeremiah 6:19-20 and Malachi 1:7-13, for example). The person whose *heart* is corrupt also corrupts his *offering to God*, regardless of how fitting the offering itself may have been (see Haggai 2:10-14, for example). Acceptable attitude and acceptable sacrifice are mutually dependent.

This idea of being "acceptable" permeates the entire New Testament gospel message. Christ did not come to merely receive people who would worship God; He came to make us *acceptable* for worship in the first place. If we are not *made* acceptable, neither is our *worship* acceptable. In Colossians 1:21-22, for example, Paul explains that Christ has "reconciled you in His fleshly body through death in order to present you before Him holy and blameless and beyond reproach"—i.e., has made you acceptable to God, if indeed you have submitted to Christ's gospel. Apart from the Son, we are unacceptable to the Father; *because* of Christ, we are made acceptable to the Father and therefore can approach Him. No one can be a seeker of God who does not ultimately submit himself to the Savior, Jesus Christ.

Acceptable worship is probably most clearly seen in Romans 12:1-2. We notice immediately that being "acceptable to God" requires Christ's mediation but is impossible without our own faithful participation. Paul writes by inspiration of the Spirit:

> Therefore I urge you, brethren, by the mercies of God, to present your bodies a living and holy sacrifice, acceptable to God, which is your spiritual service of worship. And do not be conformed to this world, but be transformed by the renewing of your mind, so that you may prove what the will of God is, that which is good and acceptable and perfect.

Acceptable worship is carried out *in the body*, but at the same time requires *the renewing of the mind*. The emphasis is not on *having* an unblemished physical body, since most of us would then be unacceptable and therefore disqualified from worshiping the Father. Nonetheless, just as the bodies of sacrificial animals had to be ideal and unblemished, so also we have to keep our physical bodies pure from any kind of moral sin (Romans 6:11-13). The "renewing of the mind" cannot occur until a person first "[walks] in newness of life," which requires water baptism as a sign of his obedience to God (Romans 6:3-4). Afterward, that person must continue to pursue the renewing of his mind which is a necessary aspect of seeking the sacred. Being "conformed to this world" renders us unfit for spiritual worship; being "transformed" is something that Christ does *to* us but never without our consent and cooperation. Thus, body, mind, and soul—the entire man—must be devoted to the worship of the Father (consider 1 Thessalonians 5:23 with regard to this thought).

Such worship, just as the bodies that we use to engage *in* worship, must be "living and holy" since the Father Himself is a living and holy God (1 Thessalonians 1:9; 1 Peter 1:16). The contrast to spiritual death or the deadness of human corruption is obvious. We are "made alive with Christ" if we have "become united with Him in the likeness of His death" (Ephesians 2:5; Romans 6:4); our *death* and *being made alive with Christ* are both accomplished through our baptism, wherein we are "clothed" (identified) with Him (Galatians 3:27). There is *purpose* to all this since we are not resurrected to "newness of life" for no good reason: we are supposed to produce *good fruit* for God. This "fruit" is good works in general (Ephesians 2:10) as well as specific characteristics of the Holy Spirit (Galatians 5:22-25). Christ has cleansed our conscience (with His blood, through baptism) for this very purpose, so that we can "serve the living God" (Hebrews 9:13-14; 1 Peter 3:21).

The phrase "spiritual service of worship" (Romans 12:1) can literally be translated from the Greek, "your logical [or reasonable] ministry [or homage]." "Logical," in this context, cannot be understood apart from a *spiritual* application; thus, "spiritual service of worship" accurately represents the original language. Also, the allusion to Levitical priests ministering to Jehovah at His tabernacle is obvious and deliberate. Paul purposely characterized the Christian's worship as a priestly activity, as did Peter (1 Peter 2:4-5). The worshiper of God is portrayed as a type of priest who brings sacrifices and offerings to the Lord's presence. This is, appropriately and necessarily, accomplished through Christ who is our *literal* high priest, "...who has taken His seat at the right hand of the throne of the Majesty in the heavens, a minister in the sanctuary and in the true tabernacle, which the Lord pitched, not man" (Hebrews 8:1-2). Imagine how sacrilegious it would be for a priest in ancient times to approach the Lord's "tent of meeting" covered with filth, intoxicated with strong liquor, and spewing profanities from his mouth. Yet this is the scenario when a Christian, his heart polluted with the filth and figurative excrement of the world, tries to approach God in prayer or service. Let not such a man (or woman) think that he will ever be received in such a wretched condition (cf. James 4:4-10).

"Acceptable" implies other conditions be met as well. Worship of Christ must be made in "righteousness and peace and joy in the Holy Spirit"

(Romans 14:17-18), not with sour, stringent, pickle-faced legalism or formality. Likewise, such worship must be made with gratitude, reverence, and awe since ingratitude and irreverence (as we have seen) always invalidate one's service to God no matter how "right" or "doctrinally correct" it might appear otherwise. Also, no person can worship God who does not love his brother or sister in Christ (1 John 2:10-11). If one will not "accept one another" as Christ has accepted him (Romans 15:7), then neither will his worship be acceptable. Finally, for this short list, acceptability of worship requires a personal contribution to the ministry itself as demonstrated by the Philippians who helped finance Paul's preaching (Philippians 4:18; see also 2 Corinthians 8:1-5 where the Philippians are among the "Macedonians" mentioned there).

Motive Is Everything

My intent here is not to delineate the full scope of "worship." Rather, it is to lay the biblical *motive* with which worship is to be carried out, beginning with Jesus' own words: "God is spirit, and those who worship Him must worship in spirit and truth." This does not exclude other motives, of course, but God is seeking after one primary motive: that which honors Him and His Word above all else.

Since God accepts only one motive and rejects all others, there must be some way a person can measure his motive in order to determine whether or not it is appropriate. If we think of "motive" as being (in this context) very closely identified with one's "faith," we can see that this makes sense. God does not accept a variety of "faiths" (i.e., any belief system that involves faith), but only that faith which is defined by *Him*. God does not have to accept your faith just because you *have* faith; rather, you must act in faith *according to how He has instructed you to act*. Jesus is, after all, the "Apostle and High Priest of our confession" as well as "the author and perfecter of faith" (Hebrews 3:1; 12:2). A person who deliberately chooses to practice his faith differently than the Author of faith has instructed will not be ushered into God's presence.[30]

A person cannot build an objective, fact-based "spiritual service of worship" upon a subjective, capriciously-defined motive. "Feelings" are not relevant here since one cannot predicate the real and logical salvation of his soul upon irrational and fickle human emotions. Sincerity alone is not sufficient to determine legitimacy for a person can be sincerely wrong. "Good intentions" are not good enough by themselves since God has told us of *His* intentions in His Word; if I refuse to abide by them, then I stand opposed to Him. As Jesus said, "He who is not with Me is against Me; and he who does not gather with Me scatters" (Matthew 12:30). Self-determined worship and godly worship are incompatible.

This brings us back to *seeking the sacred*. God's holiness cannot be compromised by sin; likewise, the pursuit of His holiness cannot be compromised by sinful motives. The sinner (i.e., an unsacred person) has no right to tell the Savior how he must be saved (i.e., made sacred). Thus, in order to seek the sacred, one's motive must be a holy one, which is to say it must be:

- **Pure**—innocent, child-like, not riddled with self-serving interests (Matthew 5:8; 18:3-4; Philippians 4:8-9; Titus 1:15, et al; see also 2 Corinthians 11:2-3).
- **Genuine**—honest, sincere, not selfish or inappropriate (Romans 2:4-8; 2 Corinthians 1:12; 2:17; James 3:13-17; et al).
- **Humble**—meek, mild, modest, lowly of mind; filled with God, not of oneself (Ephesians 4:1-3; Philippians 2:3-4; Colossians 3:12-13; et al).
- **Righteous**—in a right standing with God, living by God's truth and not by personal opinion or prejudice (John 3:21; 17:17; Titus 1:1 ["...knowledge of the truth which is according to godliness"], 1 Peter 1:22-25; et al; see also Galatians 2:11-14.)
- **Believing**—trusting in God, confident in Christ's willingness and ability to save, not wavering in doubt (John 17:20-21; Romans 15:13; 2 Timothy 1:12; Hebrews 11:6; et al).
- **Zealous**—filled with activity, diligence, desire, and enthusiasm (Romans 12:10-12; 2 Thessalonians 1:11-12; 2 Timothy 2:15; Titus 2:14; 2 Peter 1:10-11; et al).

A motive that has all these characteristics is certainly going to be acceptable to God, which means that this person will be able to worship God in spirit and truth. His life will manifest the virtues and hallmarks of a child of God since his pursuit *of* the sacred is in agreement *with* the sacred. His actions, habits, behaviors, lifestyle will all be such that brings glory to the Lord. Likewise, he will purposely avoid whatever violates God's holiness, knowing that this robs God of His rightfully-deserved honor and glory (1 Thessalonians 5:21-22).

In essence, a person's entire life becomes his worship to God. All the different realms of a believer—attitude, personal conduct, marriage, parenting, education, career, social relationships, citizenship, etc.—are conducted (ideally) in such a way that honors Christ above himself (cf. Galatians 2:20). We ought not to focus on any one particular action and say, "That is worship!" but we ought to consider the complete "package" a person has to offer. We are supposed to be, after all, a "living and holy sacrifice" (Romans 12:1) which demands *all* of what we have to offer, not mere portions or incidental acts of homage. As we are to love God with all our heart, soul, and mind (Matthew 22:37-38), so we are to *worship* God with this same all-encompassing endeavor.

Seeking the sacred is not a part-time job; it is not a hobby or a casual interest; it is not an incidental occurrence. It must be, by definition and practical application, a lifelong, passionate quest that consumes one's entire life (cf. John 2:17). The person who fails to *be* a seeker of the sacred— which is synonymous with failing to be a *worshiper of God*—leads to nothing short of his complete and irredeemable ruin. However, the one who actively and genuinely seeks after God with all his heart, soul, and mind *will not be disappointed* (Romans 10:11); his earthly existence will culminate in a heavenly one in the presence of God whom he sought *with* his life on earth. The one leads to the other: the life in pursuit *of* God here will lead to a life *with* God in the hereafter—as long as we pursue Him "in spirit and truth."

Endnotes

25   Leviticus 19:18 reads in part, "…But you shall love your neighbor as yourself; I am the LORD." The "I am the LORD" phrase, which is repeated numerously in that chapter, is not to be lightly regarded. The implication is that one rightly honors God through whatever instruction precedes that phrase; likewise, God is dishonored through failing to observe that instruction, no matter how sincere a person thought himself to be otherwise (a situation implied in, say, Matthew 15:1-6).

26   I want to be clear here: I am not suggesting for a moment that we dispense with assembling together to worship God. Rather, I am emphasizing the importance of knowing why we assemble together, so that our coming together is a part of our life worship and not the extent of it.

27   Notice how baptism, mentioned earlier as a necessary part of discipleship (Matthew 28:19), is directly linked to "uniting" with Christ "in the likeness of His death" (Romans 6:3-7). This action, then, is required if one is to "walk in newness of life" and be "freed from sin." Take baptism out of the equation here and the basis for one's spiritual freedom evaporates into thin air.

28   Whether this is to be understood as one's personal "faith" or "the faith" (as some render it) seems irrelevant in the end. If there is no personal faith in God on earth, then no one will be following "the faith" (gospel).

29   In fact, *pneuma* is the word which is also translated "unclean spirits" (as in Matthew 10:1, *akathartos pneuma*). *Pneuma* can be translated "spirit" (upper or lower case), "wind," "breath" or "soul." In John 3:6, for example, we see *pneuma* translated into both "Spirit" and "spirit" in the same verse. It is the context which dictates how (or in what case) the Greek word *pneuma* is rendered in English.

30   This discussion does not deal directly with those who have faith in God but possess only a limited knowledge of Him due to mental limitations, isolation from the gospel message, or other extreme and atypical conditions. Such people are not exceptions to what is expected of the rest of us, but actually fall into a different discussion altogether, that of insuperable ignorance. This refers to those who are not unwilling (or neglecting) to learn of God's Word, but are unable to do so because of circumstances beyond their control. This is touched on in Romans 2:25-29, but the explanation is much more involved than what that reference indicates. Nonetheless, personal faith is, even in such circumstances, something that God determines (or excuses, if He so decides) and not men.

CHAPTER TEN

What Will a Man Give in Exchange for His Soul?

For whoever wishes to save his life will lose it; but whoever loses his life for My sake will find it.   For what will it profit a man if he gains the whole world and forfeits his soul?   Or what will a man give in exchange for his soul?
Matthew 16:25-26

How much is the preservation of your life worth to you?

Actually, it may depend upon your circumstances.

Suppose (as might even be the case) you are young, healthy, well-educated, well-connected, employable, attractive, and fairly intelligent. You have your entire life ahead of you; your future is promising and your present isn't looking too bad, either. Your major concern, besides choosing between a brand new Porsche and a BMW for your next car, is landing yourself yet another lucrative deal through your daddy's real estate company or financial investment firm. A (large) new house is on the horizon, and your sweetheart agreed to a "pre-nup" in order to marry you. Life is good.

The irony is that, chances are, someone like you is not going to read this chapter, much less this book. This is because you are not thinking about God, your soul, or anything sacred beyond the retro-rustic Catholic cathedral at which you booked your $15,000 wedding. "Seeking the sacred" is not something that really interests you. And why should it? You are, after all, in a very secure and stable position in life. Sacredness—and especially that which deals with any spiritual commitment on your part—

is not only uninteresting, it is unnecessary. You do not *need* God in your world; sacredness is inconsequential for "the good life." You will, when it is politically or socially advantageous to do so, give a token nod toward the heavens, but otherwise you are entrenched in the affairs of this world and this world only.

"How much is the preservation of your life worth to you?" This is not even a relevant question to you, since your life is not being threatened. No sense in wasting time worrying about preservation of life when it is clear that your life is well-preserved. Of course, this shallow, balsa-wood mentality of yours is predicated on your present circumstances—and your over-inflated pride—and not reality. The *reality* is that self-preservation will take center stage as soon as your circumstances take a turn for the worse.

So then, for the sake of illustration, let's drastically change your circumstances.

Let's suppose that lucrative deal you were banking on falls through; even worse, the real estate market takes a serious nose-dive, as does the economy. Your falsely-inflated, superficially-wealthy investment props fall flat on their faces. Dividends plummet, shareholders cut their losses and bail, and wealthy friends cannot distance themselves from you fast enough. Your daddy's health suddenly evaporates along with his hard-earned savings as he dies a slow and messy death. The bank repossesses the BMW—the one you spent hours comparing against a Porsche while sauntering pompously through the showroom with the dealer—and you are forced to drive a used Ford Focus. Your spouse has an affair with your best friend, finds a legal loophole in your pre-nup, and leaves you—after having stripped the house of all its furniture and wealth. Meanwhile, the mortgage company threatens foreclosure. Life is suddenly very bad.

Now you find yourself truly grasping at the tattered remnants of your fragile world. "At least I have my health!" you sigh, but then there is that nagging pain in your lower back and you haven't really been feeling all that well lately. The doctor confirms your suspicions: you are facing kidney failure and are put on the long waiting list for a transplant. So now here you are, hooked up to a dialysis machine for three hours a day, three times a week, wondering how in the world you are going to pay for all this, amazed at how quickly your life has deteriorated, and then someone asks you once again, "How much is the preservation of your life worth to you?" Suddenly the question has significance; it takes on an entirely new meaning. Suddenly the question interests you since the answer will have profound implications.

For the first time *in* your life, you start thinking seriously *about* life—not just "the good life" filled with ease, luxury, and self-indulgence but *the very substance of who you are.* You take a good, long, hard look at yourself: presently, you are pathetic. There is nothing attractive or sophisticated about you anymore; you are no longer youthful, charming, and buoyant, but are haggard, exhausted, and struggling to stay alive. You wonder to yourself, "What is left of my life? Everything I once had is gone; I took everything for granted. Now little remains except for…my soul." *My soul.* "What if," you ask yourself with that mind-numbing terror that a person experiences when suddenly staring over the brink of a cliff into the roiling fires of hell, "I lose my soul as well? *What will have been the point of my existence?*"

Good question.

Your mind begins racing wildly. Whereas before you never gave "the preservation of your life" a second thought—the idea was irrelevant— now you have gone even *beyond* your physical life and begin to wonder about the preservation of your *afterlife.* This is because you believe there is little left of *this* life. You squandered everything you had for a few years of self-gratifying indulgence and dissipation; now, as your physical existence is threatened, your mind becomes fixated upon your spiritual existence. Will you squander that too? Will your spiritual life evaporate as quickly as your secular toys and investments?

What price will you now pay to rescue your soul from a wretched end? How much money—how much of *anything*? Before, when you were young, charming, wealthy, and arrogant, you would not have spent a dime toward anything spiritual. Now, however, money has no meaning; the world you are heading for has no context for earthly wealth or status. Now you would spend your entire fortune—if you still actually *had* a fortune—for something you have never yet seen or experienced: the preservation of your soul. Now that earthly wealth has lost all the glitter and sparkle that it once had, the thought of dwelling in security in the presence of God has a soul-soothing serenity to it like nothing you have ever known before.

What is it like to die forever in hell? You never took the time to consider the question before. Now it is the most pressing thing on your mind.

It is amazing how dramatic our earthly circumstances can so powerfully impact our spiritual outlook, isn't it?

The Need-to-Reluctance Ratio

This is not the case for every person, of course. There are some people—I have talked to them—who, if faced with the loss of all they have in this world, have decided to take their own lives. They figure that if there is nothing left to live *for*, there is no reason left to live *at all*. They are not thinking about their souls; they are only bent on escaping the misery and agony of *having nothing here*. Hell, they reason, cannot be nearly as bad as that. What about the grace of God? "If God were merciful," they reason in their spiritual delirium, "He would not allow me to suffer this way." Having foolishly and contemptuously shrugged off God, they would decide to take matters into their own hands. At least one of these has already done so.

Thankfully, most people are not this way. Thankfully too, a number of those who *claim* to be that way really are not willing to go to that extreme. It is one thing to talk about suicide and self-extinction when you are not actually seriously considering it. It is another thing to sit there in the dark with a cold, metallic, unforgiving barrel of a .45 Ruger pointed against your pallid, sweating temple, your finger poised nervously on the trigger. Some people—thankfully—are all talk.

Some of those who are brought to their knees through their deteriorating life's circumstances, however, will undergo an intriguing transformation. They are not converted to the Lord Jesus Christ, but they do become very *spiritual* whereas before they were very *worldly*. (Remember, "spiritual" does not mean "Christian"; the terms are not automatically interchangeable.) They begin looking at the world differently, like a child seeing a carnival for the first time. They realize that they have made a terrible mistake, a disastrous miscalculation, and now they need to "find themselves," "get religion," or simply recalibrate their thinking.

In order to be converted to the Lord, however, these people will be required to take that new-found spiritual awareness to the next step: they must realize that there cannot be a spiritual world without a supreme Spiritual Being to oversee it. Just as this physical world did not appear by accident, so one's spiritual soul did not spontaneously pop into existence: one's soul cannot be a figment of one's own imagination. The Bible speaks of one's soul with the utmost seriousness and crystal-clear reality, and God does not waste time with figments of imagination (Ecclesiastes 5:7). Those who take their soul's preservation very seriously must also take God very seriously (and vice versa). Preservation of the sacred—in this case, one's own soul—must be made a paramount and all-consuming endeavor.

But as I have illustrated, one's view of spiritual matters is heavily influenced by his earthly circumstances. I have used highly exaggerated scenarios to make the point, of course; people's lives are not always this clear-cut. Also, it is wrong to assume that all wealthy people are unconcerned with spiritual matters, or that rich people cannot be Christians. Certainly it is *hard* for "rich men" to successfully enter into God's world (Matthew 19:23-24), but not impossible. Likewise, it is wrong to assume that all impoverished or desperate people automatically start thinking clear-headedly and wisely about their spiritual future. Some of these will shake their fist at God in a teeth-gnashing, spittle-spewing tirade and then denounce whatever scrap of spiritual faith they had left. Trials, by themselves, do not make Christians.

The hypothetical scenarios I have provided above do, however, illustrate an intriguing truism of human nature. I will call this phenomenon the **"need-to-reluctance" ratio**. As the *need* to survive increases, the *reluctance* to contribute whatever is necessary toward that survival decreases proportionately. It works like this: when a person is in very favorable, comfortable circumstances, he (or she) will tend to be extremely <u>reluctant</u> to relinquish his time, wealth, energies, or even his attention toward what he perceives is an unnecessary pursuit—in this case, the preservation of his life. However, as his circumstances deteriorate and become increasingly chaotic, his <u>need for survival</u> becomes increasingly important. What was first perceived as a *waste of time* suddenly becomes a *matter of supreme urgency*. His initial reluctance (or unwillingness) to spend time, money, or effort toward preservation now has completely reversed: the will to survive—whatever the cost—becomes his most important concern.

During times of complacency, personal gratification, and the absence of external threats, people will invest their time and money in *comfort* and *pleasure*, which often translates to the amassing of fortunes or quests for power. Yet when people are faced with earthly extinction—and for the more spiritual-minded, spiritual death—no amount of money can compensate for the irreversible, irretrievable loss with which they are now faced. In view of such loss, one's existence takes on a new and radically different perspective. Things that might have once been taken for granted may suddenly have profound significance.

You don't have to be rich to experience what I am talking about. In fact, the same principles may apply toward those who are excessively tight with money as with those who carelessly spend it. For example, say you are on a walk through the city around lunchtime and are thinking about getting something to eat. You peer into a nice, family-owned deli on the corner and spy some fantastic-looking sandwiches under glass, and your mouth begins salivating. Then you glance at the price: $9.99 for a six-inch pastrami and havarti sandwich, a side, and a cup of coffee. "Ten dollars!" you exclaim under your breath. "Why, I can get twice as much at the McDonald's down the street." Of course, it won't be the same fare, but that's not the point: you simply do not want to part with that much money for what appears to be an inferior amount of food.

This would all change, of course, if your city was completely barricaded and under siege by an invading army that sought your complete ruin. Consider, for example, the horrific three-year siege of Leningrad during World War II in which people peeled their living room walls just to eat the paste from the wallpaper.[31] If circumstances were different and your life was in peril, you would easily pay ten dollars for a six-inch sandwich, even if it was made with stale bread, nearly-spoiled bologna, and wilted lettuce. In fact, if you had the money, you would pay fifty dollars for this, or a hundred, or a thousand—the *money* really would not matter as long as your *survival* was ensured in the process. The *need to survive* is inversely proportional to the *reluctance to sacrifice* toward that need. To restate the principle: as the need to survive *increases*, the reluctance to sacrifice toward that survival *decreases*. During the Syrian siege of Samaria, for example, a donkey's head sold for 80 shekels of silver—a tremendous amount of money for the nearly-useless head of an unclean animal (2 Kings 6:24-31). Likewise, a pint of dove's dung sold for five shekels. A woman even killed and ate one of her own children. (Read Deuteronomy 28:49-57 for another graphic example of this in God's promise of judgment against unfaithful Israel.) Very similar incidents (and worse) occurred during the siege of Jerusalem by the Roman army in AD 69-70 (foretold in Luke 21:21-24).

You might think, "I would *never* succumb to such horrible atrocities!" Sure, while sitting there in the comfort of your living room, sipping fine Sumatra coffee, listening to George Winston play piano, and enjoying the protection of the American government, *of course* you would never succumb to such atrocities! Who would? If your circumstances were changed—if the scenario considerably deteriorated and your situation suddenly became desperate—there is no telling what you would do to survive. No amount of comforts, amenities, extravagances, or money would be enough to give in exchange for your *survival*.

One's perspective of the *sacred* may change radically as his earthly or physical circumstances are changed for the worse. For example, you might have a certain family heirloom that has been handed down for generations - say, an original coat-of-arms, or a Revolutionary War-era cherry wood secretary, or a genuine silver tea set. In your present circumstances, you might be terribly reluctant—if not downright *unwilling*—to let go of that heirloom in exchange for, say, another year of life. But the fact is, if you are not being faced with the immediate loss *of* your life, the exchange hardly seems realistic, maybe not even conceivable. As it stands right now, that heirloom—lifeless, finite, probably man-made, and seemingly-sacred as it is—may seem *more valuable* than your own life. But now imagine your house is engulfed in an unquenchable inferno. The firemen cut a hole through the wall to find you clinging to your heirloom. One fireman tells it like it is: "You must come with us *empty-handed* or we cannot save you at all. *There is no time to waste!*" I am certain that you would preserve your life. Suddenly the entire meaning of what *is* sacred is completely recalibrated.

Your life is worth infinitely more than anything else on this earth. Life itself is suddenly more *sacred* than anything else on this earth. You were forced to recognize this fact because of the desperation of your circumstances, but God has *always* had this perspective. Your life—really, your *soul*—is your most precious possession.

Every Form of Greed

Jesus once told a fickle crowd, "Beware, and be on your guard against every form of greed; for not even when one has an abundance does his life consist of his possessions" (Luke 12:15). Have we been speaking all this time of something as base and carnal as "greed"? When it comes down to it, *yes we have*. When we tenaciously cling to things in this life simply because *we want them*, this is greed, plain and simple. "Greed" (or covetousness) here refers to that unwholesome, ungodly craving for anything that improperly takes a hold of one's heart. It is a type of spiritual slavery, a kind of emotional intoxication with which one becomes drunk and unreasonable. We have all felt this before: that deep and strangely *pleasurable* fixation and hunger for something that (we think) will bring us happiness, advancement, profit, or *completion*. Peter warns us, "...for by what a man is overcome, by this he is enslaved" (2 Peter 2:19). When we ourselves are caught in the clutches of greed, we do not *feel* imprisoned but deliriously *liberated*. There is a certain euphoric, sensual, often giddy, and sometimes even *erotic* sensation directly associated with our desire for whatever it is that has stolen our heart.

Jesus warned against "every *form* of greed," which implies that there is more than one form or kind of greed. For example, there is the dark, seedy, slimy sort of greed that compels a man to sell his mother into slavery or his daughter into prostitution for something as base and worldly as mere money. Then there is that seemingly less conspicuous greed that tempts a person to cheat on his taxes, steal a memory stick from the company office, or maybe stiff a cab driver of his fare every now and then. Then there is that virtually undetectable, imperceptible greed which compels one to hoard his personal possessions without giving God His well-deserved credit for supplying them or to refuse to let go of one's personal cravings in order to make room for the love of Christ and the "fruit of the Spirit" (cf. Galatians 5:16-25). There are indeed several forms of greed in this world, and Christ categorically condemned every single one of them.

"For not even when one has an abundance does his life consist of his possessions." This strikes at the very core of a greedy person's misperception: his *possessions* (real and imagined, even if they are fewer than someone else's) translate to the very substance of his *life*. He assumes that possessions equal life; therefore, an *abundance* of possessions equates to a fuller, richer, better *life*.

Jesus countered this, of course, with the prospect of *losing* all of one's possessions in one felled swoop, like what befell the rich man who tried to amass all of his possessions as a means of securing what we call "the good life" (cf. Luke 12:16-21). This man was not interested in the sacred, but his sole focus was on saving his own life through prosperity and self-indulgence. In his mind, preservation was automatically secured through the abundance of crops. Perhaps he even interpreted such abundance as divine *acceptance* of his mediocre spiritual status. Yet God gives blessings to direct people's attention upward, even though many are fixated instead upon the blessings themselves and not the One who provides them.

Certainly there is nothing wrong with desire itself. There *is*, however, something evil and useless in *greed*, since this may endanger one's life and most certainly jeopardizes one's soul. But the immediate *perception* might be otherwise: as long as one does not "see" any threat to his life, he may not see the point of letting go of the greed in his heart. Even worse, he *never* sees his soul (until it is too late), and may be oblivious to whatever endangers it. Even when Christ makes the warning clear and unmistakable, one may still second-guess the supernatural source of His information. Like Lot who hesitated at leaving Sodom, even though being compelled by an angel of God (Genesis 19:15-18), so a person might sit there and justify his perilous situation even though Christ implores him to act otherwise.

The real essence of this person's problem, when indeed he *has* such a problem, is that he does not perceive the loss of which Jesus is speaking. When the *loss* is not perceived as being real, then the desire to *relinquish* worldly possessions, profits, or positions remains small. A man's willingness to release the clutch he has on the things of this life is inversely proportional to his comprehension of the loss he will incur otherwise. On the other hand, when a person hears the gospel and truly believes in its message, his desire for the things of this world is converted into a desire for divine fellowship and the glory of heaven. Such a person internalizes the Spirit-inspired counsel of the apostle Paul (Colossians 3:1-4):

> Therefore if you have been raised up with Christ, keep seeking the things above, where Christ is, seated at the right hand of God. Set your mind on the things above, not on the things that are on earth. For you have died and your life is hidden with Christ in God. When Christ, who is our life, is revealed, then you also will be revealed with Him in glory.

This person may have once coveted earthly wealth and possessions, thinking that this was the summation of his life. Now, however, he has a completely different perspective: his heart is deeply embedded in the promises of God, and this life becomes less and less attractive to him. As the lure and compulsion for worldly things—i.e., greed—diminishes, his *adoration for the Lord* increases, drawing him away from that which was once destroying him. In comparing his ministry to Christ's, John the Baptist said: "He must increase, but I must decrease" (John 3:30). So it is with the one whose heart is truly given over to the Lord: Christ must "increase" to that person, while his own life "decreases" proportionately. In having made the decision to leave the world behind, he now can pursue *real* life, that which *transcends* this life.

Jesus declared unequivocally, "for where your treasure is, there your heart will be also" (Matthew 6:21). We might reword this: Wherever you keep that which you regard as *sacred*, there will be your fullest, most passionate attention. If indeed "...you have died and your life is hidden with Christ in God" (Colossians 3:3), then your treasure is also with Christ and your soul is entrusted to God (cf. 2 Timothy 1:12). Your reluctance to sacrifice *whatever is necessary* in this world for the sake of maintaining that sacred fellowship with Christ is negligible since your soul's need to survive—even better, to *flourish*—is so much greater than whatever you are called upon to relinquish. You have not yet seen the Lord, but He has given you a sufficient reason to believe. *This* world has not given you a sufficient reason to believe in *it*; "The world is passing away, and also its lusts; but the one who does the will of God lives forever" (1 John 2:17).

The Reality of Your Soul's Need for Christ

What compels you to be in one group or the other—"swallowed up by life" with the Savior (2 Corinthians 5:4) or devoured by the world? It eventually comes down to this: either you regard your soul's desperate need for the Lord as *real* or you do not. Once again, your circumstances largely dictate this but so does your attitude toward what is sacred to begin with. Consider a rich young ruler who approached Jesus with his carefully-planned, well-organized life (Matthew 19:16-22): he certainly thought highly of the Lord and His Law. The problem was that he thought even more highly of his wealth and status. The man obviously respected Christ, and he *did* love God—in his own way. While his heart was in need of God's *approval*, his soul did not see the need of God's *help*. His reluctance to let go of his worldly treasures was great simply because his need to be "saved" apart from his own personal efforts was small. He did not sense the urgency and true nature of his situation—after all, he was rich, young, and in charge. That would all change, for if his proud heart did not repent, he would leave this world and no longer be rich, young, or in charge of anything. Jesus knew this immediately; He always does. That is why He told the man, "If you wish to be complete, go and sell your possessions and give to the poor, and you will have treasure in heaven; and come, follow Me." Jesus realized that the young man's most valuable possession was not the property that he owned but his *soul*; the only One who can successfully guard the soul is Christ Himself.

Zaccheus, however, was a completely different sort of man (Luke 19:1-10). He too was rich, but not young. Perhaps his age (and maturity) affected his outlook differently than that of the rich young ruler. His reluctance to relinquish his hold on the world was considerably less than that of the other because his *need to survive* was much more real than the other's. As the gospel pricked his tender heart with its message of grace and hope, his once-tenacious clutch upon the riches of this world slowly relaxed and released. He volunteered to give up half of his wealth *and* compensate four-fold anyone whom he had overcharged. The fact that Jesus did not have to compel the man to do this speaks volumes of his sincerity. This is why the Lord received this man so gladly, because Zaccheus received *Him* so gladly.

Consider another comparison in Scripture: a different rich man and a poor man named Lazarus (Luke 16:19-31). This parable-like story (which I believe is based upon real people and events, though illustrated in earthly terms) was prompted by the self-righteous attitude of certain Jews. Just prior to the story, Jesus told them, "No servant can serve two masters; for either he will hate the one and love the other, or else he will be devoted to one and despise the other. You cannot serve God and wealth." Then Luke added, "Now the Pharisees, who were lovers of money, were listening to all these things and were scoffing at Him." So Christ responded, "You are those who justify yourselves in the sight of men, but God knows your hearts; for that which is highly esteemed among men is detestable in the sight of God" (Luke 16:13-15).

On the heels of that exchange, Christ revealed a sobering picture of two men involved in the ultimate reversal of fortune. A "rich man" enjoyed all sorts of comforts and luxuries on this earth; Lazarus, by contrast, was an impoverished beggar covered with sores. (Notice Zaccheus and Lazarus are named—they are both *known by God*—whereas the rich young ruler and the "rich man" are nameless. These latter men's personal *lessons* have been preserved for us, but their identities are forever forgotten.) Lazarus languished at the rich man's gate hoping for some compassion and help; the rich man paid him no attention, being caught up in his plastic, superficial life. Both men died, as all men eventually do, and one was buried in the earth while the other was escorted by angels to Paradise.

Finally—but too late—the rich man came to his senses. While on earth, he did not give up even a single moment of his worldly comforts so as to relieve Lazarus's suffering; now, however, he wanted Lazarus to leave the comforts of Paradise to relieve *his* suffering. Notice the stark contrast of the rich man's request: he did not ask for worldly riches, but only for a drop of water, only for a moment's relief from his torment. His reluctance to sacrifice all his worldly riches, if he had still possessed them, would have disappeared altogether once he was faced with the *reality of his unbearable loss*. The loss of his life—and everything *in* this life—was one thing; the loss of his soul was infinitely greater. This latter loss stripped him of *all fellowship with God* and every blessing that accompanies that fellowship. Once, if he had just let go of his worldly riches, his status, and his pride, then his soul would have been preserved for all eternity. As it is, this man now burns with eternal regret, his loss being worse than he could have ever imagined. His soul, which was *always* real and had *always* needed his full attention, is now irretrievably lost—his punishment, irrevocable. At this point, he would pay *anything* for a moment's respite from his wretchedness; unfortunately, he has nothing left to give. Whatever he once had he already spent on this world; the world offers nothing in return but death (Romans 6:23).

The Price of Your Redemption

How important is the preservation of your life to you? What about the preservation of your *soul*? Another way of asking this might be: How important is it that you seek the sacred—the holiness of God? The preservation of your soul and seeking the sacred lead to the same thing: the one pursuit is inseparable from the other. Seeking God's holiness—separating yourself from what is unholy *and* drawing near to His fellowship—leads to the preservation of your soul.

The preservation of your physical life, however, is not guaranteed. In fact, it is not the most important objective. Sometimes we have our priorities all backwards: we may sacrifice our souls to "save" our physical lives. This not only fails to serve our best interest, it really does not make sense. For one thing, your physical life can only be saved for as long. Even those whom Jesus healed by the power of God's Spirit eventually succumbed to an earthly death. When the end of your stay here on earth does come, life as you know it will be forever different. Then "the dust will return to the earth as it was, and the spirit will return to God who gave it" (Ecclesiastes 12:7). Regardless of how many years you lived, how many things you accomplished, how many people you knew, or how many memories you collected, at some point in earthly time *your life will cease to be*. Nonetheless, your soul will live on *forever and ever*. Eternal life is incomprehensible to us, yet it is more real than the world you see all around you.

The measure of our soul's worth is graphically demonstrated in what was paid to *redeem* it because of sin. Peter puts this in perspective for us (1 Peter 1:17-19):

If you address as Father the One who impartially judges according to each one's work, conduct yourselves in fear during the time of your stay on earth; knowing that you were not redeemed with perishable things like silver or gold from your futile way of life inherited from your forefathers, but with precious blood, as of a lamb unblemished and spotless, the blood of Christ.

The "blood of Christ" equates to *the life of God*, inasmuch as Christ *is* God (John 1:1-3). His physical blood, the essence of His human life while here on earth, represents the *divine life* that He has always possessed as God. Christ (God) died for us *not* to save our physical lives but to forever preserve our *spiritual souls*—something we could never have done on our own if we were to live for a literal million years. Silver and gold—the precious things of this world—are unable to accomplish or redeem what the pure, innocent, and divine blood of a flawless sacrifice for sins has done. God gave His life so that you might forever have *your soul* preserved.

A Most Serious Decision

As I said before, sometimes we get this all backwards. We try to control, secure, improve, advance, embellish, and gratify our physical lives through means that we have chosen, often *at the expense of* our spiritual well-being. This "saving" of our lives, in trying to preserve what we have through our own efforts and designs, is never successful. Jesus refers to this self-preservation when He said, "For whoever wishes to save his life will lose it; but whoever loses his life for My sake will find it" (Matthew 16:25). A person trying to manage his own life (for the purpose of saving it) will still die someday and lose all that he had sought to protect, preserve, and improve. If that man has not taken care of his spiritual life, then he loses that too. Having tried to "save" a very small thing (by comparison), he loses everything.

We would like to think that if people realized just how important their souls are—how *eternal* and *priceless* they are—everyone would regard their spiritual preservation with the utmost seriousness. The secular, sensual world, however, has a way of numbing people to the seriousness of their true condition. The world and its pleasures serve as a kind of narcotic to the mind, lulling folks into spiritual lethargy and complacency, anesthetizing their hearts against any pain of sin or the consequence of imprudence. Earthly *circumstances* tend to dominate people's thoughts rather than their thoughts being fixed upon God *regardless* of their earthly circumstances.

Christians are not immune to such worldly sedation. Because of this, we are to discipline ourselves for godliness, which takes great effort. "For it is for this [i.e., godliness—MY WORDS] we labor and strive, because we have fixed our hope on the living God, who is the Savior of all men, especially of believers" (1 Timothy 4:10). Our attitude should imitate Paul's: "But whatever things were gain to me, those things I have counted as loss for the sake of Christ" (Philippians 3:7). Paul sacrificed *everything* for Christ because he realized that the need for his own self-preservation was paramount. Not only this, but his gratitude toward the Lord for His having sacrifice everything for *Paul* inspired his deep love for Him. This dual incentive—spiritual preservation *and* humble gratitude—provides a powerful motivation toward seeking the sacred. One who is so motivated will not be deterred by the world or its distractions.

Of course, the world's influence is not going to melt away just because we surrender to Christ. The world's temptations, allurements, intoxicants, and demonic influences are powerful indeed; we would be foolish to underestimate them. Satan still struts around the dwelling places of man with seductive charms and wicked intent. "Be of sober spirit, be on the alert," Peter rightly warns us; "Your adversary, the devil, prowls around like a roaring lion, seeking someone to devour" (1 Peter 5:8). On the other hand, God's divine love, mercy, grace, and forgiveness are *even more powerful*, but will only help those who turn to Him in genuine faith.

God does not promise the security of your physical life, but He has sworn a divine oath to uphold your soul's preservation through the High Priesthood of Jesus Christ (cf. Hebrews 6:16-20). The loss of this world may seem tragic but only to the one who has placed everything he has *in* this world. According to Jesus, the loss of your soul is *the worst thing that could ever happen to you*. "For what will it profit a man if he gains the whole world and forfeits his soul?" As soon as that man dies, or the world dies—both are inevitable— not only does he suffer the loss of all things, he *never stops suffering*. Ask the rich man who writhes and gnashes his teeth in perpetual torment while Lazarus basks in the joy of God's fellowship. "Or what will a man give in exchange for his soul?" What Jesus means is: What is *worth* the exchange? What is *more valuable* to you than your own soul?

For those who are actively seeking the sacred, this is a question that is already answered. For those who are still waffling and debating, the answer still needs to be addressed. Jesus' question, however, is not going away: "Heaven and earth will pass away, but My words will not pass away" (Matthew 24:35). That which is sacred to God never does pass away.

Endnotes

31 The Siege of Leningrad, a World War II Axis military blockade of the city now known as St. Petersburg, lasted from September 8, 1941 to January 27, 1944. Over 600,000 civilians died as a result of the siege, which is considered one of the worst in all of modern history.

CHAPTER ELEVEN

Speaking with the Sacred

*Hear, O LORD, when I cry with my voice, And be gracious to me and answer me.
When You said, "Seek My face," my heart said to You, "Your face, O LORD, I shall seek."*
Psalm 27:7-8

You've probably read of studies where researchers "tested" whether or not prayer had any effect on healing a sick person. The researchers want to know one of two things: whether or not prayer really can heal the sick, or if prayer accelerates the healing process. In these studies then, there are usually three groups: a control group (for whom no prayers are offered); an informed test group (who knows that prayers *are* being offered for them); and an uninformed test group (who does *not* know that prayers are being offered for them).

Regardless of the results of such studies, there is something extremely disturbing in their underlying premise: reducing God's power among men to a mere cause-and-effect science experiment (like, "If I poke this nerve, then this appendage twitches"). Prayer was never meant to be measured, gauged, calibrated, or quantified; it is not to be "tested" in a clinical research context. It is presumptuous to measure God's ability to perform against human expectations. He has already *proved* His ability to perform: the evidence is not only visible and compelling, it is irrefutable (cf. Romans 1:18-20). Furthermore, the record of His activity among men and the miracles He has accomplished ought to be sufficient to believe in Him and what He is capable of doing (cf. John 5:36; 10:37-38). Putting God in the center of a circle of men, so to speak, to see whether or not He will "do something" is blasphemous.

This chapter really is not about prayer's affect on sick people today; it is on the sacredness *of* prayer. Prayer is not only our communication *with* the Sacred, but prayer itself is sacred. In order to be seekers of the sacred, we must regularly engage in sacred communication. But what *makes* prayer "sacred"? Why has God given us *this* medium of communication rather than any other? What *should* we expect from a God whom none of us have ever seen—a God whose answers to our prayers may not always be as obvious as we would like them to be? Why *should* we pray to a God who already knows everything anyway—a God who knows what we will ask before the request is even made?

These are good and fair questions. It is impossible for anyone to do justice to them in the course of a single chapter. In fact, I may not answer *any* of them to your personal satisfaction. However, a book on "seeking the sacred" would be terribly incomplete if we did not talk about praying to the Sacred God.

What Prayer Is—and Is Not

Prayer is not a rabbit's foot or any other form of a "good luck" charm. It is not an amulet which grants special powers to the one who possesses it. It is not a magical incantation that only works if the right words are intoned in the right order. It is not a prying tool which forces God's hand to give a person what he wants. It is not a magic lamp, and God is not a genie. It is not a special coin, and God is not a dispensing machine. It is not a spiritual narcotic, designed only to offer therapeutic solace to the one praying but accomplishing little else in the process. It is not a desperate, last-ditch effort of escaping one's personal ruin by invoking heavenly powers after that person's own attempts at salvation have failed miserably.

Prayer is the sacred means of communication which God has given us to use for our own good. Since He has *given* it to us (at no cost), it is a *gift*. Like all gifts which God gives to us, it is supposed to be appreciated, used wisely, and (thus) not misused. Prayer is a privilege, not a right. However, we are to *respond* rightly to the gift of prayer, just as we are to respond rightly to the gift of grace, the gift of mercy, the gift of forgiveness, and the many other gifts He gives to His children. This necessarily implies that one must *be* a child of God in order to receive this gift. We have no record of God responding to the prayers of those who are not interested in having a right relationship with Him. In fact, we see just the opposite in Scripture (see Isaiah 1:15-16; 59:1-2; John 9:31; and 1 Peter 3:7).[32] God is not obligated to hear the prayers of those who refuse to surrender their hearts to Him. Those who pray to God only when they find themselves in a perilous predicament (but do not trust God otherwise) profane the sacredness of prayer. They have no appreciation for its intended purpose, just as they have no real appreciation for God Himself.

Whatever comes from God is holy (James 1:17), and prayer is most certainly a holy gift. This should call to mind the holy food that was given to the priests under the Law of Moses and how this was to be regarded (Leviticus 22:1-3). Remember also that men are unable to create or reproduce what is sacred to God. We cannot make prayer "happen" if indeed God has not granted us the privilege of it in the first place. Likewise, we cannot replace prayer with something of our own making: we cannot communicate with God in ways other than prayer. Any attempts otherwise are not authorized by Him, are offensive to Him, and are not going to accomplish anything worthwhile.

The Process of Communication

Communication is the process by which two or more parties send information, make requests, or demonstrate emotions. Technically, communication can be verbal or non-verbal (i.e., gestures, facial expressions, body language, posture, etc.). People can communicate with one another without a single word or sound being made—we do this all the time with one another. For example, suppose you board a city bus and are looking for a seat. Next to the first available seat is a middle-aged woman who scowls angrily at you before turning toward the window, shaking her head. Adjacent to the next seat, a young twenty-something man glares at you coldly, his arms folded, his jaw set. Next to the third seat, a gray-haired, bespectacled man smiles warmly, moves his coat from the empty seat, and nods politely to you. None of these people said a word, and yet they all communicated strong messages to you. Which one are you going to sit down beside?

Communication does not really exist unless there is a complete exchange of information between at least two parties. If I talk, but no one responds to what I said, communication has technically not taken place. I *talked*, but talking and communicating are not necessarily the same things.

In order to communicate:
1. a person must *send a message* to another person (or persons);
2. this other person must be able to receive that message and *respond* to it verbally or otherwise—in other words, he must *give an answer*;
3. the first person must *receive* this response.

Only when all three of these actions have occurred in this order has communication truly been made. This works on every level: When a man's wife talks to him but he does not respond to her with any meaningful acknowledgement, that is *not* communication. On the other hand, when God speaks to us through His Word *and* we respond to this with obedience *and* God has acknowledged our response, communication is achieved. God's message is not communicated if we cannot hear it; we cannot "hear" it if there is no one to "preach" it (cf. Romans 10:14-17). Communication is not always *positive* acceptance of what is said either. A person's flat refusal to comply with the message that has been "sent" to him (such as the gospel's call) is still participating in the process of communication as long as he has received that message, has responded to it, and his response has been received.

My point in all of this is: prayer is a real, productive, and *sacred* form of communication. The fact that we *can* communicate with God is extremely crucial to understanding our *relationship* with Him. A relationship void of communication is hardly a relationship at all. People who are in a relationship but are unable to communicate with each other cannot further their relationship. Their association remains static and unproductive; once they become estranged, whatever might have existed between them dies altogether. If we were unable to communicate with God, then we could not have a functional relationship with Him. We might have an agreement in theory, so to speak, but we could not have *fellowship*. We cannot be seekers of the sacred without the communication that God makes possible to us.

People communicate on many different levels. For example, your conversation with a waitress may be extremely limited, but it is communication all the same. Communication with your boss (or employee) reaches yet another level; communication with your softball teammates might go even further. Beyond this is communication with your good friends, close relatives, your children, and your spouse, or a kindred spirit (cf. Philippians 2:20). The point is: not all communication is equal. There is nothing wrong with this in itself; in fact, this is very human, perfectly normal, and commonly observed.

We often define levels of communication by *depth*. How *deeply* we communicate with someone determines the closeness of our relationship to that person. The general term for this closeness is "intimacy," although many confuse this with something romantic or sexual in nature. Intimacy, by itself, does not require romance or sex at all; it is measured by *depth of communication*, not necessarily even physical proximity. People who jump into bed together on a first date certainly do become *physically* intimate (close), but there is no depth to their relationship since there is no depth to their communication. Such depth takes time, experience, and nurturing; it cannot be achieved in a one-night stand. Likewise, we might have a meaningful conversation with a stranger we met at the coffee shop, but one meaningful conversation is not equal to an intimate bond that two people have taken months or years to cultivate. Anyone can dig a shallow hole, but a deep hole—say, a few miles down and a thousand yards wide—takes a long time to dig. The shallow hole has a very limited capacity; the deep hole has an enormous capacity. So it is with our relationships: the short-term, shallow, or temporary relationships may be able to hold something important, but they cannot hold very *much*; deeper relationships are able to hold *many* important things, which makes them all the more special and enjoyable.

At the core of communication—and thus prayer—is *sharing*. When we communicate with someone, we share with them. *What* we share will vary according to the relationship we have with that person in the first place and/or the intent of the communication. The news correspondent on CNN shares information with his (or her) viewers. (It is not an ideal communication since there is no perceived acknowledgement or response from the listening audience.) His intention is merely to convey "news" to people, but he also cannot help but convey some of his own opinions, personality, and slant on the stories he covers. A schoolteacher, on the other hand, speaks face-to-face with his (or her) students, so that a real relationship is possible through the exchange. That teacher's intention is not merely to convey information to a mass of faceless people but to train his students to learn about and interact with the world. His position will enable him to share his own education, personal experiences and observations, and his friendship. Even so, there are limits to the relationship he can have with his students; he can only communicate so much. A friend, however, can far exceed such limited relationships—if both parties are willing. Thus, the friend is able to communicate so much more of himself than the newsperson or teacher. He shares not only information but also a manifold personality, moods, feelings, opinions, and (often) a diverse collection of memories and common interests.

The intimacy of a close friend can usually only be surpassed by that of one's spouse. Theirs is a sharing which can include everything that close friends share, as well as a physical and emotional intimacy that exceeds all other relationships. Such communication can easily transcend even the earthly context: a Christian couple can speak of (and "share" with one another) their spiritual lives in a context that nearly defies human explanation.

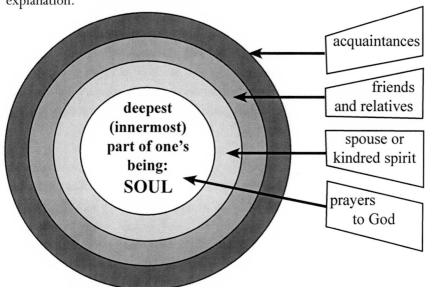

The "Core" of One's Being:
Levels of Intimacy and Self-disclosure

All of the previous examples illustrate a progressively increased amount of *self-disclosure*—that hidden part of ourselves which we are willing and/or able to share with someone else. Some things we *choose* to disclose to others; other things we choose *not* to tell (consciously, anyway).[33] Some things we are *able* to disclose to others; other things we are *unable* to communicate. There are some feelings, for example, that are beyond words, description, and (thus) self-disclosure. People may be able to sympathize— or empathize—with those feelings, but *their* feelings are not *yours*, and vice versa. We communicate facts, feelings, moods, and personality with people, but there are always limits to what we can tell them. Taken further, we can tell people what is *in* our soul, but we cannot truly reveal our soul to anyone. We have never even *seen* our soul; we cannot explain adequately to someone that which we cannot even fully understand ourselves. Self-disclosure is limited then to what a person actually knows of *himself*. One cannot communicate what he does not (or cannot) know.

There is no communication deeper, more intimate, or more spiritual than one's prayer to the Lord. God not only knows every single physical aspect of your life—down to the very cells and atoms that comprise your human body—but He also knows every *thought* and *intention* of your mind (Hebrews 4:12-13). As God told the prophet Samuel, "...God sees not as man sees, for man looks at the outward appearance, but the LORD looks at the heart" (1 Samuel 16:7). God *sees your very soul*: He knows what you "look" like even beyond what you are able to know yourself. He not only hears what you *attempt* to communicate through your own human abilities, but He hears what *exceeds* your capacity for conscious communication, but which your soul "senses" anyway.[34]

This makes prayer the most personal, intimate, and self-disclosing form of communication possible. We do not speak to God with mere words, voice inflections, emotions, or body language. We communicate soul-to-soul, so to speak: our soul communicates—communes, really—with God's Holy Spirit. God's Spirit "intercedes for the saints according to the will of God" (Romans 8:26-27), and carries our petitions to God. Thus, "through Him [Christ] we both have our access in one Spirit to the Father" (Ephesians 2:18).[35]

In this way, we are able to share with God not only what is in our thoughts but even what is in the depths of our souls. We are able to engage the sacred realm of God in a way that defies all earthly context, ability, and explanation. When you go to the Father in prayer—an expression we use to describe the experience—in a very real sense, you *go to the Father*. In the spirit, you ask permission to present yourself before the Lord in all His glory, and if indeed you are a seeker *of* God, He grants you permission to enter. You are allowed to speak whatever is in your heart, but the Light of God penetrates the very core of your being. There is no need to hide thoughts or shy away from the truth for God knows every single flexure and nuance of who you are. God's inspection of your soul is similar to a Levitical priest's inspection of animals brought to the altar for sacrifice: those which were blemished were rejected; those which were healthy and intact were permitted for sacrifice (Leviticus 22:17-25). The soul that is not cleansed by the blood of Christ cannot come before the Father; God recognizes no soul which is still stained with sin (Isaiah 59:1-2). We cannot serve as a "living sacrifice" to Him in that condition. Thus, we come *through* Christ (Romans 5:9; Colossians 1:19-20), *by* the Spirit, and *to* the Father.

You are indeed transparent to the Lord, but this is to your advantage. The Light which examines and exposes your soul is not meant to destroy you but to give you an opportunity to see yourself for who you really are. Those who practice the truth have nothing to hide (John 3:21). One whose attitude is not what it should be is enlightened by God, as long as he continues to be a seeker of the sacred (Philippians 3:15). "But if any of you lacks wisdom," James says, "let him ask of God, who gives to all generously and without reproach, and it will be given to him" (James 1:5). In other words, if anyone comes to God in prayer *with the intent of being illuminated*, then God will certainly illuminate him. This process *of* illumination will not involve a miraculous epiphany, a divine revelation, or some kind of wondrous vision, but it will happen all the same—however, whenever, and through whomever God chooses to communicate it.

God's Answer to Prayer

This leads us to a common question: If prayer is communication, and communication requires a response from the one who has received our message, then how *does* God answer prayer? The short (but accurate) answer is: *however He chooses to do so*. Since God has proved Himself capable of overcoming every earthly hindrance, every human obstacle, and every circumstantial interference, certainly He still possesses such capabilities. If He *wanted* to speak to you from the clouds in a thunderous, ground-splitting roar from heaven, He is certainly capable of doing this. To *expect* Him to do this—and then to be disappointed when He does not—is not yours to impose upon Him. God is all-powerful and exercises supreme control over all things and every element; He does not need to provide miracles in order to answer prayers. He *speaks*, and whatever needs to be done is *done*. How this happens is His decision; it is not yours or mine to dictate.

Just because you and I cannot *observe* God's response to our prayers does not mean He does not *receive* and then *answer* them. For example, when you send a letter to a friend across the country, and she sends a reply letter to you a few days later, communication has occurred but neither of you *observed* the other writing the letter. You *know* your sent letter was received because of the response. Upon your having received her response, communication was made; the cycle was completed; closure to that particular exchange of information was achieved. With regard to prayer to God, it may be hours, days, weeks, or years before you recognize the answer to your request; in fact, in some cases you may not "see" it at all. Yet you have not been asked to time every answer to every prayer; you have been asked to *believe* in the power of prayer. You have not been asked to analyze God's responses and critique them; you have been asked to *believe* that God will respond to you. No one can be a seeker of the sacred who does not believe in the dynamic activity of the sacred. Either you believe in God—and thus pray with such belief—or you do not. It is not right to pray with an "I-don't-know-if-this-will-do-anything-but-I'll-try-it-anyway" approach. As Jesus Himself said, "…All things are possible to Him who believes" (Mark 9:23). Likewise, nothing is possible for him who does *not* believe, for God's spiritual gifts are not given to unbelievers (cf. Ephesians 2:11-12).

Perhaps it would be profitable to cite James 1:5-8 now in its entirety:

> But if any of you lacks wisdom, let him ask of God, who
> gives to all generously and without reproach, and it will

be given to him. But he must ask in faith without any doubting, for the one who doubts is like the surf of the sea, driven and tossed by the wind. For that man ought not to expect that he will receive anything from the Lord, being a double-minded man, unstable in all his ways.

When we pray, we are not to "hope" that God hears us, then wonder "if" He will respond or not. Prayer needs to be made *in faith* that God most certainly *does* hear and responds to those who are seekers of His will. We do not pray to God then to *inform* Him of anything, including our own heart. God is everywhere at all times; He knows everything, both visible and invisible. Our prayers *do*, however, communicate our faith in Him. One who does not have faith ought not to pray, since prayer is, above all else, an act of faith; faith is expressed ideally through prayer. Speaking in full confidence to a God whom none of us have ever seen, expecting Him to hear our requests and trusting that He will respond appropriately *to* those requests *requires great faith*. Such faith is predicated on the evidence God has provided; it is not a blind or pointless exercise (Galatians 5:5; Ephesians 3:11-12; Hebrews 11:6). God has given us, in His Word, a *reason to believe* in prayer; therefore, it is reasonable and justifiable that we pray to Him. Just as Jesus often prayed to God, so His disciples are to pray. If Christ Himself trusted in the sacred communication of prayer, certainly we who are so much less than He can do the same.

Prayerful Entreaties

There are essentially three kinds of prayers: entreaties, appeals, and praise. An entreaty is a humble and sincere request of someone (usually one who is in a higher position than the one doing the asking) for something. Similar words are "pleas," "petitions" (Ephesians 6:18; 1 Timothy 2:1), "requests" or "supplications" (Philippians 4:6). We ask things of God that we cannot obtain or access on our own. Picture yourself as a lowly servant of a great and powerful kingdom, bowing at the feet of its all-powerful king, bringing your needs before him. Picture yourself also *knowing for certain* that this king will grant your requests in whatever way serves your best interest, since he cares for you (cf. 1 Peter 5:6-7).

Such requests must be just that: *requests*, not demands. When we *ask* for something, we should be prepared for whatever answer is given; otherwise, we might as well insist upon the one and only answer that makes us happy. It is not uncommon for people—yes, even devout Christians—to make demands of God that defy all aspects of humility and propriety. Just because God *can* do something does not mean that He *must*, or that you should be disappointed if He does not. For example, picture a Christian man who is distraught over, say, his daughter's life-threatening illness, and so he fervently goes to the Lord in prayer. The essence of his prayer is this: "Father, since I know you are *capable* of healing my daughter, I fully expect that You *will* heal her." It is natural that a father would want his daughter to recover from a sickness; however, recovery from sickness is not always *according to God's will*.

Someone gasps, "Why would God actually *allow* an innocent child to die?" How a young girl's death might work to the benefit of God is not a question I must answer in order to maintain that God has the right to make sovereign decisions, even those concerning life and death. Our concern, apart from the compassion and human emotions we have toward our loved ones, ought to be: What does God want? What is His will? "This is the confidence which we have before Him," John wrote, "that, if we ask anything according to His will, He hears us" (1 John 5:14). *All* prayers ought to be asked according to His will and not our own. No Christian should ever knowingly ask something of God that is *not* according to His will. This does not mean one cannot ask God *questions* in his search for information but that he dare not question God's *authority*.

We should not believe in God—and thus pray to Him—only when He explains to us what He is doing and why He is doing it. I have encountered this many times among Christians: an attitude of distrust and disenchantment toward God because He did not offer them (what they thought was) a suitable explanation for His actions. Someone will say something like, "I don't *understand* why God did (or did not do) this; it doesn't make sense." If left unchecked, this turns into, "*Since* God did not help me to understand this, *therefore* God does not make sense." First, the response to prayer is questioned; next, God's own authority is brought before the board of human review. This is no longer faith but is unjust and unwarranted criticism. This does not respect the omniscience and beneficence of God; it calls His goodness into question, even rebukes it. Thus, if a man is facing even such a horrible prospect as the death of his own child, he must not abandon his faith in God if He does not permit that child to live. If I were that father, I would be begging through prayer and pleading with tears for my child's life. Nonetheless, if God decided otherwise, then it would be wrong—and presumptuous—for me to walk away from the Lord simply because He did not comply with my expectations.

A "no" (or "wait") answer from God *is still an answer*. Those who claim that "God didn't answer my prayer!" often mean that God did not answer it how they *expected* Him to do so. Either we let God be God and thus let Him make God-like decisions or we assume our decisions are superior to His. We cannot have it both ways. Furthermore, we cannot allow our emotions to dictate our spiritual beliefs. We cannot practice theology only when it is therapeutically beneficial to do so. God is not asking us how we *feel* on this matter or that; He is asking us to trust Him and telling us that He will not abandon us (cf. Hebrews 13:5-6).

Prayerful Appeals

The second kind of prayer is that of an appeal. In this context, an appeal is not asking for a certain "thing" to be granted to you, but for *help*. We appeal to God in prayer to help us deal with problems and circumstances that are beyond our control. We might say that in prayer we *give* to God that which we are unable to bear on our own, and we *receive* from Him that which we are unable to acquire on our own. Jesus, for example, said that He could appeal to His Father for twelve legions of angels to deliver Him, if necessary (Matthew 26:53). Jesus, as a Man, did not have such authority, but He could appeal to the One who did. Similarly, we appeal to God for "a good conscience" through baptism (1 Peter 3:21) because we cannot obtain a good conscience apart from Him (see also Hebrews 9:13-14).

The word "appeal" (often rendered "pray" in the New Testament) is *parakaleo*, which means to implore, seek (the) comfort of, or urge someone to act. It is a form of the word *parakletos*, an intercessor, advocate, or comforter—the word used to describe the Holy Spirit's role as a protector of the disciples (in John 14:16, 26; 15:26; and 16:7). "Appeal" also has a legal connotation to it, an idea still used with reference to an appellate court (i.e., court of appeals). In this way, we appeal (pray) to Christ as our "Advocate" (*parakletos*) when we sin, since we are helpless otherwise, and He is able and willing to speak on our behalf (1 John 2:1-2).[36]

Prayerful Praise

The third kind of prayer is that of praise which easily includes the idea of thanksgiving. The "fruit of lips" is our praise to God for sharing Himself with *us* and the sharing of our gratitude for *Him* (Hebrews 13:15). Included in *all* our prayers ought to be expressions of thanksgiving to God (Philippians 4:6; Colossians 4:2).

It is a great privilege for us to partake of the sacred, one which we should never take for granted. Ingratitude is a sign not only of carelessness and self-absorption but also of disbelief. Those who do not thank God for His kindness and blessings imply that they are not convinced that He is the *source* of them. It can also imply resentment over other gifts having *not* been given (but that *should* have been given—or so it was believed). If indeed we are partakers of the sacred, we are to "Let the peace of Christ rule in [our] hearts, to which indeed [we] were called in one body; and be thankful" (Colossians 3:15). Our thankful appreciation for God then must be exhibited in our attitude and conduct toward others *as well as* in our humble prayers to the Lord.

How We Are Taught to Pray

God the Father *wants* us to communicate with Him; God the Son has taught us *how* to pray. In Matthew 6:9-13, Christ offered a simple model of the kind and content of prayer that God desires. This is often referred to as "the Lord's prayer" but really it is a *disciple's* prayer: it is typical of what a disciple *of* the Lord ought to be addressing. It was never meant to be regurgitated word-for-word as is common among many denominational religions, but is to provide us insight into what is anticipated of those who *do* pray to God. In that model prayer are elements of what should be expected in all prayers:

• **"Our Father who is in heaven":** We cannot assume equality with the Sacred God; having fellowship with God does not make us equals with Him. God is in heaven, and we are not (cf. Ecclesiastes 5:2); this sets Him far above our mundane existence and our earth-bound perceptions. The first thing a person should acknowledge in his prayers then is the fact that *God is our Father*—the Source of our being, the Sustainer of our existence—and that *He dwells in heaven*. This sets the tone and context for all that follows.

• **"Hallowed be Your name":** "Hallowed" means venerated, sanctified, or holy. In agreement with the theme of this book, we could translate this, "*Sacred* is Your name," and we would not have corrupted the text whatsoever. God is in heaven because He is sacred: He is to be revered above all that exists. There is no one who is sacred apart from God's having designated him as such: He is the source *of* sacredness. His "name" indicates not only His position as God but also His *sovereign authority* (as in Matthew 28:19; John 1:12; 20:31; et al). So when we pray, "Holy is Your name," or any expression commensurate with this, we are declaring our surrender to His will, our acceptance of His authority, and our deference to His superiority over us.

• **"Your kingdom come":** God's kingdom has always existed, but Christ has not always been its King. The manifestation of God's kingdom through Christ's redemption is what is meant here. From our vantage point in history, God's kingdom *has already* "come": if it had not, then you could not be a Christian, for there would be no church and you could not have forgiveness of your sins (cf. Colossians 1:13-14). Christ's church has been built upon His God-given authority as King over His Father's kingdom (Matthew 28:18; Ephesians 1:22-23). If Christ did not have that authority—if God had not given Him that authority—then He could not have built a church, and He could not redeem a single soul. As it is, Jesus is both Messiah (Christ) *and* Son of God, and upon that invincible, unchangeable, and omnipotent authority Christ now rules as King of kings and Lord of lords (cf. Matthew 16:13-19; Hebrews 8:1; Revelation 17:14). For us to pray that God's kingdom would still "come" does not recognize these things. At the time when Christ *stated* it, the kingdom had not yet been given to Him; now we must express this differently. The *essence* of Christ's statement is still valid, that is, that we should pray for the redemption of men's souls, which is what Jesus' statement necessarily implied.

- **"Your will be done…":** God does not have to tell us what His will is before we can endorse it. We are to adopt His will as our own, thus we are to comply with His will even above our own. Jesus did not ask for our mere resignation to the sacred here. We are not to shrug and sigh, "Well, God's going to do what He's going to do; who can resist Him?" (cf. Romans 9:19-21). We are to *pray* that His will be accomplished—through us, for us, and with our full support. In other words, our prayers should be an enthusiastic *anticipation* of God's will being performed on earth, to the success of His kingdom and the subsequent salvation of many souls.

- **"Give us this day our daily bread":** Just as God "humbled" Israel with a daily provision of supernaturally-produced manna (Deuteronomy 8:3), so we should be humbled by our complete dependence upon God's generosity. We cannot produce even a single loaf of bread from nothing, but God can produce anything He desires for His children. God may well have given us "our daily bread" even if we did not ask Him for it—this happens all the time—but when we *do* ask Him for it, we confess our complete reliance upon His kindness and grace. Such everyday kindness is supposed to lead sinners to repentance (Romans 2:4), but it should also draw seekers of the sacred even *nearer* to God. Not only should we ask God for "bread" but for protection, providence, wisdom (James 1:5), forgiveness, breath, and life.

• **"And forgive us our debts, as we also...debtors":** God *wants* to forgive us of our sins, but He will not do so unless we *ask* Him for this. God is not on some power-trip; He is not forcing us to our knees with extortion; He is not forcing us to say the magic word or cry "uncle." Forgiveness—like all aspects of salvation—is clearly *conditional*: it cannot be extended unless the one in need of it demonstrates his faith in the One who provides it. This demonstration of faith is two-fold: first, one must *be willing to forgive others* of their sins against oneself; second, one must *pray to God* for forgiveness. If one will not forgive others, then God will not forgive him (Matthew 6:14-15; see also 18:21-35). If one will not pray for forgiveness, then God cannot respond with grace. Forgiveness is not to be assumed; it is not accidental or automatic. When a person forgives others *in honor of God*, he demonstrates trust that God will compensate for whatever losses are incurred through that forgiveness *and* that He will indeed remove that person's sins.

• **"And do not lead us into temptation...":** This must be understood in the context of other passages. God is not the source of temptation (James 1:13); He does not bait people into stumbling; He does not taunt people with sin. God *can* save us from being tempted beyond what we are able to endure as long as we trust Him to do so. We cannot pray, "Save me!" and then carelessly wander into our own demise. With every temptation there is a "way of escape" (1 Corinthians 10:13), and we should pray that God will *provide* and *reveal* that "way." We should never ask God to excuse us from *being* tempted; however, this is self-defeating and is not according to His will. Rather, we should ask that He not allow us to be overwhelmed by temptation. God allows us to be tempted so that our faith can be strengthened. It is through overcoming temptations that we learn to depend upon Him all the more; this also purifies our character and teaches us endurance (1 Peter 1:6-9; James 1:2). Temptation itself is not sin; it is not a sin to *be* tempted. Temptation really is *decision time*: it is an opportunity to deliberately choose God's will over our own, desire God over our own lusts, and hope in God rather than seek instant gratification in sin.

Asking, Seeking, Knocking

So much more can be said on prayer, but the purpose of this chapter is not to provide a comprehensive analysis of the subject. On the other hand, seekers of the sacred must recognize how vitally important it is to be not only prayerful in practice but also believers in prayer. Christians are to be "devoted to prayer" (Romans 12:12; Colossians 4:2), and all such devotion is to be "overflowing with gratitude" (Colossians 2:7). It is impossible to be a seeker of the sacred without regularly immersing oneself in prayer. This also implies God's expectation of His people and our personal responsibility toward that expectation. Such responsibility cannot be circumvented or replaced by something else. No amount of good deeds, Bible reading, hymn singing, church-going, or any other pious activity can replace one's solemn and sacred communication with the Lord. Nothing we do in the flesh can compare to what is accomplished by the soul in prayer.

Jesus did not just teach us to pray, but He taught us to pray actively and tenaciously. This does not mean we are to be pushy or imposing in prayer but persistent and determined (as illustrated in Luke 18:1-8). Being active and tenacious does not mean that we refuse to take "no" for an answer from God—we are not to "test" God by questioning His answers (Matthew 4:7). Even if God *does* say "no," then we may ask, "If not this way, then *what* way would You have me go?" In this way, we have deferred to God's decision but have not given up seeking Him.

This brings us to the role of prayer in drawing near to God. Jesus taught us, "Ask, and it will be given to you; seek, and you will find; knock, and it will be opened to you. For everyone who asks receives, and he who seeks finds, and to him who knocks it will be opened" (Matthew 7:7-8; see also Luke 11:5-13). This is really a crescendo of ideas: we are not only to ask, we are to seek; we are not only to seek, we are also to knock. The one leads to the other, but the completion of the cycle eventually leads to a new cycle altogether. The rhythmic nature of our communication with God requires this. We are not told to ask, seek, and knock *once,* but continuously and perpetually, until we behold the Lord in fact and have no more need of human faith.

What does it mean to ask, seek, and knock? Prayer is not for God but for us; we do not ask God for things which we think He might have overlooked otherwise but because He wants us to appreciate His provision of such things. We cannot ask for something of which God disapproves, but the failure to ask properly—or at all—is tantamount to disbelief and selfishness (James 4:3-4). We *ask* because we *believe* in God's existence and His ability to provide whatever it is that we need. I should stress the word "need" here since people are prone to confuse this with "want." God *sometimes* gives us what we want, but He *always* gives us what we need. We must take in the big picture: what we ask for cannot always be about us but must also include God's interests which bear directly upon the interests (and especially the salvation) of others. In all of this, we are to be an *asking* sort of people—not a whining, nagging, threatening, demanding, or imposing sort of people, but those who *ask* with all humility.

Asking is supposed to lead to seeking. "Seeking" implies that something is lost, hidden, or obscure and is waiting to be discovered. Certainly that "something" is not lost to God but to us. Furthermore, God is not lost, but we are lost unless we seek after God. After we ask God to make something evident to us, to put us to good use, or to carry out His will, then we are supposed to seek after the fulfillment of that request. This means we are not to stand still and wait for God to work a miracle; rather, we are to engage in the work for which He has created us anew (cf. Ephesians 2:10). This does not mean we are to do *everything*, but that we are to do *something*. God does what *He* does; we are supposed to do what He expects *us* to do. God does not "seek" for us in the same way that we are to seek after Him. We do not "seek" apart from God either; His grace and providence lead us in the direction we should go.

Someone once asked Jesus, "Lord, are there just a few who are being saved?" Jesus replied, "Strive to enter the narrow door; for many, I tell you, will seek to enter and will not be able" (Luke 13:23-24). Does this imply that our "seeking" might be in vain, that we might "not be able" to receive salvation after all? In response to this, it is clear that there is a right way and a wrong way to seek after God. The New Testament has several passages which speak of those who sought God wrongly (Matthew 7:21-23; John 5:39-40; Romans 10:2-3; Galatians 5:1-4; et al). Jesus' own comments in Luke 13 dealt with Jews who *assumed* that they would be partakers of the kingdom of God (because they *were* Jews) but did not live accordingly and did not believe in God's Son. When Jesus said, "Strive to enter...," He meant, in essence, "You are going to have to work at this. Your status as Israelites does not grant you automatic citizenship in the kingdom of God. If you will not make the personal sacrifices necessary to follow Me, then you will forfeit your invitation into the kingdom altogether."

Likewise, we are going to have to "work" at being believers, which means we are going to have to work at prayer. Not only are we to ask for God's direction, but we are to seek after His answers. This does not mean that God is purposely trying to elude us in order to make our pursuit of Him unnecessarily difficult. It means that discipleship is already difficult and that we are going to have to think, live, act, and pray with difficulty. As Paul rightly said, "Through many tribulations we must enter the kingdom of God" (Acts 14:22). Indeed, no one skates into heaven with ease, but each disciple must bear his own cross (Matthew 10:38). No one stumbles into heaven accidentally, but each person must live and practice his faith in such a way that leads him there (2 Peter 1:10-11). We are to be seekers of God, not merely believers in His existence; we are to strive to enter the "narrow door," not amble along with complacency or indifference (Matthew 7:13-14). Such seeking and striving is part of the prayerful life of a genuine disciple of Christ.

Our seeking will always bring us to a door. What this door "looks" like, or what it opens into, may differ from person to person. Regardless, we always come to a point in our seeking after the sacred that prevents us from going any further on our own. The "door" metaphor in Scripture indicates something that either is waiting to be opened or must remain closed. In either case, Christ is the One who opens and shuts doors for those who seek Him (Revelation 3:7). He has the authority to do this; in prayer, we recognize and respect this authority. Thus, when we come to a locked door, we ask Him either to open it or leave it closed: we leave this decision to Him. Once He opens that door, however, we are expected to walk through it. How many times have people asked for doors to be opened, then failed to cross the threshold once this was done, being frightened by what lay on the other side? On the other hand, if He chooses to leave a door locked then we should not take a fireman's axe and start battering it to pieces. Both failing to enter an opened door and trying to beat down a closed door indicate a lack of faith.

Someone asks, "Why would Christ lead anyone to a closed door?" We might answer rhetorically: Why did God give to Abraham a son of promise (Isaac) only to ask him to sacrifice that son as a burnt offering? Why did God lead Israel out of Egypt only to dead-end their journey at the shore of the Red Sea? Why did Christ's disciples train for three years only to watch their Teacher's life be snuffed out in a gruesome and seemingly untimely death? In all of these examples, God led people to a closed door. God brought Abraham, Israel, and Christ's disciples to a door that could not be opened by anyone but Him. The lesson then was to prove God's supernatural ability to open doors that no one else could open. Thus, God opened the door to Abraham's future by sparing his son Isaac through a vicarious sacrifice (of a ram). God opened the door to Israel's future by parting the Red Sea. And God opened the door to the disciples' ministries by shattering the bonds of death through His Son's resurrection. If God can open these doors, can He not open doors for you?

"But not all doors are *meant* to be opened," someone says, and this is true. Christ opens doors that He wants opened, but closes doors that He wants closed. You've heard it said that every time one door closes, another opens: this seems to be generally the case. It might be even more accurate to say, however, that every time Christ closes a door, *many* others may be opened. We should not limit the One who possesses all the resources of heaven and earth to having only a few doors to work with!

Coming to a closed door is not enough by itself: you must also *knock*. This indicates that you desire entrance but are waiting for permission for entrance to be granted—or denied, as the case may be. By knocking, we defer to God's authority over our own. In humility, we recognize that Christ sees more, knows more, and controls more than we do, thus it is better that He open the door (or not) than if we made that decision alone.

What is the outcome of asking, seeking, and knocking? "Ask, and it *will be given* to you; seek, and you *will find*; knock, and it *will be opened* to you," Jesus promised (emphases mine). "For everyone who asks receives, and he who seeks finds, and to him who knocks it will be opened." Listen to what He promised: *everyone* will receive, find, and have the right doors opened who *does what is expected of him* as a seeker of the sacred. This means that if *you* ask, seek, and knock, that Christ *will indeed*—it is a guarantee!—provide you with what is in your best interest to find.

Notice I said "what is in your *best interest* to find," not always what you (thought you) were looking for. Seeking after God is an ever-changing, ever-enlightening, ever-deepening process. No one ever ends up finding in God exactly what he started searching for in the first place, yet what he ends up with is always *far superior* to this. Drawing near to God is never a disappointing endeavor but always surpasses one's expectations as long as a person draws near to Him in the way He has prescribed.

Beyond What We Might Ask

Prayer is the most intimate form of self-disclosure possible in our earthly existence. For this reason, it is intensely personal. Even when we pray as a group, each person must participate in that prayer himself. I can pray on *your* behalf, or you can pray on *mine*, but we cannot have anyone pray *instead* of us. Furthermore, your prayer cannot forgive my sins; God only forgives those who pray for their own forgiveness. Likewise, I can pray that God would help convince you to *turn* to Him and repent, if indeed you were in sin, but my prayer cannot replace your own. We cannot pray by proxy anymore than you can seek after the sacred by proxy: you are either doing this or you are not. There is no middle ground; there is no third option.

None of this is meant to *limit* prayer, however. It is only to regulate its proper usage, to show that there are right and wrong ways to pray. As to the effects of prayer, however, there are no limits. "The effective prayer of a righteous man [or woman!] can accomplish much" (James 5:16, bracketed words mine). This does not mean that you automatically get exactly what you prayed for; it means that God listens to the prayers of righteous people and promptly acts upon them. The answers to such prayers are still according to His discretion, but we cannot restrict (or doubt) the scope of His ability. "God works in mysterious ways," someone has said, and this is true. He does not have to disclose all mysteries to you, nor does He have to reveal all secrets to you. He just needs you to believe in Him. "The secret things belong to the LORD our God" (Deuteronomy 29:29). On the other hand, the psalmist wrote that "The secret of the LORD is for those who fear Him, And He will make them know His covenant" (Psalm 25:14).

"Our Father who is in heaven" is a sovereign God of unlimited power. When we pray to Him, whether the request is small or enormous, we should always come to Him with this in mind. Do not come to God then with pre-answered prayers. Who are we to restrain God, to challenge His will? Do not come to God with a few paltry options ("God, it must be this way, that way, or the other—these are the *only ones* that will work!"). Who are we to limit God's infinite resources?

Instead, as humble seekers of the sacred, we should accept the fact that God is able to exceed not only what you ask for but even what you think. His ways are higher than yours, and His thoughts are superior to yours (Isaiah 55:8-9). Therefore, His answers are better than yours—and mine. Personally, I am extremely glad that I can pray to a God who is wiser, stronger, greater, and more merciful than I am capable of being. I am comforted by the fact that our God is not a prisoner of my own circumstances but can actually *control* them. Furthermore, I am tremendously thankful that I can communicate with such an awesome God anytime I choose to, day or night, in times of trouble or prosperity.

It would be fitting to close this chapter with words far more eloquent than my own. I defer then to Paul, who wrote (Ephesians 3:20-21): "Now to Him who is able to do far more abundantly beyond all that we ask or think, according to the power that works within us, to Him be the glory in the church and in Christ Jesus to all generations forever and ever. Amen."

Amen indeed.

Endnotes

32   We *do*, however, see God listening to the prayers of the unconverted (Acts 10:1-4 is a classic example), but only because such people are *seeking* God in the first place. It is apparent that every person, in "calling upon the Lord" (Acts 2:21; Romans 10:13), offers prayers to God prior to his conversion experience.

33   Another person may be able to *read* that person's personality, moods, thinking processes, etc., but this is not something that is voluntarily offered up. Put another way: a person may indeed "communicate" more than he intended or thought possible through what he reveals in his talk, actions, behavior, etc., but since the intention is not for self-disclosure, this scenario belongs to another discussion.

34   In fact, God knows not only what you *want* Him to know (what you voluntarily share with Him), but He knows what you do *not* want Him to know (what you attempt to hide from Him).   He is able to discern even the secrets of the heart (Psalm 44:21; Luke 8:17; Romans 2:16).

35   "Both" in this verse refers to the two groups of whom Paul spoke: Jews and Gentiles (Ephesians 2:11ff.)

36   See Strong's Greek word reference #3875, *Thayer's Greek-English Lexicon of the New Testament* by Joseph H. Thayer (Grand Rapids: Baker Book House, 1977); see also "Comfort" in *Expository Dictionary of N.T. Words* by W. E. Vine (STBC, no date).

CHAPTER TWELVE

The Elephant in the Room

Hear, O Israel! The LORD is our God, the LORD is one! You shall love the LORD your God with all your heart and with all your soul and with all your might. These words, which I am commanding you today, shall be on your heart.
Deuteronomy 6:4-6

Years ago a commercial that illustrated the difficulty of confronting alcoholism made a powerful impression upon me. It portrayed a family that was trying desperately to go about its daily routine at home—watching television, sitting down for a meal, walking down the hallway—but was continually having to work around a literal elephant that was strolling through the house. No matter where this family went, the elephant was always there—in the way, pinning people against the wall, forcing an alternate route. This commercial would have been entirely humorous if indeed it did not represent a very serious and sad scenario.

This family having to maneuver around this huge creature in the middle of its home effectively portrayed the ridiculousness and pointlessness of trying to avoid a problem as huge and debilitating as alcoholism. If there is an alcoholic in their midst, family members can plant their heads in the sand if they want to but that doesn't make the problem go away. Such avoidance becomes nearly as difficult to endure as the problem itself: the one feeds the other. If the family would confront the reality of the situation, no matter how uncomfortable and painful this would be, the "elephant" would go away, one way or another.

The Real Source of Conflict

Having discussed a very ineffective and problematic means of dealing with alcoholism, I would like now to turn our attention to something even worse than alcoholism and more debilitating than *ignoring* the problem of alcoholism. I'm talking about something with which nearly every single person has to grapple at some time or another—or more accurately, what many people may not choose to identify at all. I'm talking also about that which entire families may tiptoe and dance around but are afraid to actually come out and say what needs to be said. I'm referring to that which will bring a person's life, a marriage, a household, or an entire congregation to its knees over time but which often goes undetected, undefined, or misdiagnosed as something else. I'm talking about, in a very appropriate analogy, the elephant in the spiritual living room, so to speak.

I'm talking about one's *improper love* for God.

Already someone is rolling his or her eyes thinking, "That? I don't have a problem with *love*. I have a problem with other things—motivation, self-control, or forgiveness—but not *love*." Such people don't always see the connection between one's love *for* God and their obedience *to* God. In God's sight, these two things are inseparable; in our sight, we might conveniently or unconsciously make them separate issues. We (think that we) succeed at one but fail at the other. The fact is: people who are blind to the problem fail at both.

Another person may say something like, "I cannot deal properly with my love for God because it involves other people, and I cannot control what other people do." This is a common refrain, especially among married people who allow their spouse to dictate the quality and/or quantity of their love for God. Such people assume that since there are limits on their relationship with their spouses, there must be a limit on their personal devotion to God: as the one, so the other. This is a huge miscalculation with devastating results, but many Christians think in this way nonetheless.

Still another person may bristle at the mere suggestion that their love for God is not what it ought to be. "Of *course* I love God!" he sputters.

"It's just my love for my wife or children or friends or fellow Christians that I struggle with." Sometimes this is turned around: "Of *course* I love my family and friends; it's just that I struggle with my love for God." In both scenarios, the person fails to realize that his love for God directly affects his love for his spouse, family, and brethren (and vice versa). In other words, one's love for *people* and one's love for the *Lord* are inextricably linked.[37]

At the root of every Christian's *external* failure to properly live up to the expectations of a child of God (in attitude or conduct) is an *internal* failure to properly love God. This is a bold statement, especially since it indicts virtually *all* of us in some way or another. It proposes that *all* of our sins are ultimately linked to our devotion to or worship of God in the first place. Even more inflammatory is the implication that all such failure to love God properly is not a result of our *inability* to love but our *unwillingness* to love. Reasons for this unwillingness may seem varied at first, but they always boil down to the one thing: we love *ourselves* more than we love God. Put another way: we refuse to seek the sacredness of God because we are more concerned with pursuing and protecting that which is sacred to us.

Are you still with me?

Different Kinds of Love

We have a hard time dealing realistically with the subject of love. This is in part because we do not want to admit that there is an elephant lumbering through the room, so to speak, and in part because our version of "love" does not always match up to the love that God wants us to have for Him. Someone says, "Well, I love my wife, or my mom, or my friend—so what's the problem?" The *problem* is that "our" love—really, the way in which we choose to love—is riddled and cluttered with *ourselves*. It often is fraught with self-interest, self-promotion, and self-indulgence. It often seeks personal profit, has self-determined expectations, and has self-imposed demands of reciprocation. We want to say that we love unconditionally— and maybe there are momentary instances in our lives when we actually do—but this is not typical.

This directly bears upon the subject of the sacred. As we do not "naturally" love unconditionally, so we are not "naturally" sacred people. Sacredness is not something that happens accidentally or automatically; likewise, we do not stumble into unconditional love. Human beings are selfish by nature; instinctively (if that is the right word), we are self-preserving, self-protecting, and self-serving. It is really God's divine influence—the stimulus of the sacred—that leads us out of our selfishness and into a more spiritual, less carnal way of thinking and living. Such people are (ideally) transformed by the internalization of God's love, such that we begin to love like *God*. This is, after all, supposed to be a supremely defining characteristic of Christians. As Jesus said (John 13:34-35), "A new commandment I give to you, that you love one another, even as I have loved you, that you also love one another. By this all men will know that you are My disciples, if you have love for one another."

Even those who are not Christians are influenced by God's love, either directly (by appreciating the fact that they are blessed by something or *Someone* other than blind luck or chance) or indirectly (through the influence of God's people). Indeed, God's children are supposed to be the "light of the world" and "salt of the earth" for this very purpose (Matthew 5:13-16). God's kindness and blessings are supposed to *lead* a person to repent of his worldliness and give himself to God (Romans 2:4). Regardless, God loves all people—the righteous and the wicked, Christians and their enemies— and showers that love upon all men (Matthew 5:43-45). His divine, heavenly influence then permeates the entire physical creation.

Despite the greatness and abundance of God's love, we seem to gravitate more easily to other kinds of love. The source of our "natural" love is from "below," that is, from the worldliness and selfish ambition which we have learned from Satan (cf. James 3:13-18). Satan teaches us how to sin and we sin. Satan teaches us how to lie and we lie—to ourselves, to each other, and to God. Satan teaches us how to love and we love in a devilish sort of way: we love in order to be loved, or we love in order to feel the gratification of loving, or we love as a means of self-preservation. The failure to love like *God* loves means that we end up loving like *we choose* to love, which is to say that we love like we have been taught by the world to love. Remember, "the whole world lies in the power of the evil one [Satan]" (1 John 5:19).

The failure to love like God also separates us from being identified with God. If by loving like Christ loves we are identified with Christ, then *refusing* to love like Christ loves alienates us *from* Christ. We will never know what it means to love like God loves unless we learn love from Him. We will never practice God's love on others unless we are transformed by His love for us. We are to be "imitators of God" (Ephesians 5:1) *first and foremost* in the way that we love.

Again, we (and I am part of the "we") have a great deal of subjective, prejudiced ideas when it comes to "love." This is not something we can talk about objectively at the onset; we first have to shave off all the self-imposed ideas that we have unconsciously attached to this subject. "Love" in our society has manifold meanings. It is often "whatever you want it to be." Love is often overused, abused, misunderstood, and misdiagnosed. Love in popular culture, including movies and songs, is much more often than not, self-serving, egotistical, shallow, and void of any real meaning. It is often a shallow, superficial infatuation or simply outright lust. Love in this context often means, "I want you to pay attention to me" or "I need your approval so I can feel better about myself" or even "I want to have sex with you."

Love can apparently even descend into the very depths of moral depravity. I remember reading some of the movie reviews of *Brokeback Mountain* (2006), the genre-bending, taboo-indulging, decency-shattering movie about two homosexual cowboys who sexually gratify themselves with each other throughout the course of their very worldly, sinful lives. Despite such cinematic dissipation, one *Newsweek* film critic wrote, "No American film before has portrayed love between two men as something this pure and sacred." Love, purity, and sacredness, according to this standard, obviously translate to homosexuality, sodomy, adultery, deception, lying, and a host of other satanic vices. Never have we as a society shown our ignorance of and complete disrespect *for* the sacred as when we flagrantly endorse immorality and deviancy as "love" (see Romans 1:18-28).

We love baseball, hotdogs, and apple pie. We also love God, our families, and our country. Sometimes the distinction between these two vastly different contexts of love is never adequately defined or clarified. Sometimes too love becomes so syrupy and sappy that no person worth his masculine salt, so to speak, will ever come close to affiliating himself to it. When God's love is reduced to a gushing Hallmark-card sentiment, we have to wonder: is *that* what God meant, or is that simply what we have *chosen to believe*? I'm not impugning every poetic expression of love here; however, Jesus' love for us was not a mere poetic nicety. Jesus' love led Him to say some very difficult rebukes (Matthew 23), compels Him to discipline His own followers (Revelation 3:19), and sent Him to the cross (John 3:16). There's nothing flowery or syrupy about any of these things.

Maybe this is also a difficult subject because we are just too proud to deal with it on a personal level. I mean it's one thing if we speak generally of people's love for God not being what it ought to be, but it's quite another thing for someone to question *my* love or *your* love for God. We simply do not want *our* love called into question; when this *is* done, it portrays us as frauds and hypocrites. Of course, it is possible that some of us *are* frauds and hypocrites! But much more likely we simply are not aware of some of the shortcomings of our relationship toward God. Or maybe we *are* conscious of our shortcomings and are thoroughly embarrassed by them. In other words, perhaps we are so embarrassed by our lack of love for the Lord that we do not want to deal openly with this lacking. Yet while trying to project a different, more positive impression upon others, we may be suddenly confronted with the fact that we cannot always hide such inadequacies any longer. Certainly we are unable to hide *anything* from God since "all things are open and laid bare" to Him (Hebrews 4:13).

Maybe we are simply embarrassed by the fact that we have to struggle with godly love at all. At first, such love may appear so easy to put into action: just be nice to people, don't kill anyone, forgive those who have done us wrong, and be a faithful churchgoer. However, if we have been trying to do even these "simple" things for any amount of time, we realize these are not really simple things at all. It is not easy to love as God loves. Practicing godly love is all-consuming: it consumes our time, our energies, and our lives. Such love is sacrificial: we must sacrifice our comforts, our prejudice, and our pride. In fact, which one of us could ever master that which Paul has so eloquently described (1 Corinthians 13:4-7)?

Love is patient; love is kind and is not jealous; love does not brag and is not arrogant, does not act unbecomingly; it does not seek its own, is not provoked, does not take into account a wrong suffered, does not rejoice in unrighteousness, but rejoices with the truth; bears all things, believes all things, hopes all things, endures all things.

Such love takes a lifetime to master, if we ever master it at all. Many of us struggle with this kind of love because we have rarely seen it shown to us by anyone except God Himself. We have few tangible examples of pure, wholesome, selfless love from which we can draw. This is especially true if we have been raised in a loveless home devoid of parental affection, warmth, or genuine acts of godliness. When our parents' "love" has so mangled or misrepresented God's holy love, it may take us years or even decades to finally learn what it means to love *like* God. Even among the spiritual family of believers, godly love may not necessarily be the norm but the exception. I don't mean to imply that we are purposely trying *not* to love, but the fact is that godly love is difficult, unnatural, and therefore (in its pure form) uncommon.

Regardless of our struggle with our love for Him, God's love for us is unquestionable and unconditional. "For God so loved the world, that He gave His only begotten Son, that whoever believes in Him shall not perish, but have eternal life" (John 3:16). This is one of the most well-known and profound statements in all of Scripture. In one sentence, God's entire Plan of Redemption is laid out and explained, Christ's ministry and sacrifice are put into context, and man's love for God is deserved and expected. And yet even though God has done so much for us, we struggle with doing even a fraction as much for Him. Jesus rebuked the Pharisees, for example, not because they tithed even small herbs with excruciating exactness, but because in doing so they *failed to accomplish the more important things.* "... For you pay tithe of mint and rue and every kind of garden herb," He told them, "and yet disregard justice *and the love of God*; but these are the things you should have done without neglecting the others" (Luke 11:42, emphasis mine). The Pharisees were, in a very real sense, professional ecclesiastics; even so, they did not love God properly. It is no wonder then when we also get some of the mechanical aspects of Christian living down pat but fail to imitate God's finest quality: *love.* In other words, this is not just a Jewish problem nor was it limited to the people of the first century. It is a *human* problem, and that means that all of us must strive to overcome this same oversight.

"God is love," the apostle John told us (1 John 4:8). We might think that this means that God is filled *with* love, or that He is quick to *show* love, or that love is kind of a default, reflexive action on His part. While all these things are true about God's love, John is not providing a mere attribute of God. Instead, he is describing God's essential nature: God IS love, which means that any thought, behavior, practice, or penchant that is not *of* godly love or not born *of* God's love *cannot be of God*. Put another way: "By this the children of God and the children of the devil are obvious: anyone who does not practice righteousness is not of God, nor the one who does not love his brother" (1 John 3:10). On the other hand, "the one who abides in love abides in God, and God abides in him" (1 John 4:16).

The Ugliness of the Failure to Love

I am constantly confronted with the everyday irreverence of those who have no fellowship with the Lord. It is difficult for me not to consciously think of the damage they inflict upon their souls every time they carry on as ungodly people. Such people are spiritually-unrefined; they do not acknowledge God's blessings; they do not speak of things of God or a love for Christ; they are oblivious to the meaning of "the word of the cross." I often find myself somewhat mesmerized by these people's insolence and imprudence. I am amazed (but not in a good way) with how saturated they have become with wickedness and demonism. Such people are unholy and profane: their language is filled with expletives and curses; they gossip, judge unfairly, and condemn without flinching; they indulge in vices and indiscretions; they mask spiritual emptiness and desperation with façades of bravery, arrogance, meanness, or self-pity. They are living ghosts of the visible world; they are dead even while they live (cf. 1 Timothy 5:6); they pursue sad and pathetic lives, with nothing to look forward to except hopelessness.

Such is the sad state of unconverted souls (as Paul also observed in Ephesians 4:17-19). It is easy for those of us who *do* have a relationship with the Lord to commend ourselves by comparison: we are not like *them*; we do not say what *they* say; we do not do what *they* do. Their lives are filled with the ugliness of sin and rebellion; *our* lives are not filled with such ugliness, since we are Christians, after all.

Not so fast, I quickly remind myself.

I am told by the Lord Jesus to love God with all my heart, soul, and mind (Matthew 22:37). To love God in this way is, of course, pleasing to Him; He is honored by my humble decision. However, how does He regard my *refusal* to love like He loves? What does my proud and deliberate *resistance* of His divine influence in my heart look like? Is my life still a "fragrant aroma" to Him (cf. Ephesians 5:2) when I purposely and callously *choose not to love Him* in the way that He deserves to be loved? How does that look—is it not an ugly, repulsive thing to Him? How does that smell—is it not like the stench of putrefying meat left out to rot in the summer sun?

It is easy to think that, because we are going through the motions of true believers, we are already far better than those lost, worldly souls I described a moment ago. If we are *sincere* in our pursuit of the sacred, we *are* in a far better position than those poor souls. (And if we are sincere, we will make great effort to share the gospel *with* those souls.) But if we refuse to love God like God loves us, what is commendable about that? If we refuse to love others like God loves them—even if they are our enemies (Luke 6:35-37)—what is praiseworthy in that? If we refuse to love *our own souls* as God loves Himself (in the sense that He ultimately serves His own best interest), what good is that? In fact, am I any better than those lost and forlorn souls who do not have a relationship with the Lord if I choose not to *love* like the Lord?

This is the question that needs to be asked, plain and simple: How can I genuinely and effectively be *seeking the sacred* if I resist the sacred love of Him who is the source of all goodness and holiness? A pursuit of the sacred without living according to the sacred love of God is like seeking good health and long life while drinking poison and injecting filth into my veins. What I *profess* and what I *do* are not only incompatible but are self-destructive.

Christians are not commanded only to love God, we are commanded *how* to love Him. When Jesus said, "A new commandment I give to you, that you love one another, even as I have loved you" (John 13:34), He told us *how* to love: *as He has loved us*. His love serves as the perfect portrayal of what our love should exemplify. Furthermore, I cannot impose my standard of love upon God, but must accept His standard of love for myself. It is not my place to tell God how I intend to love Him anymore than it is my place to tell Him how I plan to worship Him. The fact is *my* love—my self-defined, self-determined, self-imposed love—is *not good enough* to be given to the Lord, no matter how well-intentioned I may think it to be.

Furthermore, I am to love others—*especially* fellow believers—as God loves, not as I choose to love. The apostle John taught that "everyone who hates his brother is a murderer" (1 John 3:15). We might easily exonerate ourselves of this crime by saying, "But I don't hate my brother—I *love* the children of God!" By implication, John goes on to say that anyone who *refuses to love his brother like Christ loves him* "hates" his brother. Put another way: anyone who purposely, spitefully, or negligently *withholds love from his brother* also "hates" his brother. To "hate" in this context then means to withhold godly love from someone, even from God Himself. John later says bluntly, "If someone says, 'I love God,' and hates [withholds love from— MY WORDS] his brother, he is a liar; for the one who does not love his brother whom he has seen, cannot love God whom he has not seen" (1 John 4:20).

What a horrible thing to realize that God's own people can be infected with the ugliness of sin with regard to that which seems so good and wholesome in itself: *love*. What an awful admission to make that among God's own people are murderers and liars due to the very fact that they refuse to love like the One who made them God's people in the first place!

The Link between Sin and the Failure to Love

Not all sin is defined by doing *wrong* things. Sin is *also* refusing to do *right things* (James 4:17) and especially refusing to do what Christ has commanded. When Jesus said, "love one another, even as I have loved you" (John 13:34), He wasn't just gushing with pious, religious sentiment. He was telling us, "I expect *you* to love like *I* love; in the case of your refusal to do so, you *cannot be My disciple*."

Though the external sin is certainly wrong, it is not an isolated problem; the real *source* of the problem is what goes on in the heart. A person is spiritually dysfunctional when he tries to improve his life only by quitting bad behaviors and addictions. By doing only this, he neglects the fact that his heart *does not yet love God as He is to be loved.* It is *this*—first and foremost—that leads to all other sins and wicked behaviors. With this in mind, we might reconsider every external sin—uncontrolled anger, sexual impurity, malice, lying, addictions, etc.—to be a manifestation of one's internal failure to love God as He is to be loved. When one learns *what* love is, *why* he is to love in this way, and then *how* he is to love, he will certainly master the rest of his life as well. Certainly he will not be able to control everything that happens *to* him—no one can—but he will be in full control of how he *responds* to whatever happens to him. This is possible because it is truly Christ who lives in and controls his heart (cf. Galatians 2:20).

Unfortunately, we often fail to make this connection. We tend to focus only on external behavior, trying to correct this as best as we can. We are not inclined to examine the nature of our heart and especially the quality or substance of our love for the Lord. Thus, when we have tried and tried to be seekers of the sacred through our own self-determined means (i.e., trying to "fix" whatever we can through our own human effort), we turn to finding other things, circumstances, or people to blame. "This can't be something *I* am responsible for," we reason, "since I have done everything in *my* power to resolve this conflict." We say this, but the truth may be that we have not honestly examined our love. We may assume that since we love at all, therefore our love is sufficient. The problem must be elsewhere.

Even when we *do* blame ourselves, we may misdiagnose the problem. For example, we may say, "I love God very much—I just have some 'anger issues' (or something like that)." In this way, we fail to realize that our "anger issues" are directly related to our (lack of) love for God; we have conveniently and subjectively separated and compartmentalized the two things. After all, "anger issues" stem from a lack of self-control; the lack of self-control (ultimately) manifests a lack of trust in God's control; lack of trust is a lack of faith; lack of faith always implies a lack of love. Thus, what we have diagnosed as an "anger issue" or something similar really turns out to be a *lack-of-love issue.*

Anytime we are dealing with the nature of God, we are dealing with moral issues. Since "God is love"—*love* is who *He* is—therefore our love for God is as much a moral issue as honesty, sincerity, sexual purity, or the respect for human life. The *failure* to love God thus represents a moral weakness on our part. We don't like to regard it in this way (I certainly don't!), but this is truly what it is. This particular moral weakness, however, breeds other moral weaknesses and also allows other such weaknesses to continue unabated. Even if we succeed in crushing the life out of one particular moral weakness—say, lying or swearing—we still have not dealt with "the" moral weakness that spawned it. Like a weed's root system that will simply not go away just because you pulled off the top of one of its plants, so this problem will reappear in a different form, in a different place, at a different time.

Once again, we naturally seem to recoil from admitting that it is our *love* that is the problem. A person may finally confess that he (or she) has a drinking problem, a penchant for pornography, or a streak of bitterness since these are very *human* problems. Such deficiencies and shortcomings are common to the sinful condition of man; to admit them simply admits that we are, despite becoming Christians, still human. However, to confess "I have a weakness in my love for God" is not something that *Christians* should ever do (or so we reason). It's one thing to realize we are still fighting against worldly habits; it is a far more serious matter to admit that the world may still have a controlling interest in our *hearts*. This contradicts our very identity *as* Christians and calls into question our integrity to God—and to ourselves.

The Link between Grace and Love

We cannot treat our love for God as a peripheral concern. Without a proper love for God, everything else falters, reeks, implodes, and *fails*. One's spiritual life may look good on the surface (just like a good layer of frosting on a cake or a nice paint job on a car), but what is underneath may be spoiled or corroded with rust. That person cannot reduce his improper love for God as an "incidental problem"—one which he will address when he gets around to it—but he must recognize that resolving *this* problem will resolve a multitude of other problems.

As far as Jesus is concerned, one's love for God is a fundamental, core-of-discipleship issue. In John 5:39-43, for example, notice Jesus' emphasis to the Jews, and consider its application to Christians. In essence, He said, "You study your Bible, thinking that by doing so you will be saved. Yet your unwillingness to *give Me your love* ('come to Me') will be your undoing. I'm not concerned with *your* perception of reality, or what others think of you; I am most concerned with *where your heart is*." These Jews had religion, they had a craving after spiritual things (Romans 10:2-3), they had an elaborate temple with which to conduct their elaborate sacrifices, but they did not have a love of God within themselves. Religion, zeal, self-righteousness, and all kinds of sacrifices do not by themselves constitute *love*. These things cannot *replace* genuine love for God; there *is* no substitute for love. You either love God or you don't. Without love, you cannot be Jesus' disciple. Without love, any other expression of religion, worship, sacrifice, or piety is empty, useless, and worthless.

The Jewish religious system was not destroyed only because the Jews themselves failed to honor God's covenant. Jesus did not call His people an "evil and adulterous generation" (Matthew 16:4) only because they were steeped in pride and self-indulgence. Jerusalem was not leveled to the ground in judgment (cf. Luke 19:41-44, fulfilled in AD 70) only because the Jews conspired to crucify their Messiah. No, the ultimate reason for the demise of the Jews and their nation was that they failed to love God with all their heart, soul, and mind (compare Deuteronomy 6:4-5 with John 8:42, for example). Their *failure to love* resulted in all other failures; their resistance of *God's love* prevented them from seeing Jesus for who He really was.

As it happened then, so it happens today. A person will not be lost only because he has not become a Christian. A Christian will not forfeit his spiritual inheritance only because he fails to comply with the covenant (gospel) that he once promised to uphold. He will not be severed from Christ and fall from grace (cf. Galatians 5:4) only because he sought to justify himself rather than be justified by God. He will not be forever separated from the community of believers only because he refused to assemble with his brethren and participate in the work of the kingdom. No, the ultimate reason for his—or anyone else's—final demise will be this: he failed to love

God as He was to be loved. His failure to love leads to all other failures; his rejection of God's love prevented him from loving Christ and his fellow man.

Let's illustrate this in another way. In the world of chess, for example, when a player makes a serious error early in the game, he will spend the rest of his time either trying to compensate for that mistake or he dies a slow and inglorious death as his opponent exploits that error to his own advantage. Of course, chess is just a game, and even though a player makes a serious mistake, his opponent is also able to make his own serious mistake, such that there is not an absolute conclusion to the matter until checkmate is actually achieved.

The spiritual realm is like this chess game except that the outcome is absolutely predictable, assuming a certain mistake is made and never corrected. If a person fails to love God—really, if he fails to love like God loves—then he will spend the rest of his life trying to compensate for that failure even though he might be oblivious to the error itself. He will never be successful at this, of course, because the error (sin) is fatal to his soul. Satan will continue to play against him, and Satan is a master strategist: left to ourselves, we are no match for him. He is a grandmaster; we are novice chess players. Either way, Satan knows that our failure to love God will be our undoing. He knows that nothing else we do will ever compensate for that deficiency. He also knows that he will be able to outmaneuver us until the very end.

God also knows this, but He is able to do something that supersedes the confines of the game: He is able to *correct our mistakes* and give us an opportunity to make right decisions from this point forward. Satan wants us to believe that there is no hope once the fatal error is committed; God wants us to know that *He is able to overcome fatal errors.* This generous action of God's is called *grace* and is more powerful than all the scheming and manipulation Satan can muster. In the chess game analogy, God actually stops the game, rearranges the pieces to our advantage, and then allows the play to continue. Satan cannot stop Him because God's power and authority are infinitely greater than Satan's.

Grace describes God's activity in the life of the believer through the work of the Holy Spirit, but this is made possible only because of Christ's work and intercession. Jesus Christ is, in essence, the personification of God's grace. Appropriately, Christ reigns upon the "throne of grace"; He is our "help in time of need" (Hebrews 4:14-16); it is He to whom we bring all our troubles and failings. He is patient and willing to transform us as long as we give to Him our obedient faith (Ephesians 2:8-9). Because of His grace and our faith, we are drawn into a deeper, more intimate relationship with God.

I want you to see the great paradox going on here. First of all, if we give our love to God—the very best love we are able to give—then God's grace will forgive us of whatever ways we have *failed* to love. This is not license to love God less than we ought; it simply acknowledges the fact that we often fall short in our efforts to imitate Him (Romans 3:23). Since we love Him, we put our faith in Him; since we put our faith in Him, He saves us by grace. Our imperfect love coupled with God's abundant grace actually bring us to the mature person that God expects us to be (cf. Ephesians 4:13). (If the reader would like to read more about the subject of "grace" please refer to my book, *The Gospel of Grace*, Louisville: Religious Supply, 2008.)

For this reason, when God's grace is active in our lives, then "love is perfected with us." Furthermore, "There is no fear in love; but perfect love casts out fear, because fear involves punishment, and the one who fears is not perfected in love" (1 John 4:17-18). We do not have to fear judgment, punishment, or Satan's overwhelming stratagems if indeed we have made God the highest object of our finest love. The more we experience God's love through His grace, the greater our love for Him is, and thus our love becomes more and more like His love.

Of course, we will continue to make mistakes—fatal errors in the game, so to speak—but we are allowed to call upon God's grace as often as is necessary, as long as we continue to *believe* in His grace. And each and every time God will pause the game, rearrange the pieces, and then allow play to continue. In the end, we will actually defeat our opponent (Satan and his lies), *not* because we are such great players but because the grace of God saves us from all our inadequacies and failures.

How Real Is Your Love?

In order for us to deal rightly with our fellowship with God, we first have to be serious about what fellowship requires. We have to be real about who God is and who we are. In doing so, we have to give Him real faith, since we expect from Him real grace. We cannot look outside of ourselves for the real source of interference in our pursuit of the sacred. Outside interferences most certainly will exist, but these cannot (by themselves) defeat us.

What I mean is this: our spiritual success or failure is really not determined by those things which are outside of our control. God measures our faith not by the number of obstacles we face, but by the presence and quality of godly love that fills our heart. We cannot measure our Christianity, so to speak, by what others do to us (or fail to do *for* us), our circumstances, our crutches, alleged personality defects (however we choose to define them), or anything else. No one is prevented from loving the Lord with all his heart, soul, and mind; no one can stop us from loving Christ with such scope and intensity; there is "no law" (boundary or legal restraint) against love (Galatians 5:22-23). Thus, we need to deal with the core of our relationship with Him. We need to ask ourselves, privately and honestly: How much do I love my Lord Jesus Christ? What is He truly worth to me—what am I worth to Him? How far am I willing to go to demonstrate my love to Him? What is *preventing* me from loving Him with all my heart?

We know that no person, earthly hindrance, natural phenomenon— not even death itself—can sever us from God's love for us (Romans 8:35-39). But what about our love for God? What will we *allow* to separate ourselves from Him by letting that person, thing, or circumstance interfere with or compromise our love for Him? All other loves boil down to self-serving masquerades of "how to enjoy life on my terms" or "how to get others to meet my expectations" or "how to have my cake and eat it too." These are all various forms of self-delusion and manipulation (control) of others for our own gain or advancement. For any of us who might be playing "Christian," we must get serious about who we are, what we are doing, and what is expected of us. Failing to love the Lord leads to the ruin of our soul. This must never be an acceptable alternative to seeking the sacred.

We must also not be afraid of what the Light of God exposes as we determine to love God completely and uninhibitedly. Consider Peter, the impetuous, firebrand disciple who pledged to die with Jesus if necessary. His love for the Lord was unquestioned: he most certainly *did* love Him. However, his was not yet the *quality* or *depth* of love that was necessary in order for him to continue on in his relationship with his Master. Christ first had to expose some of Peter's weaknesses in order for Peter to learn this. Thus, Jesus told him that he would deny Him three times and that Satan demanded to sift him like wheat (Luke 22:31-34). Think of the impact that must have made upon Peter! Here he thought his love for the Lord was so strong that he could defy the entire Jewish Council, the Roman army, and death itself! The fact is Peter later fell to pieces at the casual interrogation of a *servant girl* (Mark 14:66-72).

After His resurrection, the Lord confronted Peter concerning this. Notice that Jesus did not ask, "Peter, will you ever deny Me again?" or say, "Peter, you're not yet strong enough to face another confrontation like before." Instead, He asked, "Simon, son of John, do you love Me?" What a powerful thing to ask!

This is the question we need to ask ourselves: "Do I love Him?" We cannot merely ask, "Am I a faithful churchgoer?" or "How often do I say my prayers?" or "How many wicked habits do I abstain from?" We must get right to the heart of the matter: *our love for Him.* If we do not love Him as He is to be loved, then nothing else we claim really matters.

You will not like such intense self-examination, but this must be done if you are going to be a seeker of the sacred. Whatever hinders your love for God must be identified and then removed. This is not a painless process. It is likened to being pruned (John 15:1-6), cutting off your right hand, or gouging out your right eye (Matthew 5:29-30). What He reveals to you in the process may not only be uncomfortable but very disturbing. You may find out things about yourself that you did not want to know—possibly things that you did not know even existed. Nonetheless, such examination separates those who truly *belong* to Christ from those who *think* they belong to Him but have allowed themselves to be deluded by Satan. As Jesus said (John 3:20-21),

> For everyone who does evil hates the Light, and does not
> come to the Light for fear that his deeds will be exposed.
> But he who practices the truth comes to the Light, so that
> his deeds may be manifested as having been wrought in
> God.

Our refusal of the Light's examination (and purification) of our souls equates to a refusal of Christ Himself, since He *is* the Light (John 8:12).

This is what you must do to initiate this examination process: First, you must pray sincerely and specifically to *allow God to examine your heart* and expose whatever is there that needs to be removed. (Likely you already are familiar with some of these things, but He will undoubtedly reveal more than you presently know.) Do not pray the standard requests (e.g., "Please let me draw closer to You") or the vague, cliché prayer ("Help me to apply these things to my life"). Pray to Christ that you *earnestly desire* for Him to fill your heart so that you may enjoy intimate fellowship with Him *and* so that you may better serve as His disciple. Also, confess to Him that, in order for this to happen, you will strive to love Him as He has loved you (John 13:34-35). Thus, *whatever you have allowed to prevent your love for Him to flourish, whatever you have put ahead of your love for Him,* ask Him to reveal this to you and help you to remove this obstacle from your life.

Having prayed that kind of prayer, you need to do *your* part in fulfilling it. You must do what you are *able* to do to remove stumbling blocks from your heart. The grace of God will do whatever you are *unable* to do, but He will not do what you are *unwilling* to do. Whenever you pray for God's help, recognize that God does not help those who put little or no effort toward their own salvation. You cannot save yourself no matter how hard you try; this is why you need grace. On the other hand, God cannot save you without your *faith* (John 3:36; Hebrews 11:1-2, 6). God tells you what your faith ought to *look* like, but it is your responsibility to *express* that faith in obedience. Otherwise, all you have is a "dead" faith (James 2:26).

Next, you need to stop trying to reform your spiritual life from the outside-in (if indeed you have been doing this). True spiritual transformation must begin in the heart since this is where your love for Christ is (1 Peter

3:15, "Sanctify Christ as Lord in your hearts..."). Stop saying things like, "If I stop doing this [sinful behavior]—or if I start this [godly behavior]—then my love for God will improve." The truth is, *no, it will not*. The apostle Paul told us that his great service to God, country, and his fellow man would be rendered null and void if he did not have love (1 Corinthians 13:1-3). Doing good works (or quitting bad habits) is *no replacement* for your unconditional love for God. These are necessary, of course (1 Thessalonians 5:21-22), but these are not good enough *by themselves.*

It is common for preachers and churches to try to transform Christians by focusing first (if not only) on their external behavior: "Do this! Don't do that! Stop this! Start that!" This misrepresents the gospel of Christ and sounds like those man-made impositions Paul warned Christians to avoid in the first century: "Do not handle, do not taste, do not touch!" Such restrictions were meant to *replace* the righteousness that comes through Christ, not to comply *with* that righteousness. No wonder he says, "These are matters which have, to be sure, the appearance of wisdom in self-made religion," but have nothing to do with the real substance of a relationship with Christ (Colossians 2:21-23). Think about it: if your car's engine has died, then repainting the car or reupholstering its interior is not going to make it run any better. First things first: you must fix the engine. Our love for Christ is the engine that drives all other loves and our everyday behaviors. Our love for Christ either *prohibits* what we do or *conditions* what we do. Our life on earth must be directly influenced by our love for Him. It should never be the other way around!

Finally (for our short list, anyway), you must follow the Master. He is the One whom you love, after all; He must be the One whose presence and will dominates your life. Jesus has invited us to come to Him (Matthew 11:28-30) since He has much to teach us and we have much to learn from Him. He has also told us that there is no other way to be His disciple than to follow Him (Matthew 16:24). Following any other "master," any other impulse of the heart, or any other love is not going to bring you any closer to the Father.

The Best Decision You Can Make

When an alcoholic is in the home, the entire family suffers. While the individual family members may be able to excel in their own ways, nonetheless the alcoholic will put an undue strain upon their personal lives, the family relationship, and their ability to contribute beyond themselves (to church, community, country, etc.). Ignoring this scenario, or pretending that it does not exist, only makes this suffering worse: there can be no resolution for those who refuse to acknowledge the problem in the first place. Getting the problem solved, however—even after it is confronted— is often a very painful and traumatic experience; yet it is in the best interest of all parties involved to do this. The alternative is simply unacceptable.

Now imagine a congregation of Christians who profess to be seekers of the sacred. They have all the right trappings of a healthy group: Bible classes, thought-provoking sermons, a commitment to conducting themselves in decency and order (cf. 1 Corinthians 14:40), etc. It's just that they have not given their hearts fully to the Lord: they do not *love* the Lord in the way that He has asked them to love Him. It is not as though they do not love the Lord at all but that they have allowed other loves and other passions to interfere with their devotion to Christ.

Are these people truly seeking the sacred? Are they sincerely devoted to "drawing near" to God in holiness? Or is there an elephant walking up and down the aisle of the church building every Sunday, awkwardly bumping into people, crashing into pews, and sideswiping lecterns while everyone pretends not to notice? If so, would you call this group a functional church? What would Christ say of this group—especially once they were informed of their problem but continued to live in denial? Will their "lampstand" remain, or will it be removed (cf. Revelation 2:1-5, "But I have this against you, that you have left your first love")?

Admittedly, practicing Christ-like love is demanding and sacrificial. It often goes unappreciated by others, makes us vulnerable to others' abuses, and is not always immediately satisfying. However, if we want to live life to the fullest, we must learn to love God to the fullest. If we wish to seek the sacred, we must fully commit ourselves *to* the sacred. If we desire to live *with* the Lord, then we must learn to love *like* the Lord. This means we cannot be searching for ways to cut corners, skip steps, or allow stumbling blocks to clutter our paths. On the other hand, this is the most realistic, positive, and dynamic way to live. Jesus said, "...you will know the truth, and the truth will make you free" (John 8:32). Certainly the cost of freedom is great, but the failure to accept this cost is infinitely greater.

Someday, when this life is over and you are standing there in absolute awe as you behold the presence of God *face to face*, your heart completely filled with joy, your life completely void of sorrow, pain, doubt, or fear, you will realize then just how important it was to have made the decision to love God with all your heart, soul, and mind. You will have no remorse; you will not look back upon whatever you had to sacrifice with any sort of regret. You will realize then that *this was the best decision you ever made*, and that now—as you enter into an eternity of glory and peace—there was no decision more important than this one.

Someday you will no longer need to walk by faith (2 Corinthians 5:7), and you will no longer need God's grace to complete you. Someday you will *be* complete, and you will worship God in fact, not in faith. For now, we love God without having seen Him (1 Peter 1:8). Likewise, we worship in faith; we hope for redemption; we desperately need grace, mercy, patience, perseverance, and all the other things that *anticipate* a life with God in His heaven. But "the greatest of these is love" (1 Corinthians 13:13) because love is an eternal constant, an enduring quality of God's covenant with His greatest creation, that which transcends this life and flows without measure into the life to come.

"God is love," and someday you will not only be able to enjoy God's *love* forever, you will be able to *see* Love.

Endnotes

37   I am deeply indebted to Dr. Larry Crabb for helping to open my own eyes to this subject, and I highly recommend two of his books: *Inside Out* (NavPress, 1988) and *Finding God* (Zondervan Publishing, 1993).

CHAPTER THIRTEEN

Grappling with Heaven

Do not let your heart be troubled; believe in God, believe also in Me. In My Father's house are many dwelling places; if it were not so, I would have told you; for I go to prepare a place for you. If I go and prepare a place for you, I will come again and receive you to Myself, that where I am, there you may be also.
John 14:1-3

A discussion concerning "seeking the sacred" would definitely be incomplete without talking about *heaven*. Surely heaven is the epitome of man's existence; being *in* heaven is the ultimate goal of every genuine believer. The anticipation of living amidst a throng of angels, the joy of beholding Christ, and dwelling in the presence of God is almost *too wonderful* to even contemplate. As surrealistic as this dream of delight may sound, Christ has promised this future for those who are seekers of the sacred. Such people will obtain "an inheritance which is imperishable and undefiled and will not fade away, reserved in heaven for you, who are protected by the power of God through faith for a salvation ready to be revealed in the last time" (1 Peter 1:4-5). This is a very powerful and impressive promise indeed!

Despite this, not all Christians seem impressed. Some talk of heaven as though it were mere fantasy; others believe heaven exists, but they do not believe that *they* will ever be there. When I speak enthusiastically about heaven, some respond with, "Yes, I'm looking forward to that too," but it comes out wooden and unconvincing, like they just read it from a teleprompter. Or they will simply look at me with the classic "guppy look"—that glazed, detached, glassy wide-eyed stare that churchgoers give to preachers when the sermon is simply making no connection with them. At best, I might get a soft, non-committal sort of "Hmmm."

Maybe these people were just distracted with something else, I tell myself. Maybe they really do not understand that it is okay to *experience great joy* over the anticipation of being immersed in glory and unfathomable expressions of love! Maybe, in some forgotten memory, I also have responded with indifference—or fear—to someone else who spoke of such supernal delight, and he too walked away wondering, "What is his *problem?*"

Well, what *is* our problem when we refuse to be excited about a future life that is so breathtakingly wonderful that it cannot even be described in human terms? Is the sacred home of God really so bland or uninspiring that we are uninterested in talking about it? Is basking in the sacred presence of God not enough to elicit our most profound responses? Is the thought of experiencing an eternal embrace in the sacred arms of the Savior not enough to cause our eyes to sparkle and our hearts to tremble with wordless rhapsody?

The subject of God's sacred heaven is ironically one of the pressure points of why a person resists *seeking* the sacred. Some will not pursue seeking the sacred simply because deep inside they are grappling with heaven. This is a bizarre conundrum, one that I've been thinking about for some time. My analysis of the situation is hardly comprehensive or universally-applied, but I have noticed some common patterns concerning how human nature struggles with the spiritual realm. Even if you personally are not one of those who *are* grappling with heaven, I think you will find this discussion intriguing all the same.

Struggling with the Reality of Heaven

Let's begin with the most obvious difficulty people have with all "spiritual" subjects: the inability to put our finger on intangible and invisible things. This play on words is intentional: we are humanly if not consciously disconnected from the invisible world. We know heaven *exists*, but we have a hard time *identifying* with anything we cannot see and touch. For example, if your dream vacation is to visit the Bahamas, you can obtain brochures and search websites about this place. You can look at pictures of its resorts, even talk to people who have visited them. In other words, the Bahamas is a place that can be researched and "seen" before going there; but the Bahamas is not heaven—not even close. Heaven is infinitely *better* than the Bahamas, and yet there are no brochures to peruse or websites to visit to learn more about it. The Bahamas may be a sacred spot for some people, but heaven is *God's* sacred home: there is nothing on earth with which to even compare it. This makes our grasp of heaven all the more difficult; this complicates our seeking after the sacred.

Furthermore, we are asked by Jesus—Someone whom we have never personally met—to give up what appears to be the security of this world and *believe that He will take care of us.* We are asked to abandon our trust in everything that we *do* see, hear, and touch, and put our trust in a future which we cannot see, hear, or touch. We are asked to sacrifice whatever is sacred to us here on earth for a sacred home with God in an existence that defies human comprehension.

In all fairness and honesty, this is a lot to ask.

Jesus knows this, of course, which is why He places such a high value on *faith.* "The righteous man" does not live by God's full disclosure of the sacred; neither does he live by crossing his fingers and hoping he will end up in heaven. Instead, "the righteous man shall live by faith" (Romans 1:17). Our entire walk with Christ on this earth is by faith, not by knowing everything there is to know of Christ's world (cf. 2 Corinthians 5:7). We are not talking here about "blind faith" which is nothing more than pure fantasy, but that which is based upon divinely-revealed evidence, empirical observation, and historical facts. We are not merely asked to believe in God, but are given a convincing *reason* to believe. Likewise, Jesus has given *us* every reason to believe in the invisible world of the sacred, and we have no good reason to doubt Him. While it is human nature to expect tangible proof of heaven, the fact is that we already have sufficient proof in the person of Christ. We are not asked to believe in heaven without any evidence of it; on the contrary, we are *compelled* to believe in heaven because of the reality of who Christ *is* and what He has *accomplished.* Faith in Christ should necessarily lead one to believe in His heaven.

To further increase our faith, Jesus described the heavenly world in language we can understand. He painted the realm of the sacred with shapes and metaphors that keep it from sounding so alien or mysterious. He said, "The kingdom of heaven is *like* . . ." or "To what shall I *compare* the kingdom of heaven?"[38] In His revelation to John, Jesus gave us a view of heaven as a crystal city resting on a twelve-layer foundation of the most precious materials on earth, its gates made of enormous, priceless pearls (Revelation 21:9-21). He showed John streets of gold, rivers of living water, and a crystal sea in front of the throne of Almighty God Himself (Revelation 22:1-2). These are not actual descriptions of literal objects, but they certainly tell of an existence more wonderful than anything we have known on earth.

Even so, the revealed information is relatively scarce. This prompts someone to ask: If God *really* wanted to whet our appetite for a future in His celestial palace, why didn't He provide more specific details? Likewise, if Jesus wanted to convince us of the wonder of heaven, why didn't He talk more about it? Without more facts about where we are going, some find it difficult to justify the kind of sacrifices Jesus requires of us to get there. In the absence of more information, many have chosen to believe that heaven cannot be anything more than a glorified earth. Of course there will be rainbows, unblemished scenery, excellent food, and the finest music; but, in essence, heaven will be a mere collection of everything good and enjoyable here on earth. One popular end-of-time doctrine teaches that "heaven" really *is* a rejuvenated earth, and that only select people (144,000 of them) will get to live with God. A "heavenly" earth is still better than what we have now—or so it is argued.

Yet there is still that nagging disappointment that we cannot see heaven's glory *first* or experience its beauty if even for a *moment*. Would it be too much trouble for God to provide everyone with a sneak preview of where He wants us to be? Jesus spoke of "dwelling places" there (John 14:1-3); why can't we see them? The apostle Paul was given a glimpse of Paradise (2 Corinthians 12:2-4); why can't we at least see what he saw?

Are *you* disappointed? Are these things *necessary* in order to be a seeker of the sacred?

Now the other side of the picture: While we may fantasize about what we expect to find in heaven, we also dream about what we do *not* expect to find there. Once again, heaven is depicted as a glorified earth but not an entirely different experience than what we know *on* earth. For example, some say heaven will be wonderful because there will be no: pollution, traffic, skylines marred by power lines, diseases or sickness, ugly people, having to go to work, pay bills, or taxes, and so forth. While I believe all this is essentially true about heaven, this fails to convey the joy of what it must be like in Paradise. It is belittling to the sacred realm of God to describe it in this way. For example, one individual, after cleaning up a messy bathroom at the church building, exclaimed seriously but irritably, "In heaven, we won't have people missing the garbage can when they throw away their paper towels!" What an inspiring reason to look forward to the afterlife!

Is this how you measure the sacred realm—by what is *not* there, by what is *missing?*

Of course, by comparing the sacred realm with our physical world imposes an earthly limitation upon a spiritual existence. If our view of heaven is limited to this earth and its perspectives, it is likely because our view of God is limited to the same. God is not God just because He is better than us nor because He does not share our faults; He is God *regardless* of us and is therefore not *comparable* to us. Likewise, heaven is not heaven just because it is better than our present world nor because it does not share our world's shortcomings; it is heaven *regardless* of our world and is therefore not comparable to it. If our view of God is limited (I'm not talking about what we cannot *know* but what we choose not to *explore*), then so is our view of a future with God. Having such a limited view severely diminishes our anticipation of the sacred. In other words, if we view the sacred as being only slightly better than our world, we will not be compelled to *give up* this world in order to seek it.

Now if you *want* to wax philosophically about streets of gold and mansions just over the hilltop, that's fine by me. If this helps to whet your appetite for the eternity to come, then so be it. In my imagination, I relish these same thoughts. For example, I have imagined that in heaven we will all be children—not immature humans but *perfect* humans who have regained forever child-like innocence and will never lose it again. We will have all the energy of perfectly healthy children but more power and wisdom than all of the angels. I picture us being cared for as the most special of all God's creation, for in fact we will be the only remnant *of* God's physical creation. We will no longer be male or female or requiring physical needs. We will not be mere survivors but spiritual immortals; we will reign as victors and conquerors with Christ. We will still enjoy life as *children*—not just "life" like we know here but life as it was *meant* to be known. Everything we do will have the thrill of having experienced it for the first time. We will embrace the fullness of life as *Christ* now enjoys it but without the curse of sin and the burden of human frailty. We will not measure time and therefore will never age in years nor will we ever succumb to the infirmity or cynicism of old age. Instead, we will enjoy—no, we will be continually *enthralled* with— "He who is the blessed and only Sovereign, the King of kings and Lord of lords, who alone possesses immortality and dwells in unapproachable light, whom no [mortal] man has seen or can see" (1 Timothy 6:15-16). It is not as though Christ will be literally standing by watching us while we soak up all the energy that heaven provides, but He will be everywhere and in everyone. Christ will be our breath, our sunlight, our joy, and the essence of our fellowship. He will be *everything* that we experience. We will be swallowed up in life, immersed in light, filled with joy and comfort, basking in the warmth of the Father's infinite love....

As good as this seems, it is merely the product of my imagination. I think it is true *in essence,* but the literal truth is beyond my ability to grasp. This is "heaven" as I envision it—or at least one version of it; in a sense it is "a" heaven. Regardless, what makes heaven special is not "what" is there but *Who* is there: God the Father, God the Son, and God the Spirit. In the end, it really is of no concern to me what I will look like in heaven, what I do there, or what I will see. In the end, if the Source of all that is sacred is there, then that will be far more heaven than I could possibly ever imagine.

This perspective is the key to a deeper, purer understanding of heaven itself. It is not the mere home or company of God that we seek but His *fellowship*. The dynamics of fellowship do not only place people in the same *context* but actually *bind* them together. All the scenery, streets of gold, mansions, and rainbows are very nice, to be sure, but these are nothing without the inexpressibly wonderful fellowship with God that begins *right here on earth*. The greatest joys of human existence have never been dependent upon scenery and special props; rather, they are found in the intimacy of kindred spirits. Consider the watching-the-sunset-alone situation: you can enjoy a gorgeous, breath-taking sunset all by yourself, but you can enjoy it *intensely* if standing beside someone whom you love deeply and who loves you deeply. The sunset doesn't have to change but the relationship factor changes everything. In heaven, we will not merely be in *proximity* to God; we will be *in* God and He will be *in us*.

One's intimate, spiritual fellowship with Christ is what brings heaven to life. Take away your fellowship with Christ and your hope of heaven evaporates. Such fellowship cannot be replaced by streets of gold, harp-playing angels, and mansions just over the hilltop. Without the One whom we love deeply and who loves us infinitely, heaven (for us) ceases to exist altogether. Without Christ, there can be no beauty, no contentment, and no joy. Our souls would languish in misery and despair, loathing our very existence, filled with unspeakable pain, shattered with irreparable ruin. Without the Light of God, we would live in absolute blackness, waiting forever to die but living indefinitely without meaning or purpose. That is not heaven but is *hell*.

Christ is not just *in* "the heavenly places" (Ephesians 1:20); He *is* heaven. He is not *in* the sacred realm; He *is* the Sacred. We will not "go to heaven" as though going to another country; we will come to Christ. He will be forever the object of our existence and adoration. Paul himself never described heaven as a city of gold but always focused on *Who is there*. He understood that when we leave this body and this earth, we will "be at home with the Lord" (2 Corinthians 5:8). He wrote, "[I have] the desire to depart and be with Christ, for that is very much better [than remaining on this earth]"; and yet, "we who are alive [at Christ's coming] and remain will be caught up together with them in the clouds to meet the Lord in the air, and so we shall always be with the Lord" (Philippians 1:23; 1 Thessalonians 4:17, bracketed words mine).

Think about that idea: "we shall always be *with the Lord*." It will not matter when or where that will be or what else or who else will be there; only that the Lord is there. That fact alone is sufficient for a lifetime of seeking the sacred. Is that sufficient for you?

Struggling with Completion

This next discussion may not be as obvious and familiar as the preceding one. In fact, it is somewhat of a paradox within a paradox: we struggle with seeking the sacred because we are incomplete people, yet it is our incomprehension of the *concept* of completeness that keeps us from striving *toward* the sacred. Put another way: since being a "complete" person is only a theoretical premise and not an earthly reality, we may grapple with a world (heaven) in which everyone and everything actually *is* complete. Such an existence just does not make logical sense to earthbound people riddled with human frailty.

It is no secret that we live in an imperfect world. It is imperfect because, if for no other reason, it is unable to sustain any ideal state for long, if at all. There is no such thing as a "perfect" man or woman, physically speaking; even the ultimate human specimen has some blemish or flaw, however imperceptible, and carries within him (or her) the seeds of his own destruction.[39] Likewise, our physical universe, according to every applicable law of science, physics, and thermodynamics, is aging, slowing, cooling, and deteriorating. As soon as something is born, it is inevitable that it will die. As soon as something is made, it eventually disintegrates into the primary components from which it was once formed. This may sound depressing, of course, but it is simply a fact of our world: nothing which comes from *man* or through a *physical process* lasts forever. Houses fall apart, cars break down, children grow up and lose their innocence, spouses get wrinkles and liver spots, coffee gets old and bitter, and death brings an end to us all.

Unfortunately, we not only know all this, but this is all we know. We have to *imagine* a world different than this since (in our universe) it just does not exist. So when God tells us of a world—*His* world—in which there is no aging, slowing, cooling, deterioration, or dying, we may doubt the possibility of it all. Try as we might to wrap our minds around this concept, it does not seem realistic. The human mind is incapable of rationally embracing impossible scenarios such as life without end (or deterioration of any kind), undiminished energy, unlimited friendships, infinite joy, or *perfection* in every possible way. These are foreign to us. We can "see" the concept but may not be able to picture ourselves in that existence. We know no other world than this one, and this one is most certainly incomplete.

Not only is nothing *perfect* here but nothing is ever *finished* here. I'm talking about this in the big-picture sense, not in individual accomplishments. For example, a person may finish his college degree, but man will never stop acquiring knowledge; a football game will certainly run out of time, but men will never cease to compete against one another; a person's life has a definite end, but humanity will continue to be replenished with children who relentlessly begin the cycle of life all over again. Each generation pursues the works and efforts of the last generation. Every year is, in many ways, much like all the years before it: lunar phases and tidal forces unendingly exert their influences on the world; seasons end but do not disappear altogether; every natural living thing eventually dies, but life itself cannot be suppressed or eradicated. Like Solomon wrote some 3,000 years ago (Ecclesiastes 1:8-10),

> All things are wearisome; Man is not able to tell it. The eye is not satisfied with seeing, Nor is the ear filled with hearing. That which has been is that which will be, And that which has been done is that which will be done. So there is nothing new under the sun. Is there anything of which one might say, "See this, it is new"? Already it has existed for ages Which were before us.

All these things will continue in our world until *God* brings the entire system to a close.

People will never stop building, learning, exploring, searching, collecting, or asking questions. It is our nature to seek to improve ourselves, our world, and our understanding of the unknown. This quest will never be complete; we will never finish this massive project; we will forever be engaged in this cyclic system of asking questions, seeking knowledge, applying knowledge, and then discovering the mysteries and questions that lead to the next search. One of the most profound things that we *have* discovered is that we will never finish discovering things.

Our own selfishness is partly to blame for this: our natural propensity to misuse, abuse, and corrupt (through greed and lust) whatever we do compromises our efficiency and interferes with our objectivity. For example, you can be sure that if men put their heads together, we could invent a car engine that would be tremendously more fuel-efficient than what is now available on the market. Corporate greed, enormous oil profits, market competition, the "need for speed" and power, etc. all complicate any meaningful advancement forward. It *may* happen eventually but only because enough money can be made on the project, not for the sheer altruistic value of the thing itself.

The truth is we're okay with that. We may complain about "the system," but "the system" is also the way of the world. In fact, we *are* "the system." Furthermore, none of us sit around bemoaning how "incomplete" the world is; we continue instead, in our own small way, to grapple with our own individual incompleteness. We all strive *after* completeness, but we have this gnawing feeling, at the same time, that we are not really going to finish anything. Once today's job is done, there will always be tomorrow's; and next week has its own projects, and next year, and so on. Finally, we get to retire, but we realize that even in retirement there is a certain exasperating sense of inadequacy and incompletion. We look back over our lives and wonder at all the things that never got done, but we know that we will never have the time or strength or health to do them all *now*. What is unfinished at the end of our lives will be unfinished forever; even if someone completes the things we ourselves began, it will remain for *us* unfinished, and that person will have his own unfinished business that will carry over into the next generation. We may not like this human dilemma, we may recognize the problem, but this is the world as we know it. Consciously or not we even perpetuate our own incompletion because (ironically) it seems to be the most advantageous thing to do at the time.

What if we were able to exist in *another* world where all the inherent deficiencies, inadequacies, and limitations of *this* realm were absent? What if we really *could* experience completion in all of our being—in body, soul, and spirit (cf. 1 Thessalonians 5:23)? What if we were able to escape the gravitational-like pull of greed, lust, and self-destructive thinking so that we could actually be 100% efficient with our time and energy? What if we no longer had to compete with other people for our own meager piece of the world but *every person* was given *the entire world*, so to speak—with no one lacking in anything?

What if? Sound impossible? "With people this *is* impossible, but with God *all things* are possible" (Matthew 19:26, emphasis mine).

God has, because of man's sin, subjected this physical world to futility. Yet the "children of God" (believers) will not always endure such futility (Romans 8:20-21). This life is filled with trouble (Matthew 6:34), trials (James 1:2), and tribulations (John 16:33), but God's world—His heaven—has none of these things. Heaven is not a work-in-progress; it is not a recycling, seasonal, ever-changing existence; it is *perfect* in form and *complete* in purpose. Just as Jesus Christ is complete—and He *is* our heaven—so our existence "in Him" will be complete.

Herein is the rub: since we do not really understand what "being complete" *means*, we may reject the entire premise *of* such completion. If this incomplete, imperfect world is all that we know, how can we latch onto a world that is so completely foreign to ours? *We have nothing by which to compare it.*

Yet God has proved—from the Creation to the cross—that He is capable of bringing about the final completion of a given work, *as long as it is a work of God* and not of man. He is not only the Creator; He is also the Great Finisher: He will bring this world and its system to an end. The world will not be "created" again; that is a done deal, a finished project; this is why God "rested" when it was accomplished (Genesis 2:1-3). Christ will not have to die again since His death was "once for all"—the absolute finality of what was required for the redemption of men's souls (Hebrews 10:10). Whatever *God* begins, He ends; just as He (Christ) is the *beginning* of all things, so He is the "summing up of all things" (Ephesians 1:9-10). Concerning God's plan of redemption, Christ said, "It is done. I am the Alpha and the Omega, the beginning and the end" (Revelation 21:6).

This is an impossible task for men: to be the beginning and ending of *anything.* We have not begun anything worthwhile, and we will not bring about the end of anything worthwhile either. The only thing we have been able to "create" is *our own death* through sin (cf. Romans 6:23; James 1:15); the only thing we have been able to "end" is our fellowship with God *through our sin* (cf. Ephesians 2:1). In other words, we cannot complete anything good, but Christ can and will—not only for Himself, but He will be the completion of all who believe in Him. And yes, He will bring about the destruction of all who resist Him.

Whenever man *tries* to achieve completion, God is there to remind him of his limitations. We have the account of the tower of Babel (Genesis 11:1-9) and the statue of Nebuchadnezzar's dream (Daniel 2:31-35) to illustrate this. It is not as though He is afraid of us becoming too strong or too much for Him to handle; rather, man's existence is not to be completed here *on earth* but *in God.* If man *could* be made complete here, there would be no need for Christ or heaven; man would become his own god and could build his own heaven. God did not create us so that we could rival Him. He created us so that we could *love* Him—and be the object of *His* love. In loving Him, we are able to *draw near* to Him in fellowship. It is not surprising then that immediately after the tower of Babel event God called Abraham and conferred upon him a promise (Genesis 12:1-3): man, through Abraham's "seed,"[40] would be *able* to reach heaven. Through Christ, who is the fulfillment of that promise, we are able to achieve what has been and always will be impossible for us: *to live with God in His world.* Christ provided the necessary sacrifice for man's sin which was beyond what man was able to do for himself *and* serves as both King and High Priest of God's kingdom, which is infinitely superior to the collective of man's kingdoms. These accomplishments were Christ's mission; He did not come into the world to complete any other project; He did not come to solve any other problem. He did not build any towers to heaven; He did not intend to unite the nations with "world peace." His purpose was to "give His life a ransom for many" (Mark 10:45) and thus bring to *completion* man's search for God.

This is what God did for us, but this is also part of what makes our unhesitant response to God so difficult. Many of us are like the tower-builders of Babel, trying to make a name for ourselves; or we are like the arrogance of world leaders, trying to bring men together under one indissoluble empire. Since we grapple with the idea of God bringing us into *His* heaven, we feel we must create our own instead. Since we do not always trust Christ to be *our* completion, we must strive for completion through our own strength—on our own terms. We struggle to come into the world at birth; we do everything possible to resist leaving the world in death. This world is our home so any other world seems completely alien to us. From birth to death we writhe and squirm and struggle to make *this* home "work"—that is, to stop writhing and struggling—even though we are certain that it will never work. Thus we are a living contradiction: we doom our own efforts by the very knowledge that our efforts will ultimately be doomed. We are defeated by our own successes: the more we advance in knowledge and science, the more impractical self-determination becomes.

This brings us back to the concept of the *sacred*. Only those things which are truly sacred—in other words, that come from God—last forever. Love, grace, mercy, forgiveness, salvation—these things originate with God, thus they (or their effects) are eternal. These last forever because, as they are used to *define* God and are used *by* God, they are entirely complete already. God is not partly loving, He *is* love; He is not partly gracious, He *is* grace; and so on. God does not practice half-way love but gives love *in its completion*; and so with all gifts that He bestows upon His children, every "spiritual blessing...in Christ" (Ephesians 1:3). God's kingdom, and the church which has been built upon the authority of that kingdom, will last forever. Heaven will last forever because it is where God is. Christ "is the same yesterday and today and forever" (Hebrews 13:8): He is eternal because He is altogether complete. Things cannot *be* this way in the physical world because this world is under a curse due to sin, and God cannot make perfect that which is devoted to destruction.[41]   Man is unable to either escape this curse or rise above it; he cannot transcend the divine imposition placed upon him.

Thankfully, even though God is indeed going to destroy the world, He is not going to destroy those who *belong* to Him. He makes distinction between "the world" (the realm and spirit of the ungodly) and those who are "in Christ" (cf. 1 Thessalonians 4:13-18; 1 John 2:15-17). Those who are "in Christ" will be taken to where Christ is—they will not only "see" heaven but will experience the incomprehensible experience of being forever in fellowship with the Lord. This will be our completion; this is the full summation of our existence. Just because we cannot conceive of such completion does not mean it will not happen. We do not have to know how everything works in God's kingdom in order to believe in the power and authority of that kingdom. Remember how Nicodemus (John 3:1ff) struggled with comprehending heavenly things? Remember too what Jesus told him: "The wind blows where it wishes and you hear the sound of it, but do not know where it comes from and where it is going; so is everyone who is born of the Spirit" (John 3:8). I believe what Jesus meant was this: "Nicodemus, just because you do not know where the wind comes from or where it goes *does not mean* you do not believe in wind or cease to benefit from it. So it is with the workings of the Spirit: just because you cannot see Him, or what it is that He accomplishes within you, *does not mean* you cannot believe that He exists and will *bring you to completion*."

What will it be like to live in such completion without anything left to look forward to beyond that life? God says, in essence, *that thought will never bother you* once you are there. Therefore, let us not only accept this premise, let us *relish* the thought. Let us set aside all inhibitions, doubts, reservations, and self-imposed limitations concerning what we think heaven will be like. Let us not think of the sacred as being bound to our expectations but far exceeding them. It is not something we were meant to understand until the time when we are safe in the arms of Jesus. "Beloved, now we are children of God, and it has not appeared as yet what we will be. We know that when He [Christ] appears, we will be like Him, because we will see Him just as He is" (1 John 3:2). Yes, exactly: *we* will be like *He* is—perfect, complete, absolutely flawless. Just like the world in which He lives.

Our Struggle with the Absence of Conflict

This third discussion is related to the preceding one but has distinct differences. Suppose we begin by illustrating it with some rather unlikely scenarios:

- Imagine you observe several siblings over an extended period of time. You witness absolutely no rivalry, no competition, and no arguing among them. Every one of them is immediately and completely satisfied with their helping of food, portion of gifts, and allotment of attention given to them by their parents. There are no disputes over who gets what or why one gets more (or less) than the other. It is an ideal family life, a perfect childhood, characterized only by quiet cooperation and unfeigned contentment. (And every person reading this that has grown up with brothers or sisters is shaking his or her head, saying, "Yeah, *right!* Never in a million years!" But wait, there's more.)

• Imagine a movie about a sweet young married couple who are head over heels in love and living out a perfect, frictionless life. There are no problems, no worries, no confrontations, and no disputes between themselves. They are not wealthy, not unrealistically intelligent, not even the best looking people you ever saw, but their relationship is absolutely free of *conflict*. Their lives seamlessly flow from one quiet, contented scene to the next. (Someone is already saying, "Then what's the plot? And why would I want to sit there and watch *that* for an hour and a half?" Exactly. What would we do with ourselves besides squirming in our theater chairs, unhappy that "nothing's happening"? But bear with me for one more illustration.)

• Imagine you apply to work for a major corporation whose sole reason for existence is simply to be *in* existence. Making money is not its objective; if it happens, so be it; if not, that's okay too. There are no aggressive advertising campaigns, no rivalries with other companies, no interoffice competition for dominance and control. There is no one vying for anyone else's position no matter how seemingly lowly their own position might be. Everyone is happy with the status quo; the company itself is happy to *be*. The pay is nice, but no one is really concerned with it either. After all, the only reason anyone is working there is because they are happy to be working. (Having discovered all this, would you want a job there? Or will you think to yourself, "These people are *crazy*! Without being more competitive—indeed, without being competitive *at all*—they are not going to survive!")

These silly scenarios are intended to drive home a serious point. Sometimes, when dreaming about heaven, we might be sidelined with the *unreality* of it all. After all, are we really supposed to live blissfully for a million gazillion years with our fellow brothers and sisters in Christ without ever fighting or complaining about one another—*ever?* This hardly seems possible, especially since we can hardly seem to get through an entire Sunday without some kind of rankling in our own congregations, much less with the saved of all human history. Or we might think, "Well, if everything's going to be perfect and happy in heaven, what's to look forward to?" Perfect contentment can, after all, grow rather tiresome and dull, especially after the first few million years. Certainly we will long for a kind of Spartacus-like rebellion among some angelic discontents, or perhaps some upset when one brother finally loses it and goes "postal" with a heavenly saber, or—*something.* Or we might think that our "job" in heaven will be meaningless and eventless, without any break in the monotony of "just" serving God and sitting through thousand-year-long "church services." After a few millennia of this, we might long for the titillating excitement of office politics and water cooler gossip; we might ache for just a few moments of human drama. Or we might drool with anticipation for some kind of competitive sport—a softball game, bowling match, badminton contest, *anything.* To sit there in the midst of unending contentment might be, ironically, quite discontenting. For some, the "sacred" might actually be *boring*—or so a person may be led to believe.

The real struggle here is with the concept of "struggle" itself. That is, we are so used to competition and challenges that we simply cannot conceive of what we would do with our time—or our sanity—without them. Historians, literary critics, sociologists, philosophers, moralists, dramatists, and economists have been telling us forever that the world operates in a perpetual state of *conflict*. Conflict, as it is used here, refers to struggles for recognition, advancement, dominance, or survival. Conflict is the inherent function of the fallen human condition; likewise, the natural world has been directly affected *by* that condition. There is conflict, competition, and rivalry, in some form or another, in every sphere of humanity and nature. Good literature, as well as good theater and cinema, is filled with all sorts of conflict: love triangles, betrayals, rebellions, revolutions, promotions, demotions, etc. These are the things that make human drama enjoyable in the first place. In life, there are protagonists and antagonists; what is there in heaven? Satan and his demonic minions will have been banished forever; we will not need archangels to fight our battles anymore; what is the point then of our existence beyond merely *being* in existence?

How then are we supposed to live in the absence of all conflict?

Heaven is hardly something to anticipate if all we see in it is an endless tedium of repetitive liturgy and incantations. Here we are used to church services and men acting in official capacity *in* those services. We might easily imagine that heaven will be more of the same, but this is unsupported by any biblical view. Church—and its "services"—is for *here on earth*, for *human beings*, not citizens of heaven. Once in heaven, we will be *in the literal presence of God.* There is *nothing* boring or tedious about that! Just one glimpse of the Father in all His majesty and glory will put an end to any such reservations. Christ had lived in the presence of the Father from all eternity (John 1:1-2), and yet His longing to return to that glory was unmistakable. After having completed His ministry here on earth, He said with great anticipation, "Now, Father, glorify Me together with Yourself, with the glory which I had with You before the world was" (John 17:5). Having experienced first-hand all the competition, rivalry, and conflicts of this life, He longed without hesitation to return to His Father's world.

Someone says, "Yes, but Jesus is the Son of God. He is the *object* of everyone else's worship!" This is true, but will we not all benefit from whatever glory He enjoys? In fact, He has promised to share His glory with us so that whatever *He* enjoys *we* will enjoy as well. "'Behold, I stand at the door and knock,' He says. "If anyone hears My voice and opens the door, I will come in to him and will dine with him, and he with Me. He who overcomes, I will grant to him to sit down with Me on My throne, as I also overcame…" (Revelation 3:20-21). This is an amazing offer, an incredible incentive! Not one of us deserves such honorary treatment, and yet the Son of God promises that *every soul in heaven* will be partakers of divine glory![42]

    Imagine yourself sitting in the supernatural presence of the Creator of the entire universe. His Son—your Savior!—is sitting at His right hand, and He invites you to come and sit *with* Him! You are not an overnight guest in the celestial palace either—you are a very special family member! You are attended by angels who minister to your every request; *they* are *your* servants. You are surrounded by the glory and beauty of heaven to which the glory of this earth cannot even compare. Since you trusted in Christ the King in your earthly life, He now trusts you to sit in the midst of the *Source of all life*. You will be bathed in light, caressed with endless music and songs more beautiful than anything ever heard on earth. Your vision will be filled with glory, your heart pounding with excitement, and your soul swallowed up in God. You will not just be in *proximity* to the Father, but you will *dwell in Him*, and He will dwell in you. Faithful believers of all time will be there to share in your honor; *every one of these* will be as dearest friends. Fellowship in heaven will be immediate, intimate, and more enjoyable than whatever we could have experienced here on earth. You will not be in *competition* with these holy ones; you will be just as joyful for their victory in Christ as they will be over yours! You will never again experience sorrow, heartache, pain, discomfort, fear, loss, separation, or death of *any* kind *ever again*. You will never again experience the burden of being human again—no more: taxes, subjugation, poverty, continually having to refill that which is always running empty, striving after that which continually eludes you, grasping after wind, and gasping for just another breath of life. Furthermore, whatever you will have in heaven will *never be taken away from you*—in fact, just as God is infinite so will your joy be infinite and forever refreshed, rejuvenated, and replenished. Your "moment in the sun" will never last for only a moment or even a lifetime but for *the rest of your endless existence*.

    Does this sound boring to you?

    All this is just a faint shadow of the reality of what the sacred life will be like. To be with God, in His world—not in faith, as we now know Him, but in fact—will far surpass the most vivid depiction of the best kind of life imaginable. Serving the Lord will not be an endless repetition of prostrations and incantations. Serving the Lord in His heaven will be *infinitely better* than the most adventurous fishing or hunting trip, *better* than sipping the perfect cup of coffee on a stormy afternoon while cuddled up with the finest book ever written, *better* than discovering a priceless treasure ship while scuba diving in shallow, crystal-clear waters, *better* than falling in love with the most beautiful (or handsome) person on the face of the earth (even though this person loves you back as though you were the same), *better* than the most fantastic sensual or sexual experience you could even imagine. The eternal joy and fulfillment of being in fellowship with God transcends the incidental joy of all these things—once again, it is too wonderful to even be *compared* with them.

Someone says, "Yes, but you still haven't really addressed the 'absence of conflict' problem." But I have! You see, with all our senses flooded with such wonderful things going on all the time, each moment being as exciting and exhilarating as the one before, do you really think any of us will be sitting around bemoaning the absence of conflict? Will any of us be longing to reinstate the conflicts and struggles of this life? These conflicts represent our *imprisonment*—and heaven is our *escape* from that captivity! It is unlikely that the desires of this world (if one actually *does* "desire" conflict) will even enter our minds once we have left this world behind. We will not miss that from which we have been liberated. We will not be like the faithless among Israel who, while waiting to enter the Promised Land, longed to return to Egyptian bondage because the food was better there (Numbers 11:4-6; 20:4-5). We will no longer be wandering in the wilderness awaiting entrance into our Promised Land; we will be in the presence of God, the *Source* and *Fulfillment* of all promises!

The passions, conflicts, struggles, and antagonisms of this world will one day be gone. This is because all the things which *cause* conflicts will also be gone: pride, greed, envy, jealousy, covetousness, and self-ambition. The internal war of the spiritual nature of man versus the carnal nature of man will be gone (Romans 7:22-23). The unseen struggle within—"the fleshly lusts which wage war against the soul" (1 Peter 2:11)—will be gone. The curse which God has placed upon humanity, which forces a conflict with nature, will also be gone (Revelation 22:3).

Earthly and internal conflict will be replaced by heavenly *peace*. This will not be a temporary peace, like a breather between conflicts, which is all we may now experience. This will not be a false peace, like when a person feels "at peace" with himself, even though he stands condemned by God. This will not be an unseen peace, which a Christian is able to experience in his heart even though he is otherwise embroiled in the conflicts of this life. No, but this will be "the peace of God, which surpasses all comprehension" (Philippians 4:7)—not experienced through the eyes of faith but as *the full reality of one's complete existence*. This will be what it means to be "swallowed up by life" (2 Corinthians 5:4): completely immersed in joy, completely enveloped in the glorious bliss of Christ's love and the warmth of His fellowship. This earth will no longer be our home, but *heaven* will be our home, and nothing—not "rust or moth," thieves, loss, time, or the devil himself—can ever threaten us again (Matthew 6:19-20).

The "peace of God, which surpasses all comprehension" is certainly something that the believer can now experience in faith. Yet while we are in this earthly body, it is impossible for us to revel in this peace in the same way that we will be able to do in heaven. As Paul wrote, "For now we see in a mirror dimly, but then face to face; now I know in part, but then I will know fully just as I also have been fully known" (1 Corinthians 13:12). "Then" we will "know fully" the peace of God since we will behold *God Himself*, the Source of all peace. "Then" we will not miss the absence of conflict but will be immersed with the exhilaration of *being fully and boundlessly alive in Christ*.

"The first things"—those which are corrupted by sin *and* are elemental in nature—will pass away (1 John 2:15-17). After this, God will "make all things new" (Revelation 21:4-5). So it will be with our conflicts and struggles: they will pass away and never be known to us again. Better things await the child of God—much, much better things. The sufferings, trials, and conflicts of this world will not even be comparable to the joys and experiences awaiting saints in the world to come (cf. Romans 8:18; 2 Corinthians 4:17). This world is dying, as are its problems, pleasures, and limitations; "whatever is becoming obsolete and growing old is ready to disappear" (Hebrews 8:13).

The Anticipation of Heaven

For now, we look forward to all these "new things" in faith. We have faith that God created *this* world (Hebrews 11:3). We also have faith that with this same power and authority He will create for us *another* world which is far superior to this one (2 Peter 3:13). Nonetheless, even in the midst of faith, there may linger human doubt. It is natural to have *some* doubt—faith would not be "faith" otherwise—but it is wrong to let those doubts overcome our faith. Faith in God is predicated on facts and evidence; doubts are based on human fears and what is unknown to us. Where God has provided sufficient evidence for faith we cannot choose to doubt instead. Has God provided sufficient evidence of His heaven? Most certainly He has—*have faith* in what He has told you. Has He told you exactly what to expect there, all the details of His world? No, He has not—He does not have to—but *do not let this fact nullify what He <u>has</u> told you.*

We cannot see and touch the sacred *yet*—but we will someday if we remain faithful until the end (Revelation 2:10). We will be made complete in the sacred realm if we trust in the One who completes us. We will no longer experience the conflicts and struggles of this earthly life in the sacred life—which is a *good* thing, not a disappointment!—as long as we finish our struggle here first. Accordingly, Peter wrote, "After you have suffered for a little while, the God of all grace, who called you to His eternal glory in Christ, will Himself perfect, confirm, strengthen and establish you" (1 Peter 5:10). God will provide nothing less for His obedient children.

As you devote your time then to seeking the sacred, dream deeply and meditate intensely on all the beautiful sights, sounds, joys, and experiences that await you in the Great Beyond. I cannot tell you exactly what to expect there, but I am supremely confident of this: *God is there, and that is enough.*

Endnotes

38 The "*kingdom* of heaven" is not literally "heaven," but refers instead to Christ's rule and authority (Ephesians 1:22-23). Nonetheless, it is cited here as being as difficult for us to grasp as heaven itself. Furthermore, one who is a genuine citizen of the *kingdom* will certainly enjoy *heaven* from which the King rules.

39 This does not nullify the perfect offering of Christ's bodily sacrifice. Jesus' body was perfect in that it was whole, of sound health, and uncorrupted by sin; He was a unique specimen. However, his body would have still succumbed to death, if He had been allowed to live a full, natural life; likewise, it was not invincible to injury or pain, and obviously could be put to death. But because nothing happened to Him except for what His divine will permitted (something we cannot do for ourselves), He once again is a unique case and defies being classified by what is common to all other men.

40 By a singular "seed," God meant a particular descendant—a specific man: Christ (cf. Galatians 3:16).

41 The concept of things "under the ban" [lit., devoted to destruction] can be seen in Deuteronomy 7:25-26 (concerning the Canaanite objects of worship), Joshua 6:17-18 (concerning Jericho), and Matthew 22:7 (concerning Jerusalem; see also Luke 19:41-44). Whatever is contaminated with sin or used for sinful purposes must be either cleansed or destroyed; since this world is saturated with the sin of man, God has no recourse but to destroy it entirely (2 Peter 3:10-12). What God destroys is not to be rebuilt but is to remain destroyed. For example, once Jericho was destroyed, it was not to be rebuilt as a fortified city, but left open and without walls (Joshua 7:26; see also 1 Kings 16:34); an even stronger case is the obliteration of Sodom and Gomorrah, which God made impossible to rebuild (Genesis 19). Consider also what Paul said in Galatians 2:18, "For if I rebuild what I have once destroyed, I prove myself to be a transgressor." God is not going to destroy the world and then rebuild it as before; He is going to destroy the world in order to make an entirely *new* dwelling place for man which will be spiritual in nature, no longer physical (cf. 1 Corinthians 15:46-48; 2 Peter 3:13; and Revelation 21:1-5).

42 This does not mean we will *become* divine, but that we will be specially treated *by* the divine. There is nowhere in the New Testament that indicates that we will become "gods" or that we will share God's divinity. A reference to us being "partakers of the divine nature" is found in 2 Peter 1:4.

Conclusion

This writing of this book has spanned about five years. I did not work on it continuously for that entire period of time because this project had to be set aside many times for other things: work, a 2,500-mile move across the country, several dry spells where it seemed I couldn't write anything worthwhile, and the mundane, miscellaneous business of life.

In the beginning, I did not intend for this to become a published work. It served as more of an outlet for some of my private thoughts and personal observations, but it eventually began to serve a more practical and relevant purpose. As I wrote about things important to myself, I would hear fellow Christians talking about those same things not long afterwards. The things that were important to me—but seldom discussed—were important to them too. It became apparent to me that a collection of these expanded ideas (or essays) would be welcomed by those who were of like mind. I assume that you are among those people, that you also find these explorations and ruminations to be valuable to your walk with Christ. Or maybe someone gave you this book to read because they *want* you to walk with Christ—or to cordially challenge you to take that walk to a higher level.

Certainly we can *all* make improvements in our relationship with God. Even Paul admitted that he had not yet "arrived" as a fully mature Christian even though he was an apostle: "Brethren, I do not regard myself as having laid hold of it yet; but one thing I do: forgetting what lies behind and reaching forward to what lies ahead, I press on toward the goal for the prize of the upward call of God in Christ Jesus" (Philippians 3:13-14). This gives me a great deal of comfort. If the apostle Paul had to struggle with seeking the sacred, then certainly my own struggle is validated, and so is yours.

When the cosmic curtain of this earthly drama is pulled aside, the only things that will matter are *your soul* and *God*. When finally freed from the confines of this human realm to embrace the sacred without need of faith or hope, your soul—if you die a faithful Christian—will be completely immersed in the Light of God. Having reached that never-ending euphoria, you will never have to return again to the shadowy world of earthly imperfection, spiritual darkness, and human vice. You will never again have to endure the anguish of *knowing* the Sacred but being unable to be *with* the Sacred. Once re-united with the Source of your life, strength, and existence, you will never have to feel pain, wrestle with sin, or leave.

Being with the Sacred will not be a momentary, fleeting experience—like a brief epiphany or the thrilling memory of last night's spectacular dream. Instead, it will be that which has no end and will appear to have no beginning. Those who are in the presence of the Sacred will not measure time or mark days on a calendar. Once we are there, it will be as if we had always been there, as if we had existed forever in the throes of spiritual bliss. We will have no regrets for what we left behind; we will long for no other existence. Once the Savior's arms embrace us and we feel His energy and power radiating throughout our being, we will experience *life* like we never knew was even possible. We will no longer merely *be* alive, but we will dwell forever with the Source of life. We will eat of the Tree of Life, we will drink from the River of Life, and we will breathe in the Spirit of God.

Isn't this what you want? Isn't this what you have always wanted?

*   *   *

Dear reader, I wish you well in your drawing near to God. My sincere prayer for you is that you will take the things we have discussed from the Bible to heart. There is a "narrow way" that leads to life, "and there are few who find it" (Matthew 7:13-14). This "way" is the path to the sacred, the road to heaven; it leads us directly to the throne of God. This "way" is narrow because it is difficult and selfless. It does not embrace everyone's views or accommodate everyone's opinions; this was never its purpose. This "way" has no room for one's baggage or "issues": you are told to leave those things at the cross. This "way" is not meant to make you comfortable: it is meant to save you from your self-inflicted demise. Discipleship is not meant to be fun, easy, or entertaining. Being a seeker of the sacred does not mean you are merely religious; it means you are resolved to follow Christ wherever He goes (Matthew 16:24).

On the other hand, God's power, beauty, majesty, and sacredness are incredibly compelling incentives for seeking Him. I have shared with you some of my insights on this; perhaps you have even better ones; or maybe I have helped you to "see" God more clearly through my own. The most important ambition you can have in this life is to give yourself over entirely to the search for God and His holiness. I have long admired those men and women who radiate with an intimate friendship with the Lord, one that is tempered with reverence and awe and yet transcends their closest relationships on earth. On the other hand, it is disturbing that so many people do not know God and do not make much effort to get to know Him. Even Christians may go through years and decades of churchgoing and religious service without ever really having (and enjoying) a healthy relationship with the Lord.

Admittedly, sacred fellowship with God is not something easily or quickly attained. Just when "mega-churches" promoting "designer worship" and "feel-good" religion are reaching full-throttle, the gospel quietly but resolutely implores us to take time and energy away from ourselves (and our religious pretenses) so that we can earnestly pursue God in all His sacredness. This is an unpopular message, and any book that echoes this resolve—like the one you're reading does—will also be unpopular.

Thankfully, the Sacred God has never been a purveyor of popularity. Seekers of the sacred themselves are rarely popular for the very fact that their identity with Christ alienates them from those who are not. Likewise, the one who genuinely seeks God's holiness "in spirit and truth" exposes those who *claim* to be identified with Him but are not. In fact, the more passionately and diligently you seek the sacred, the less popular you become among those who refuse to do this—and they will be many.

Then again, this is part of the cost of discipleship. Your faith in Christ cannot be dependent upon popularity or peer approval. It can only depend upon the immutable promises of God and your conviction in those promises. In the end, remember, all that will matter is *your soul* and *God*. Let others go their way; you must not follow them. Let the world do what it will; do not imitate its arrogant obstinacy. "It is the Lord Christ whom you serve" (Colossians 3:24): never forget this. Never abandon your resolve to serve Christ. This is where we separate the men from the boys. This is where we separate the secular from the sacred. This is where we separate the casual churchgoer from the true believer.

We opened this book with God, in essence, looking into your heart and asking you a most important question. I have been alluding to this question throughout this entire book, and it continues to be posed to each one of us. Even though you are finished with this book, you are never finished dealing with this question for it must be asked every day for the rest of your life. How you answer it will bear upon your eternal future; therefore, be as honest and forthright as you can. The question that God asks, once again, is this:

Do you know Me in the way that I want you to know Me?

More Bible workbooks that you can order from Spiritbuilding.com or your favorite Christian bookstore.

BIBLE STUDIES

Inside Out (Carl McMurray)
Studying spiritual growth in bite sized pieces

Night and Day (Andrew Roberts)
Comparing N.T. Christianity and Islam

We're Different Because..., with Manual (Carl McMurray)
A workbook on authority and recent church history

From Beneath the Altar (Carl McMurray)
A workbook commentary on the book of Revelation

1 & 2 Timothy and Titus (Matthew Allen)
A workbook commentary on these letters from Paul

The Parables, Taking a Deeper Look (Kipp Campbell)
A relevant examination of our Lord's teaching stories

The Minor Prophets, Vol. 1&2, w/PowerPack (Matthew Allen)
Old lessons that speak directly to us today

Esteemed of God, the Book of Daniel (Carl McMurray)
Covering the man as well as the time between the testaments

Faith in Action: Studies in James (Mike Wilson)
Bible class workbook and commentary on James

The Lion is the Lamb (Andrew Roberts)
Study of the King of Kings, His kingdom, & His return

Church Discipline, with Manual (Royce DeBerry)
A quarter's study on an important task for the church

Exercising Authority, with Manual (John Baughn)
How we use and understand authority on a daily basis

Communing with the Lord (Matthew Allen)
A study of the Lord's Supper and issues surrounding it

Seeking the Sacred (Chad Sychtysz)
How to know God the way that HE wants us to know Him

1st Corinthians & 2nd Corinthians study guides
(Chad Sychtysz) *Detailed studies to take the student through these important letters*

TEENS/YOUNG ADULTS

Transitions, with PowerPack (Ken Weliever)
A relevant life study for this changing age group
Snapshots: Defining Moments in a Girl's Life (Nicole Sardinas)
How to make godly decisions when it really matters
The Path of Peace (Cassondra Givans)
Relevant and important topics of study for teens
The Purity Pursuit (Andrew Roberts)
Helping teens achieve purity in all aspects of life
The Gospel and You (Andrew Roberts)
13 weeks of daily lessons for Jr High and High School ages
Paul's Letter to the Romans (Matthew Allen)
Putting righteousness by faith on an understandable level

WOMEN

Reveal In Me... (Jeanne Sullivan)
A ladies study on finding and developing one's own talents
I Will NOT Be Lukewarm, with PowerPack (Dana Burk)
A ladies study on defeating mediocrity
The Gospel of John (Cassondra Givans)
A study for women, by a woman, on this letter of John
Sisters at War (Cassondra Givans)
Breaking the generation gap between sisters in Christ
Will You Wipe My Tears? (Joyce Jamerson)
Resources to teach us how to help others through sorrow
Bridges or Barriers, w/Manual (C. DeBerry & A. Kmitta)
*Study encouraging harmony between younger/older
sisters-in-Christ*
Learning to Sing at Midnight (Joanne Beckley)
A study book about spiritual growth benefiting women of all ages
Forgotten Womanhood (Joanne Beckley)
*Workbook which covers purity of purpose in serving God as a
woman*

PERSONAL GROWTH
Compass Points (Carl McMurray)
22 foundation lessons for home studies or new Christians
Marriage Through the Ages, with Manual
(Royce & Cindy DeBerry)
A quarter's study of God's design for this part of our life
Parenting Through the Ages, with Manual
(Royce & Cindy DeBerry)
Bible principles tested and explained by successful parents
What Should I Do?, with Manual (Dennis Tucker)
A study that seeks Bible answers to life's important questions
When Opportunity Knocks, w/PowerPack (Matthew Allen)
Lessons on how to meet the Jehovah's Witness/
Mormon who knock on your door

SPECIAL INTERESTS
In the Eye of the Hurricane - AUTISM (Juli Liske)
A family's journey from the shock of an autistic diagnosis to victory
I Cried Out, You Answered Me - DEPRESSION
(Sheree McMillen)
What happens when faith and depression live in the same home
Her Little Soldier - DIABETES (Craig Dehut)
The journey of a young man suffering from Juvenvile Diabetes
For However Brief a Time (Warren Berkley)
A son's human interest tales of his father in a time now gone by
Family Bible Study Series, with Curriculum Guide
(Ken Weliever)
16 quarters of Bible class curriculum for families and congregations

*All PowerPacks include PowerPoint presentations +
Teacher's Manual

Breinigsville, PA USA
29 September 2010
246387BV00002B/69/P